lonely planet

THE BIKEPACKERS' GUIDE TO THE WORLD

Contents

Introduction 04

What is bikepacking? 08

Africa, Asia, Oceania

Atlas Mountain Race (Morocco) 12
Bikamino (South Africa) 18
Congo Nile Trail (Rwanda) 22
Lesotho Traverse (Lesotho) 26
The Bartang Valley (Tajikistan) 30
The Border Roads (China) 36
The Kazakh Corner (Kazakhstan) 42
Shiretoko Loop (Japan) 46
Goldfields Track (Australia) 52
Alps 2 Ocean (New Zealand) 58
The Mawson Trail (Australia) 62
Attack of the Buns (Australia) 68
Kahurangi 500 (New Zealand) 72
Hunt 1000 (Australia) 78
Tour Aotearoa (New Zealand) 84
Munda Biddi (Australia) 90
Murray to the Mountains (Australia) 96
St James Trail (New Zealand) 100
Tasmanian Trail (Australia) 104
Tour D'Top End (Australia) 110
More to ride 116

Europe

Adriatic Crest (Croatia) 120
Burrally (Spain) 124
Caucasus Crossing (Georgia) 128
Danube Cycle Path
  (Germany, Austria, Slovakia & Hungary) 132
The Hebridean Way (Scotland) 138
Hope 1000 (Switzerland) 142
Isar Cycle Route (Germany) 148
Jura Traverse (France) 152
Bikepacking Kjölur (Iceland) 156
The Meuse Cycle Route
  (France, Belgium & the Netherlands) 160
Mjølkevegen (Norway) 166
Trans-Cambrian Way (Wales) 170
Trans-Dolomiti (Italy) 174
West Kernow Way (England) 178
Wild Atlantic Way (Ireland) 184
The Wolf's Lair (Italy) 188
King Alfred's Way (England) 194
Montañas Vacias (Spain) 200
Tuscany Trail (Italy) 204
La Vélodyssée (France) 210
John Muir Way (Scotland) 216
Vuelta de Vasco (Spain) 220
More to ride 224

Americas

Ruta Maya de los Cuchumatanes
  (Guatemala) 228
The Baja Divide (Mexico) 232
The BC Trail (Canada) 236
Camino dél Puma (Peru & Bolivia) 240
Colorado Trail (USA) 244
Green Mountain Gravel Growler (USA) 248
Oregon Timber Trail (USA) 252
Ruta Chingaza (Colombia) 256
The Tahoe Twirl (USA) 260
Tree to Sea Loop (Canada) 264
The Great Allegheny Passage (USA) 270
Katy Trail (USA) 274
Kenai 250 (USA) 278
Cowichan Valley 8 (Canada) 282
Finger Lakes Overnighter (USA) 286
Trans Ecuador Mountain Bike Route
  (Ecuador) 290
More to ride 294

Index 298

Introduction

As the term hints, bikepacking is essentially backpacking, but carrying your luggage on your bicycle instead of on your back – which enables you to be almost as independent as when backpacking, but also go further and faster (and maybe have a bit more fun). There's nothing especially new about bikepacking: it is also known as cycle touring and has a very long history. Britain's Bicycle Touring Club was founded in 1878 and saw oak-thighed cyclists pedalling from one welcoming hostelry to the next. The first person to cycle all the way around the world was Thomas Stevens, who departed from San Francisco in 1884 and returned to the US in 1886. Annie Londonderry, the first woman to pedal around the planet, left Boston some 20 years later.

The bicycle has always been a great liberator for travellers but never more so than today, whether you think of yourself as a traditional cycle tourist or new-school bikepacker. Modern technology – including lightweight but durable packs that can be strapped to any bike, high-tech navigational aids, and bikes that get more capable (if also more complicated) every year – means that bikepacking the world (or a small portion of it) has never been easier. But taking a trip by bicycle can still be an intimidating prospect, and that's where this book comes in: hopefully it will share a sense of what is possible for those intent on two-wheeled travel.

There's a first time for everything, and even the most seasoned bikepacker started somewhere. They were likely feeling a familiar combination of excitement and trepidation. Excitement because what is more thrilling than embarking on an adventure where you are voyaging under your own steam, both completely in control of your destiny and at the mercy of events? And trepidation because you can't help feeling a little exposed setting off on a bicycle, carrying everything you might need for the next few days or weeks.

But one of the great qualities of bikepacking is that it teaches you more about yourself than you'd expect – and most of the time you'll surprise yourself with the situations you can manage. There are few better ways of gaining resilience, confidence and the ability to think on your feet.

Why bikepack?

There's a lot that's great about touring by bicycle. People riding bikes (rather than driving) feel more connected to the places they visit. They can interact easily with people and are more dependent on local services, meaning that the money they spend stays in the community. Beyond the human interaction, bicycles can also help you reach amazing places: from wild landscapes such as New Zealand's Heaphy Track (left) to little-visited villages.

It's also a supremely flexible mode of travel – if you want to stay a little longer in a place or skip it entirely, you can. You're the boss. You can stay overnight in hotels or hostels as a 'credit-card' tourer and eat at pubs and cafes throughout. Or you can strap a sleeping bag and lightweight tent to your bike, carry a small stove and coffee maker and be almost entirely self-sufficient. Your choice.

And the environmental aspect can't be ignored today. Cycling is a very sustainable way of getting around, especially when coupled with a joined-up public transport policy that permits bikes on buses and trains. It's also perfectly possible to have epic adventures in your backyard without flying at all.

About bikepacking

One of the obstacles for fledgling bikepackers is to know where to go, how to get there (and back) and what the experience might entail. This book pulls together a lot of information about more than 75 bikepacking routes and there are many online resources to help you plan a trip, whether it's your first or fiftieth. See page 9 for more on this.

Bikepacking is certainly not a perfect pastime. There's a perceived high cost of entry with new bikes and kit costing as much as $5000 or more, so it can be viewed as the preserve of the privileged few (although, sometimes, any bike will do, so long as the wheels turn). And while men and women participate with equal enthusiasm if not quite yet numbers – arguably the most celebrated bikepacker currently is female – racial representation has hardly started. But electric bikes are opening the door for older and less well or able people to take part, and bikepacking is an open and welcoming community that embraces new enthusiasts and shares information, advice and support – so long as people ride responsibly, clean up after themselves and don't give the activity a bad reputation.

If that sounds like something you'd like to be part of, find inspiration in these pages, pump up your tyres and head out on the open road or trail.

What is bikepacking?

The spectrum of bikepacking styles ranges from experienced and adventurous types who are comfortable camping in the middle of nowhere to casual weekend cyclists who prefer a bed at night and a fresh-ground coffee in the morning. How you define yourself will determine what kit to carry.

Types of trip

For bikepackers, there is such a thing as Type Two fun. This is an experience that isn't necessarily enjoyable at the time but is the story you tell on getting home and the memory you recall a year or more later. Type Two experiences are not uncommon in self-sufficient bikepacking: you could find yourself pushing up an unrideable hill for five hours or stuck in storm. But at the other end of the spectrum there are credit-card cycle tourers, people who travel light because they're staying in inns or with hosts overnight and eating in pubs and cafes. For this style of bikepacking you just need toiletries, a change of clothes and some spares and tools. Both groups enjoy themselves.

But it's likely that the more experience and confidence you gain at the easier end of the spectrum, the more interest you'll have in pushing beyond your comfort zone and tackling one of the longer and more challenging routes in this book.

Logistics

Bikepacking brings certain constraints that don't affect backpackers. Getting to the start of the route with your bike requires some planning. Can you fly with your bike? Can you take a bus or a train with your bike at your destination? Do you need to pack your bike into a box or a bag? If so, what do you do with the packaging when you set off? And what can you do about security for your precious bike on the road?

Packing a bike

There are typically two options: the recyclable box, usually donated by a local bike shop; and the bespoke bicycle bag. The bike bag will be easier to wheel down a concourse, but what do you do with it when riding? There are a few possibilities: sometimes you'll find a friend or acquaintance to take care of it for a few days or weeks. Or you can ask a local hotel to store it for you (for a fee usually) or use one of the luggage-storage apps that connect you with a person or business that can look after the bag. However, the bike bag

option only works if you're able to return to the same place to pick it up again. What if your ride is one-way and across an entire country? Another option is to pack your bike securely into a cardboard box. Once you've assembled the bike, you can recycle the box and be on your way. This presupposes that you will carry everything that you packed into the box, and also that you will be able to source another box at the end of the trip. The third option is to leave your bike unprotected: this works for some but probably not if you mind your bike being damaged.

Navigation

Before you get to the start of your route, you'll need to figure out how you'll navigate your way along it. There are lots of great options today. At the easiest end of the scale, some official rides are signposted, such as many of the EuroVelo routes. But even so, it's advisable to have one or two backup options. The most foolproof are paper maps: they don't run out of batteries or require software updates, but they may be bulky or not sufficiently detailed.

Global Positioning System (GPS)

Modern mobile (cell) phones can use GPS and several good apps, such as Gaia or RidewithGPS, allow users to plot or upload and follow routes. The disadvantage of using a phone is that they burn battery life quickly. You can carry a battery charger pack or use solar-powered chargers or even a dynamo hub to mitigate this. A dedicated GPS unit, such as those made by Garmin or Wahoo, will offer better battery life.

Sleeping

If you're not planning on booking accommodation every night along the route then you may need to carry camping kit. At a minimum this can be a lightweight sleeping bag and maybe a sleeping mat for insulation and comfort. If the circumstances (weather, warmth, security) allow you to sleep under the stars then stringing up a simple tarp might suffice; a bivvy sack will protect you a bit more from the elements. The next step up is a small tent that weighs as little as your budget allows. (If you're riding with a friend, you can share the burden of carrying it.) Brands like Big Agnes make tents designed for bikepacking.

Eating and drinking

Similarly, how much cooking kit you carry will be determined by the type of trip you're taking and how far off-grid you're going. For some tours – if you have the budget – you can get away with eating at cafes and other places for the whole time, so a stove is not needed (although a compact coffee-maker is often appreciated). But if you're riding far from towns then a lightweight cooking set comprising a stove (there are several varieties), a frying pan and maybe a saucepan, a drinking mug and a utensil with which to stir and eat might be necessary. Buy the most compact and lightweight kit you can afford: the weight adds up.

Water

Water is an essential, wherever you are, and you will need to plan ahead to carry your daily amount. In arid regions that may mean increasing the carrying capacity of your bike by adding mounts for extra water bottles or using a backpack with a bladder. You should calculate your daily requirements, which will be several litres. If you're in an area with abundant fresh water then you

can purify your drinking water. There are several methods of doing this, such as using a filter, purifier, chemical treatment or even a battery-powered ultra-violet device like the Steripen. There are pros and cons to each.

Hygiene

If you're cycling long distances, bodily hygiene is essential to avoid infections and illnesses. Firstly, there's the basic hygiene around food preparation. If you can't wash your hands with soap before preparing food, at least use a sanitiser gel. Boiling utensils generally sterilises them. For the rest of your body, it will be your butt that receives the most wear and tear if you're sitting on a saddle for hours at a time. There are a few things you can do to avoid saddle sores. A good pair of padded cycle shorts is essential; they must fit properly to avoid any friction or chafing. You should also find a saddle that suits you. Next, don't sit around in sweaty shorts – change out of them as soon as possible, and wash your skin thoroughly. If you do have some chafing, use a treatment like Sudocrem to help the skin repair. An anti-fungal cream is also a useful addition to a first-aid kit.

Waste

Dealing with human waste is an unavoidable and important part of bikepacking know-how. Traditionally, advice has been to carry a trowel and dig a hole at least 200ft (60m) from a water source, using biodegradable toilet paper sparingly. However, with the increase in numbers of people visiting the great outdoors in recent years, that's no longer a sustainable option in some popular places; it turns out that poop doesn't break down as quickly as you'd think. The solution is to pack out your poop in a WAG bag, which stands for 'waste alleviation and gelling'. Chemical crystals make your waste inert so it can be carried out and disposed of responsibly at the next opportunity.

Spares and repairs

Bikepackers ought to be able fix most mechanical problems as there might not be any help nearby. That means carrying a basic tool kit with some common spare parts, and knowing how to use it all. The most essential skill is being able to fix a flat tyre. There are two types of tyre: tubeless, in which a fluid sealant sloshes around inside a tyre and blocks small punctures; and tyres with an inner tube. Many bikes use tubeless technology today; if yours does, you'll need to carry rubber plugs to push into larger holes, a tyre boot in case a tyre is slashed, and some spare sealant to top up the tyre. Research and learn the useful techniques for fixing punctures in tubeless tyres. For tubed tyres, the process is easier: either replace or repair the inner tube with a patch. For both fixes you'll need a high-quality pump, such as those by Silca. Other common problems include broken chains (carry a chain-breaker tool and spare links) and broken spokes (carry some spare spokes and a spoke key). Depending on the length of trip, spare brake pads are often useful, too.

How to bikepack

The learning curve for first-time bikepackers is steep. But a few tips on what type of bicycle to use and how to pack it for a trip will help you get on your way.

The first task of planning what to pack for a trip is deciding what sort of bikepacker you are. If you go down the route of carrying a stove, pots and pans, a tent and sleeping bag, you'll need to be very organised, somewhat resilient and also able to invest in lightweight kit. Your bike will also influence where you ride. You can even commission custom bags designed for exactly your size and style of bike. Ultimately, however, the bikepacking community is usually ready to help with advice and second-hand gear.

Pack heavier items lower on the bike for better stability.

Use handlebar bags for easy access to snacks and navigation kit.

Try to pack lighter items higher up, such as sleeping bags and clothing.

Ensure bags are firmly fixed and follow all instructions.

Reduce punctures by using wide tyres with tough sidewalls.

Choose a bike with the widest possible range of gears for hills.

Carry spare parts, such as chain links and spokes, in case of failures.

Modified mounts can allow for extra capacity to carry water bottles.

Types of bikepacking bike

The best bike for cycle touring is the bike you have – a new generation of bikepacking bags with Velcro straps can be attached to most bicycles. But having a bike purpose-built to be comfortable and capable of longer adventures will mean making fewer compromises, and the investment will quickly pay itself off. The key features to consider are a robust wheelset and gearing with a wide range (a small ring option at the front and large cogs on the cassette at the back). Some bikepackers will prefer hub gears for lower maintenance and also a steel (rather than carbon fibre) frame so that it can be repaired on the road. Here are some types of bike to consider.

Gravel

The terminology is a little misleading but these are great do-it-all bikes (below). They have drop handlebars, giving the option of multiple hand positions, but a slightly more upright stance for comfort. Most can take a wide range of tyre widths so you can change according to whether you're riding mostly on or off-road. Suspension is a rare

option, but they'll generally have a wide range of gears, powerful disc brakes and be able to carry lots of bags. They're a good all-round choice but will be out of their depth on very rough tracks.

Mountain

Mountain bikes, like the example on the left-hand page, are the ultimate in all-terrain transport. Broad, flat handlebars provide stability and space for mounting bags. Knobbly tyres, up to 3" wide, give grip and cushion off the road. And ultra-low gearing helps the bike to be pedalled up hills. Many models have suspension at the front (hardtails) or front and rear (full suspension) but it's not necessarily preferred by bikepackers. They're also very robust, especially when made from metal rather than carbon. The trade-off is all the extra weight to pedal around and the fact that they'll be slower on smoother surfaces.

Touring

The traditional choice is the touring bicycle (above), which may have drop or flat handlebars, smoother tyres and mounts for panniers. Largely superseded by gravel bikes today, they're an elegant and comfortable choice for speedy progress if you're riding mainly on surfaced roads.

About this book

Many people contributed to the *Bikepackers' Guide to the World* and you can read about them in the Acknowledgements on page 303. Their efforts resulted in a collection of more than 75 cycling routes (some of which the contributors crafted themselves through many miles of trial and error).

We've scored each route out of five, one being relatively easy and five being for experts. Factors such as the isolation of the location; the facilities and supplies you might find (or not) on the route; the type of terrain and riding surface; dangers such as altitude, climate and wild animals; and the experience required for the trip were taken into account. Several routes rated one or two follow rivers or rail trails with little elevation gain, or gravel bike paths, and take in towns, villages and cities in which to rest and recover. Moving up to routes rated two or three and you might find more rugged terrain, fewer settlements for supplies, and more physically arduous stages. And routes with a score of four or five offer an extremely challenging experience and require careful preparation. Find a table of the routes and their ratings on page 301.

It's sensible to start with easier trips and gain experience and skills before moving on to harder challenges. But the beauty of independent bikepacking is that the learning curve is steep, so you will surprise yourself with what you can accomplish quite quickly.

We hope to help novices not only with the ratings but also by suggesting ways of getting to and from the start and end of each route (often the biggest headache), and hazards to consider. Almost every route in this book has an online presence, often with downloadable maps for navigation devices. The most comprehensive resource for researching a route is bikepacking.com, where an active community can offer advice and updates on current trail conditions.

Contents

Africa, Asia, Oceania

Atlas Mountain Race (Morocco)   12

Bikamino (South Africa)   18

Congo Nile Trail (Rwanda)   22

Lesotho Traverse (Lesotho)   26

The Bartang Valley (Tajikistan)   30

The Border Roads (Tibetan Sichuan)   36

The Kazakh Corner (Kazakhstan)   42

Shiretoko Loop (Japan)   46

Goldfields Track (Australia)   52

Alps 2 Ocean (New Zealand)   58

The Mawson Trail (Australia)   62

Attack of the Buns (Australia)   68

Kahurangi 500 (New Zealand)   72

Hunt 1000 (Australia)   78

Tour Aotearoa (New Zealand)   84

Munda Biddi (Australia)   90

Murray to the Mountains (Australia)   96

St James Trail (New Zealand)   100

Tasmanian Trail (Australia)   104

Tour D'Top End (Australia)   110

More to ride   116

➜ Distance: 720 miles (1159km)   ➜ Ascent: 54,350ft (16,566m)   ➜ Difficulty: 5

Atlas Mountain Race

Morocco

Morocco's Atlas Mountains are both an accessible introduction to Africa and an extreme environment punctuated by oases. Pedalling (and pushing) from Marrakesh to Agadir through the southern part of the range is a risk-filled challenge that's not to be undertaken lightly.

Plan and Prepare

Logistics

The start of the route in Marrakesh can be reached by flights from cities around the world. You can also travel overland: ferries from Spain and Gibraltar arrive at Tangier, from where there are ONCF rail services to Casablanca, sometimes on Africa's first high-speed trains (2-4hr); at Casablanca, you change for Marrakesh (3hr). In the south of Morocco, transport is less convenient and you may want to hire a car to return north.

Hazards

Multiple risks are present, and wilderness experience is vital. Dehydration and sunstroke are very real possibilities. Navigational failures or being unable to fix a mechanical problem can leave you stuck far from help, and there can be big distances between villages. Surfaces are mostly uneven, to the extent of having to push your bike. Days are very hot and nights very cold.

Gear

This is a rugged route, so a 29er hardtail mountain bike would offer the best combination of features, including front suspension, stable handling and wider, tougher tyres to minimise the risk of punctures. You'll need to carry as much water as possible: at least two water bottles plus a bladder, and a water purification system (you'll mainly be topping up from towns and villages).

Info

The Atlas Mountain Race (atlasmountainrace.cc) takes place in February due to the cooler daytime temperatures – although nights can drop below 32°F (0°C). From May the temperatures are searing hot and don't cool down until November.

A few of the routes in this book are derived from bikepacking or ultra-endurance bike races – and this is probably the toughest of these. Designed by the creators of the Silk Road Mountain Race through mountainous Kyrgyzstan, the Atlas Mountain Race invites the world's hardiest bikepackers to tackle a large swathe of Morocco's southern Atlas, racing south from Marrakesh through dry and deserted mountains to the coast at Agadir via a handful of towns and villages, including rock-climbing hotspot Tafraoute and other oases. The region is a heartland of the Berber people, many of whom still live in these mountains herding livestock between pastures, and who never underestimate their harsh conditions: a local saying is 'where there is water there is life'.

The landscape of shattered rock intimidates, but every once in a while a village around a water source appears, the green of the trees a shock against the rust-red cliffs. The race route follows historic (and now disused) colonial gravel roads that have eroded into rubble and sand in places. The going is tough, so much so that out of the 190 starters of the inaugural race in 2020, only 130 finished. Among the competitors, the winner completed the route in about four days but many aim for six or eight days, which is still at least 93 miles (150km) per day up and down steep tracks. But without the pressure of a ticking clock, a slower pace allows for more appreciation of this remarkable place and its people.

Marrakesh to the Atlas

Pedalling southeast out of the bedlam that is Marrakesh, it's not long before the car horns fade and the route starts to climb. It's uphill all the way into the mountains; after 31-43 miles (50-70km), valley towns such as Tidili Mesfioua and Tighedouine promise waterfalls, food and accommodation.

This is now the Atlas range for real: after about 72 miles (116km) the climb to one of the highest spots tops out at 8200ft (2500m), high enough to feel shortness of breath. Many of the racers will be pushing their laden bikes at this point. The next highlight is historic: the evocative, now-abandoned kasbah of Telouet (right), once home to one of Morocco's most powerful pasha families. Based at a trading crossroads frequented by merchant caravans, the El Glaoui family gained great wealth and influence, but overplayed their hand when Moroccan independence dawned in the 1950s.

The route now continues east, deeper into the mountains, ignoring the turn-off into the Ounila Valley and Aït Ben Haddou. Passing another kasbah, Toundoute, the rough path eventually meets the N10 main road.

Deeper & higher

For the arduous 60 miles (97km) between Imassine and Afra, the route is truly remote and racers have to be self-sufficient; the reward is a sense of solitude and heady views across a high mountain plateau. At Afra, another intersection with a main road and about 217 miles (350km) from the start point, the trail turns west and the gradients level off a little. The riding surface ranges from tarmac to sand. The town of Tazenakht, famed for its woven rugs, is one of the busier settlements on the route and an opportunity for racers to resupply before heading off into the mountains again, for 106 miles (170km) of tough riding on both surfaced and unsurfaced roads until the oasis village of Aguinane. Of several small settlements passed along the way, Aguinane is the most spectacular, a cluster of palm trees sandwiched between rock cliffs. The difficult descent to the valley floor here is a precursor to the coming challenges.

A Berber heartland

Each year, as the Sahara seasons change, Berber nomads pack their camels, gather their families (and their flocks of sheep) and begin the trek to the higher Atlas pastures. Although a majority of Moroccans identify as Berber and a quarter speak the Berber language, this nomadic way of life is vanishing fast. Most Berbers now live in urban areas, though the Atlas Mountains remain their cultural stronghold. And life is getting tougher for nomadic Berbers: not only are Sahara borders with countries such as Algeria and Libya becoming more tightly controlled, despite the ever-shifting sands, but water sources such as rivers and oases are drying up as the climate changes.

Toward Tafraoute

The route now turns towards the coast, following an undulating and mostly unpaved road that ascends to 5742ft (1750m); the only road to be crossed is the P1805 to Igherm. In this largely uninhabited mountain landscape, far from help, water and food, the riding becomes more challenging; about 47 miles (75km) from Aguinane, the tiny Berber village of Ibn Yacoub is a welcome sight. About 109 miles (175km) from Aguinane, immediately after a treacherous climb and descent, Issafn is a small town with shops, cafes and a bus service to Agadir (if an escape route is required). The stretch to the next major settlement is similarly hard and hazardous, covering two huge climbs of up to 6000ft (1829m) over a mostly unpaved 95 miles (153km). There is a shortcut via a marked road off to the right, via Ifsfass and Tazalaght, but it's still an arduous journey. But with the goal of Tafraoute ahead, spirits will rise.

With its quartzite cliffs and granite boulders, Tafraoute (top left) has long been a base for Atlas adventures, attracting climbers like Joe Brown and Chris Bonington. The town has developed to meet the needs of incomers and offers accommodation from campsites to chic homestays. Calories can be replaced with plates of home-cooked couscous with lamb, prunes and vegetables, or bowls of nutritious harira soup. But for racers, the final 100-mile (161km) stretch to Agadir (lower left) beckons.

To the coast

The good news is that there's more tarmac on this last leg and more descent than ascent. Rock fields are replaced by vast plots of vegetables destined for European supermarkets. But there are still sneaky tricks to watch out for, such as long sandy stretches. But once at Agadir, riders can sink their toes into the sand of the 5-mile (8km) Plage d'Agadir and toast their epic journey through Morocco's Atlas.

Atlas Mountain Race

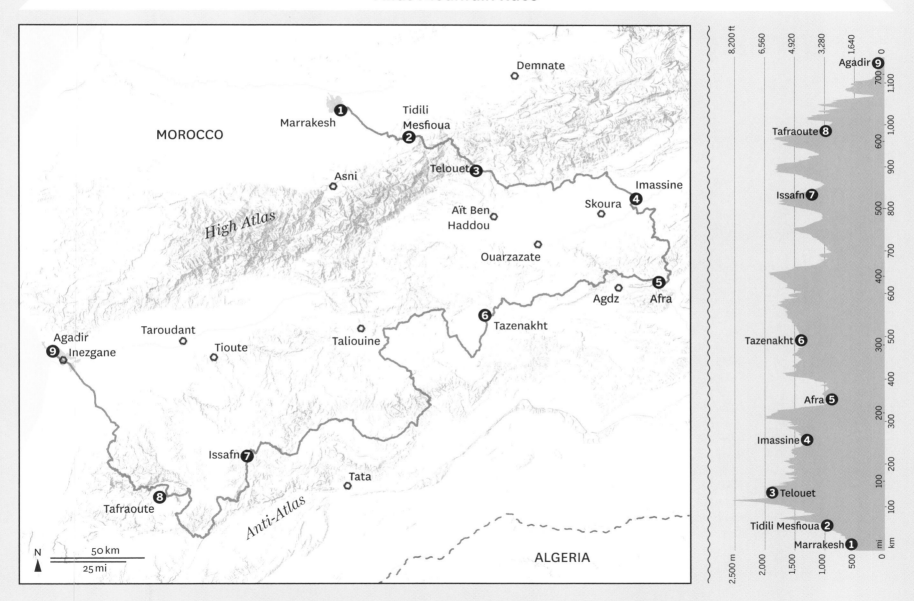

MOROCCO

Demnate

Marrakesh ❶

Tidili
Mesfioua ❷

Telouet ❸

Asni

High Atlas

Aït Ben
Haddou

Imassine
❹

Skoura

Ouarzazate

Agdz

Afra ❺

Tazenakht ❻

Taroudant

Tioute

Taliouine

Agadir ❾
Inezgane

Issafn ❼

Tata

Tafraoute ❽

Anti-Atlas

ALGERIA

N

50 km
25 mi

8,200 ft
6,560
4,920
3,280
1,640
0

Agadir ❾

Tafraoute ❽

Issafn ❼

Tazenakht ❻

Afra ❺

Imassine ❹

Telouet ❸

Tidili Mesfioua ❷

Marrakesh ❶

2,500 m
2,000
1,500
1,000
500
0

700
1,100
1,000
600
900
500
800
400
700
600
500
300
400
200
300
100
100
0 mi
0 km

→ Distance: 294 miles (473km)   → Ascent: 19,400ft (5913m)   → Difficulty: 3

Bikamino

South Africa

Tour South Africa's overlooked and sparsely populated Namaqualand for endless gravel trails, nights under the stars, cold surfing in the Atlantic and, if you time your trip right, a taste of South Africa's Wildflower Route in bloom. You can be as self-sufficient as you please.

Plan and Prepare

Logistics

The loop starts in the Northern Cape at O'kiep, about 355 miles (570km) from Cape Town, the nearest international transport hub (it's almost as close to Windhoek, Namibia). Buses travel this route via Springbok (you may need a taxi from Springbok), but your bike will need to be packed and boxed.

Hazards

Namaqualand is generally safe, but there are a couple of varieties of dangerous snake to watch out for: cobras and adders. Even if the weather is cool, the sun is very strong so protect your skin with long, loose sleeves and high-factor sunscreen. Traffic levels are low but mining vehicles tend to travel very fast on the deserted roads, so be aware of their presence. There's no phone coverage for most of the route.

Gear

The route is suitable for a gravel bike (if kitted out as robustly as possible) or a mountain bike. It's cold at night and some places are far from settlements, so carry adequate survival gear including a tent and sleeping bag as well as a stove, food and water. Make sure you can fix punctures and other basic mechanical problems.

Info

The route was developed by Open Africa, a rural tourism enterprise, in conjunction with event organisers EcoBound, who can offer supported trips; see bikamino.com for details. Avoid travelling during the southern hemisphere's summer months (December to February). The wildflowers bloom in early spring, around August and September, but remember that temperatures will be chilly at this time of year.

Come August and the veld of Namaqualand, in South Africa's Northern Cape, begins to be speckled with colour. It's wildflower season, and with the coming of the spring rains, some 3500 flower species, including warm-orange Namaqualand daisies, unfurl their petals for the brief but bright display that heralds the start of another year. There's no better way to immerse yourself in this sea of colour than on a bicycle, where all your senses are engaged. A pair of South African organisations have created a cycle tour of this little-visited region that loops through Namaqua National Park and along the Atlantic coast for several hundred miles.

The trail can be followed independently or with support, including food and accommodation, from the local operators. This is an exceptionally quiet region of South Africa, lying along the west coast near the Namibian border and a long way from anywhere. But the terrain is fairly easy going, with just one ascent that hits an elevation of 4400ft (1341m). Most riders will plan on taking 10 days or so for the full route although it's possible to cut it short if need be. Most of the route is on dirt roads and gravel, although there are a couple of long stretches along tarmac highways

To the coast

The trail starts in the former copper mining town of O'kiep, inland and just north of the regional hub of Springbok. Copper was first discovered here in 1855, making it South Africa's oldest mining town. In the early days, Cornish miners came over from Britain to work the pits. The mines are long since closed but the local geology is still interesting – just be wary of abandoned mine shafts if you explore off the beaten path. The route heads west to the Atlantic Ocean; Nigramoep makes a handy stopping point after 30 miles (48km).

© Jacques Marais

On the flower trail

Namaqua National Park isn't the only place in the area where you can see seasonal blooms. On the way up from Cape Town on the N7 highway, stop at the Hantam National Botanical Garden near Nieuwoudtville, which is known for its collecton of flowering bulbs (also known as geophytes), including the dazzling blue blooms of the Pride of Nieuwoudtville (*Geissorhiza splendidissima*). The gardens are equally beautiful in autumn, when the amaryllis burst into flower. Between the Botanical Gardens and Namaqua National Park, northwest of Garies, the Skilpad Wildflower Reserve at Kamieskroon blazes with orange and pink in spring. Lots of hiking trails lead into the wilderness.

Early on, you'll catch your first sight of the region's distinctive quiver trees; actually succulents, their branches were used by the San people as arrow quivers. The open landscapes are scrubby but spectacular: the deep canyon carved by the Schaap River is an early feature and entails a climb up to the Nigramoep farmstay, where you can stop and camp, or continue on. After the Kastelsberg Pass you'll join South Africa's longest gravel road between two towns. There's another long pass to conquer before you weave your way to the coast at Kleinsee, home to a De Beers diamond mine that was closed in 2011, causing the place to become something of a ghost town. Kleinsee is now on the 'Shipwrecks and Daisies' touring route, though the *malmokie* (sea mist) might mean that you don't see much.

From Kleinsee, around 105 miles (169km) from the start, the Bikamino turns inland (and uphill) to the Namaqua National Park.

Into the national park

The landscape starts off sandy but trees and shrubs eventually appear and the track keeps going upwards, with views over the hills as a reward. After about 55 miles (88km), you'll be deep in the national park and can spend the night at the Luiperdskloof safari lodge, which is perfect for stargazing. The route then bears back down towards the coast through the park. Surf (and seafood) beckon at Hondeklipbaai, where it's tempting to linger. From here, the route zigzags inland and back to the coast, but remains mostly flat and within the bounds of the national park all the way to the Groenriviermond campsite, although it's slow going on the sand. The birdlife here is exceptional. This is the most southerly point of the full route; the trail turns north up to Garies and then Kamieskroon, where it switches to a tarmacked highway for the last 45 miles (72km) back to O'kiep.

Bikamino

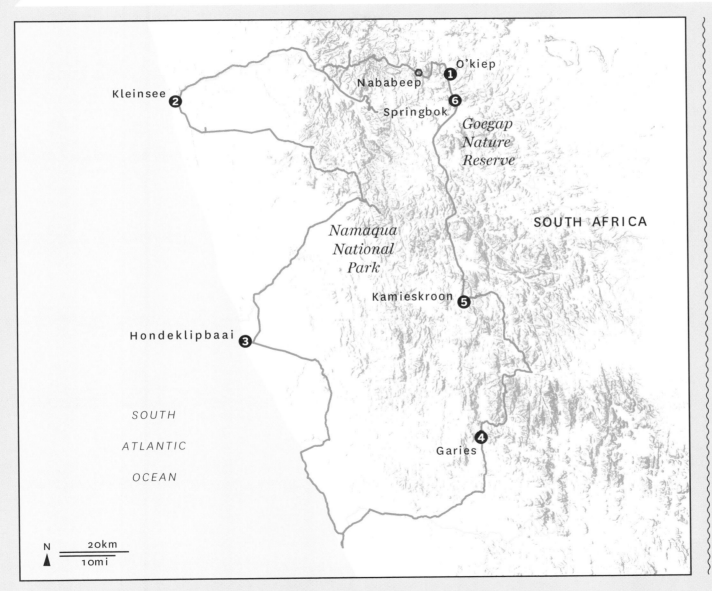

O'kiep **1**

Nababeep

Springbok **6**

*Goegap
Nature
Reserve*

Kleinsee **2**

*Namaqua
National
Park*

Kamieskroon **5**

SOUTH AFRICA

Hondeklipbaai **3**

SOUTH

ATLANTIC

OCEAN

Garies **4**

N
20km
10mi

4,593 ft 3,937 3,281 2,625 1,968 1,312 656 0

Springbok **6**

Kamieskroon **5**

Garies **4**

Hondeklipbaai **3**

Kleinsee **2**

O'kiep **1**

1,400 m 1,200 1,000 800 600 400 200 0

➡ Distance: 158 miles (255km)   ➡ Ascent: 19,100 ft (5822m)   ➡ Difficulty: 3

The Congo Nile Trail

Rwanda

Discover rural Rwanda on an official hiking or biking route along the shore of Lake Kivu on the country's western border. Accessible and easygoing, this is a great introduction to bikepacking in Africa.

Plan and Prepare

Logistics

The start point is Gisenyi, which lies right on the border with the Democratic Republic of the Congo about 95 miles (152km) from the capital, Kigali. Regular bus services will carry bicycles, but expect to pay extra if they're unboxed. Kamembe is the end of the trail and about 150 miles (241km) from Kigali, with regular bus connections and a ferry back to Gisenyi. There are also flights from Kigali to Gisenyi.

Hazards

Because the route borders the DRC, take note of current local advice on safety. Rwanda is typically secure, but travelling after dark on roads can be risky. Take the same precautions with your personal property as you would in any country. Mosquitoes are prevalent and malaria is present throughout Rwanda, so take the recommended malaria prophylaxis. Always purify water (against viruses and parasites) or drink bottled water.

Gear

The route is rideable on a gravel bike or mountain bike, with some sections now becoming paved. Tyre clearance for mud is recommended. And aim to be self-sufficient with puncture protection (whether or not you're running on tubeless tyres) as there are plenty of thorns. A complete tent is preferable to a bivvy. Also carry wet-weather gear and mosquito nets, plus your preferred cooking equipment.

Info

Avoid Rwanda's wet seasons (March to May and September to December), as some paths and roads will be impassable due to mud. Better options are mild but drier May and June, or during the northern hemisphere winter (December to February). Accommodation is in basic campsites or lodges; plan these ahead with a tour operator such as Rwandan Adventures in Kigali, where you can also rent bicycles. There's more info at visitrwanda.com and africanparks.org

Back in 2009, Rwanda's tourism board decided to encourage visitors to explore more of this beautiful country. So the Congo Nile Trail was designed, linking the dirt roads along the eastern shore of Lake Kivu, one of Africa's Great Lakes. The full trail, which extends south from Gisenyi to Kamembe at the foot of the lake, was intended for both hikers and cyclists. Hikers will clearly take longer than bikers (maybe 10 days as opposed to five), depending on how much of the trail is tackled, but both groups will appreciate the lush jungle scenery and lakeside life. Villages along the way (about a million Rwandans live near the lake) can provide food and other essentials. Accommodation is typically in designated paid-for camping spots that may not have any extra facilities.

Recently, the southern stretch of the route has been paved, allowing for more vehicular traffic, which puts some people off. Many hikers and bikers now stop at Kibuye (after 60 miles/96km), but the trip into Nyungwe Forest National Park will allow for some wildlife-spotting in the jungle.

Leaving Gisenyi

The northern half of the trail hugs the lake. Gisenyi is a large resort town but the rest of the settlements are typically fishing villages, with a fleet of boats pulled up on the shore. An introduced fish species, the sardine-like sambaza, is a staple of local restaurants and delicious after a day's ride, served deep-fried with a squeeze of lemon or spicy pili-pili sauce, and a chilled bottle of Mützig lager on the side. Dirt roads also pass through plantations of coffee and banana, the former crop often dried by the roadside and the latter's broad leaves offering welcome shade. Many riders aim to reach Kinunu on the first day, a ride of 26 miles (42km).

Lake Kivu

On the surface, Lake Kivu seems serene – but it hides a strange secret. It's one of Africa's deepest lakes and its location top of the East African tectonic rift means that there are hot springs at its base that discharge warm water filled with explosive gases that can't escape due to the lake's depth. The cooler water at the top is also less dense, meaning that it too can't circulate. But should a shift in the tectonic plates move the water, a quantity of dangerous gas could be released – which has happened before – poisoning surrounding villages. Scientists believe that it may be possible to extract the methane for energy and so reduce the risk of an eruption, though this hasn't yet been achieved.

On to Kibuye

Heading out of Kinunu, with the lake on your right, the red-dirt track starts to climb and descend steeply. Your destination is Kibuye, a well-developed town on the shore of the lake where many hikers and some bikers end their trip and take a taxi or bus back to Gisenyi. There's plenty of accommodation with gorgeous lake views, but first there's 40 miles (64km) to conquer (you can break the journey at Musasa if preferred). The tropical birds and trees – including wild guava, mango, avocado and pineapple – keep spirits high. You'll rarely be alone on the route, with kids walking to and from school and adults travelling from village to village. English and French are widely spoken, but a cheery *muraho* (hello) in the official language of Kinyarwanda is always reciprocated.

Into the highlands

After a lakeside rest at Kibuye (budget permitting – rooms in town are cheaper), the route turns inland through highland tea plantations to reach the Nyungwe Forest National Park, a dense and ancient forest. If you can spend some time here, you might spot some of the 13 primate species, 140 varieties of orchid or 332 bird species. There are also canopy walks (right) and waterfalls; if you're coming this far, it makes sense to purchase a permit and explore the park further. But the route for riders is tough, with an often-muddy surface and steep, slippery hills, fallen trees and more. Note too that there have been reports of armed groups of men at the forest entrances in recent years; check with local authorities and consider booking a guide and accommodation (Nyungwe is managed by African Parks). The high country hovers at an elevation above 6500ft (1980m), but you'll descend out of the park down to lake level at Ishara, before continuing on a tarmacked road to the endpoint at Kamembe.

The Congo Nile Trail

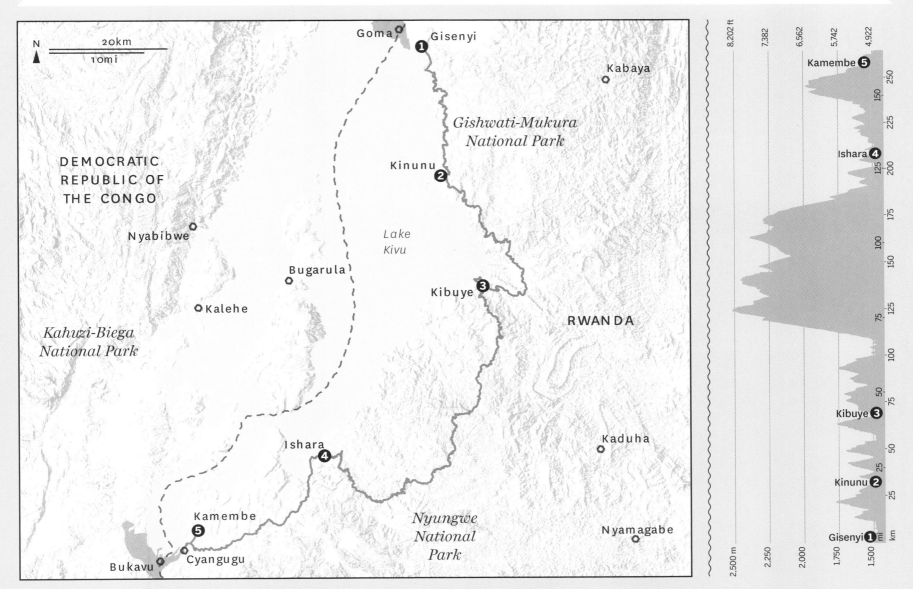

→ Distance: 311 miles (500km)   → Ascent: 44,000ft (13,411m)   → Difficulty: 4

Lesotho Traverse

Lesotho

Cross from side to side of the diminutive, oblong-shaped highland nation of Lesotho on a challenging but rewarding African route, taking in the spectacular Sani Pass, world-class waterfalls and mountain trails.

Plan and Prepare

Logistics

This route starts in Lesotho's capital, Maseru, on its western border with South Africa and served by daily flights from Johannesburg. The closest major city is South Africa's Bloemfontein, 95 miles (153km) west, with a bus service to Maseru (2-3hr). At the other end of the trail, over on Lesotho's eastern border, the Sani Pass descends east to the South African town of Underberg; from here, taxis cover the 2hr, 80-mile (129km) hop to Pietermaritzburg, from where buses run to Durban.

Hazards

There are few natural dangers in Lesotho, although venomous snakes are present. Malaria is not typically an issue but do check current advice. Altitude sickness is a possibility given the higher elevations. On the trails, mud can be a problem after heavy rainfall. Thunderstorms blow in regularly during the southern hemisphere's summer (December to March) and can be dangerous if you're in an exposed location.

Gear

A well-maintained and reliable bike is essential, given how far you are from assistance or obscure spare parts. A hardtail mountain bike is ideal. Ensure that you're able to carry plenty of water (perhaps with bar- or fork-mounted bottle cages). Tyres should be as puncture-resistant as you can manage – you'll encounter lots of thorns along the way, so carry spares and puncture-repair supplies whether you have tubeless or tubed tyres.

Info

Summers experience heavy rains so try to ride before December; spring starts in October. Alternatively, aim for autumn (April-May). Winter (June-September) is very cold and the days are shorter. There are high elevations so prepare for cold, windy and wet weather. There's little phone (or internet) coverage. Note too that you will likely be entering South Africa and Lesotho, so plan for visas accordingly – follow your country's travel advice. For more info, see visitlesotho.travel

It's not for nothing that Lesotho is known as the 'Mountain Kingdom'. The lowest place is at an elevation of 4593ft (1400m) and the land tilts all the way up to the highest point in southern Africa, the 11,424ft (3482m) Mt Thabana Ntlenyana (or 'beautiful little mountain' in the local language of Sesotho). This high-plateau nation is enclosed completely by South Africa – the chances are that you'll enter or exit via a South African city such as Bloemfontein to west or Durban to the east. Long the lands of African chiefs, the region was annexed by Britain in 1868 when threatened by Boer encroachment. Almost a century later, in 1966, Lesotho became independent. With a population of barely two million spread across an area the size of Belgium, this is a land of adventure that is also relatively accessible.

This traverse of the country, designed by Logan Watts of bikepacking.com and plotted in part by Darol Howes, co-founder of the Lesotho Sky mountain bike race, meanders across the nation from the capital via the mighty Maletsunyane waterfalls to the famous Sani Pass. There's no reason why you couldn't do it in reverse, if the logistics were preferable – there's more than enough ascent in either direction.

Towards the falls

As Lesotho's capital fades into your bike's rearview mirror, your goal is the marvellous Maletsunyane waterfall, which cascades for 630ft (192m) from a basalt ledge. It's a staggering sight but you'll likely take a couple of days to cover the 90 or so miles (145km) to get there. One possible place to stop is the town of Roma (the name refers to the Catholic mission here). It's set in a fertile valley, and traders still ride their horses into town. Alternatively, keep going until Ramabanta, about 60 miles (96km) into the journey.

Biking in Lesotho

Unlike much of Africa, Lesotho is very welcoming to cyclists and, with its abundance of dirt trails and steep slopes, has become a mountain-biking hotspot. The off-road Lesotho Sky stage race takes place over five days each September, with the support of local communities. The organisers also established the Sky League, a race series that promotes local cycling talent, and trains local guides who can help keen mountain bikers discover more of Lesotho's trail-laced landscape. One top route follows the Sani Valley's Mkozama River, beneath the pass. There are also great trails at Afriski in the Maluti Mountains to the north, Lesotho's only ski resort and another business supporting sustainable tourism.

From here on, the route starts ascending more dramatically until you reach Semonkong (the 'Place of Smoke') in the Thaba Putsoa or Blue Mountains. The settlement is named for the spray that rises from one of Africa's highest waterfalls, Maletsunyane (left). Anywhere else in the world and the falls would be mobbed by sightseers but, arriving by bicycle, you might have it to yourself. From here the route dives deeper into the interior of the country on mostly dirt roads: only a couple of thousand miles of roads are paved in Lesotho (similarly, of the 28 airstrips, three are tarmacked). Elevations touch 9750ft (2972m) so expect shortness of breath and some chilly nights – lodging in hostels is possible at points along the route. The trail descends to a still-high 7000ft (2134m) as you pass through tiny, one-shop villages. Most of the Basotho people are farmers and herders leading a virtually self-sufficient lifestyle, with their cattle, sheep and horses gathered around conical-roofed homes.

Up to the Sani Pass

After a few more days on the road, the route lines up for the Sani Pass. There's long been talk of tarmacking this ribbon dirt that weaves upwards to the South African border, and plans look like they may soon proceed. But for now it's a challenging gravel track that demands a 4WD – or quads of steel and plenty of perseverance if you're pedalling up. In adverse weather and after land slips it can verge on impassable. The average gradient is relaxed, but gets to 25% in places. Once at the top you can rest at the highest pub in Africa, the excellent Sani Mountain Lodge, which straddles the border between South Africa and Lesotho and offers views over the jagged peaks of Unesco-listed uKhahlamba-Drakensberg Park. The road then descends for about 30 miles (48km) past mountains and lakes down to the South African town of Underberg.

Lesotho Traverse

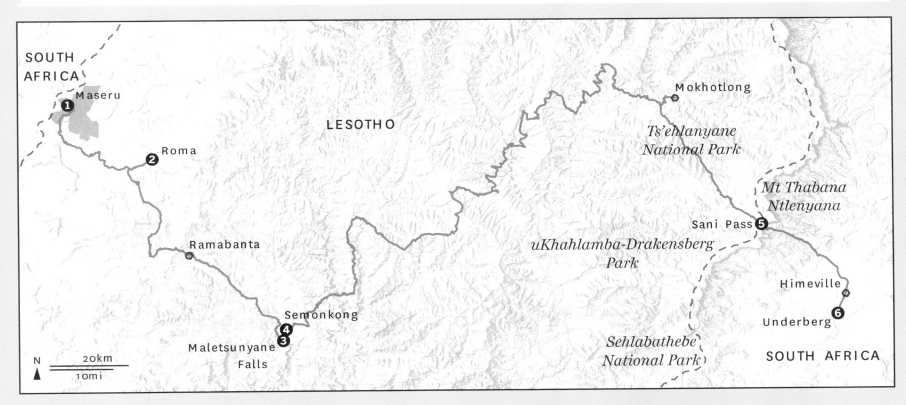

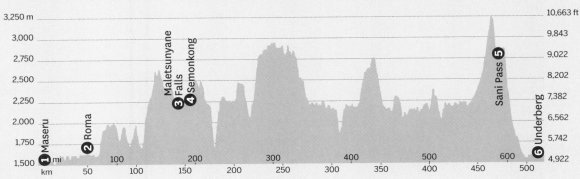

→ Distance: 258 miles (415km)   → Ascent: 21,114ft (6436m)   → Difficulty: 3

The Bartang Valley

Tajikistan

Tajikistan's Bartang Valley is the most adventurous way across the Pamir Mountains – if you can complete it. With high mountains, desert moonscapes, numerous water crossings and some of the planet's most far-out wild camping – plus legendary Bartangi hospitality – it's one for the bucket list.

Plan and Prepare

Logistics

Airport access is from Osh (Kyrgyzstan) and Dushanbe (Tajikistan). The route can be done in either direction, but is much easier east to west. It starts in the Kyrgyz border-town of Sary-Tash and ends at Rushon on the Pamir Hwy in Tajikistan, an easy 40 miles (64km) from the provincial capital of Khorog; take shared jeep taxis onward to Dushanbe, a very long, hard 300 miles (483km) away.

Hazards

With much of the route over 12,000ft (3658m), altitude sickness is a real concern. Take ample time to acclimatise. Water levels at crossings in the Bartang Valley itself are unpredictable and range from 'minor inconvenience' to 'serious danger'. Exercise caution, and ask about the conditions ahead when you can. Landslides are a regular danger in the valley, too, so be on your guard.

Gear

The fatter your tyres, the faster you'll be on the Bartang's rough road surfaces. Weather on the high Murghab Plateau is unpredictable; be prepared with adequate shelter and clothing. Clear water is available all along the route, but should be filtered or purified. Low-riding panniers will make life much harder at water crossings – consider a light, high-riding setup. Bring a battery pack for electronics.

Info

A Tajik e-visa and Gorno-Badakhshan Autonomous Oblast (GBAO) permit are required for the route; purchase online (at www.evisa.tj), and print out a copy once granted. Conditions in the Bartang are notoriously unpredictable. Even from July to August (the best time to attempt the route) snowmelt can result in serious flooding. The caravanistan.com forums are the best place for up-to-date information on current route conditions.

The Bartang Valley offers the best of Central Asia, with otherworldly landscapes, remote villages – and a dollop of danger to get the blood flowing. It's also a route where success is by no means guaranteed: gather as much up-to-date info as you can before departing, and be prepared to turn around if conditions get too dicey.

From no-man's land to the Murghab Plateau

The route begins in the tiny crossroads border-town of Sary-Tash in southern Kyrgyzstan. It's not the kind of place in which you'd be inclined to linger, but it's the best town on the route in which to organise supplies. From Sary-Tash, head 15 miles (24km) south on the M41 highway to the Kyrgyz border post at Bor-Döbö. Once you've been stamped out of the country (queues can take an hour or more), head off on the rough, beautiful road into no-man's land, which climbs 2700ft (823m) over 12 miles (19km) to the Kyzylart Pass, at a gasping 14,048ft (4282m).

From there, cruise downhill to the Mad-Max-looking Tajik border post. It was once known for scams and bribes, but of late seems to have cleaned up its act. Queues at the border can take an hour or more, but once that's done, you ride out on to the high, wild desert of the Murghab Plateau.

Located in the rainshadow of the Trans-Alai mountain range, the plateau has the look of a moonscape: barren, wind-whipped and an absolute pleasure to ride. The road proceeds on warped tarmac for 15 miles (24km), climbing gently to another pass, then descends to the sublime deep-blue of Lake Karakul (right), created by a massive meteorite impact sometime in the last five million years. A glorious lake vista opens up before you as you speed down into a mountain-ringed landscape of sand dunes and emptiness.

Into the wild

The tiny village at Karakul, 12 miles (19km) further on, feels like the end of the world: a handful of bombed-out-looking buildings and tangles of rusted metal beside an ethereal mountain-ringed lake. There's not much to do, but the atmosphere is sublime, and with a number of homestays it makes a good place to stop for the night.

From Karakul, the Pamir Hwy continues south; after 20 miles (32km), the trail leaves the road and turns southwest, following the scars of jeep tracks across the plateau. Roughly 15 miles (24km) further on, it joins and follows a stream for 12 miles (19km) to a prospective campsite. The trail then breaks west, then north, then west again across the desert, continuing through river crossings to the edge of the Murghab Plateau, where a huge, sublime vista of the Bartang River – and a steep switchback descent – await. There may (or may not) be local officials here selling $3 permits for Pamir National Park (through which the route passes), and they may (or may not) try to overcharge you.

The Bartang River Valley

'Bartang' translates as 'narrow passage', and for the next 120 miles (193km), the route follows the course of the river through a steep-walled canyon, losing nearly 6000ft (1829m) of elevation. This is where things get interesting. Though all crossings of the great Bartang River itself are bridged, there are dozens of side-stream crossings from here to the end of the valley, and the river itself may overflow the road in places.

Upon joining the river, follow the rough track gradually downhill for 20 miles (32km) to Khudara – the most remote inhabited village in the Bartang. Khudara has several family homestays, and makes a good place to stop for the night.

The Bartangi People

'The one who has not been to Bartang has not been to the Pamirs at all', wrote Russian traveller and scholar Pavel Luknizki in the 1930s. A road was only completed through the Bartang in the 1990s, but the Bartangi people have thrived in this gorgeous but hostile landscape for a thousand years, irrigating the dry brown uplands with snowmelt to build isolated green oases. They're also famously hospitable, and cycling through the Bartang, you're likely to receive many invitations to tea from local people. Though the various Bartangi dialects are often mutually unintelligible, Russian is the lingua franca here, and learning a few words will go a long way – as well as delighting your hosts.

Deeper into the valley

From here, the road closely follows the course of the river, the wild canyonlands punctuated by occasional climbs and dotted with oasis villages. Depending on conditions, the road may be blocked by landslides (you'll need to carry your bike over, if you can) or flooded at its margins by the high water of the river itself, which at the time of writing reached over 3ft (1m) deep in places. You'll also want to keep your wits about you when riding, as from the edge of the road it's often a long, unprotected drop to the raging waters below.

Any of the villages that you pass will likely have a family homestay where you can stop for a meal and find a bed for the night, but the large village of Basid, 30 miles (48km) downriver from Khudara, makes a worthy goal. It's past the biggest climb in the valley, a long, sharp, winding detour of more than 1000ft (305m), and boasts excellent homestays and even mobile phone reception.

The home stretch

As you gently descend into the lower reaches of the Bartang Valley, the quality of the infrastructure improves, though the river may still be over the road in places. Nonetheless the big climbs are over, and with the exception of a few stretches of wading, it's largely smooth sailing to the mouth of the valley 30 miles (48km) below. You rejoin the M41 Pamir Hwy at the market town of Rushon, 1.25 miles (2km) below where you left it four days earlier. From here, you can continue your adventures cycling other popular routes around the Pamir Hwy (including the Wakhan Corridor on the Afghan border), or else ride to Khorog, a few hours away, to catch a jeep onward to Dushanbe or back to Kyrgyzstan.

The Bartang Valley

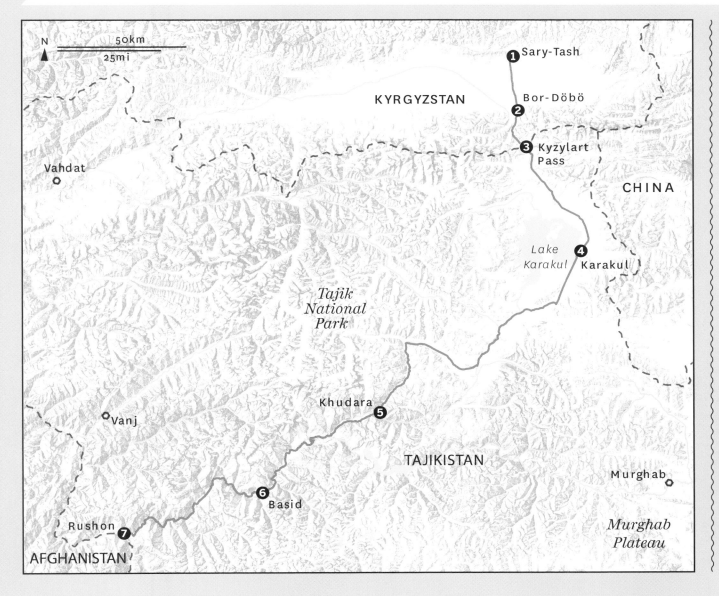

N
50km
25mi

KYRGYZSTAN

① Sary-Tash

② Bor-Döbö

③ Kyzylart Pass

Vahdat

CHINA

Lake Karakul

④ Karakul

Tajik National Park

Khudara **⑤**

Vanj

TAJIKISTAN

Murghab

⑥ Basid

Rushon **⑦**

Murghab Plateau

AFGHANISTAN

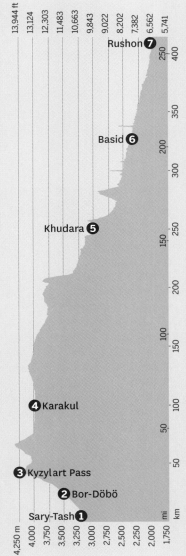

13,944 ft
13,124
12,303
11,483
10,663
9,843
9,022
8,202
7,382
6,562
5,741

Rushon **⑦**

Basid **⑥**

Khudara **⑤**

④ Karakul

③ Kyzylart Pass

② Bor-Döbö

Sary-Tash **①**

4,250 m
4,000
3,750
3,500
3,250
3,000
2,750
2,500
2,250
2,000
1,750

→ Distance: 269 miles (433km) → Ascent: 31,624ft (9369m) → Difficulty: 3-4

The Border Roads

Tibetan Sichuan, China

A remote, high-altitude dirt-road adventure through Tibet's Khampa heartland, with jaw-dropping mountain scenery, gilded Buddhist temples and the chance to experience genuine Tibetan culture away from China's big cities. Come for the 16,000ft (4877m) passes; stay for the momos.

Plan and Prepare

Logistics

Chengdu is the closest international airport, a two-day journey by bus (Chengdu-Kangding, then Kangding-Ganzi) from the start of the route at Ganzi. The city of Yushu, at the end of the route, has good domestic air connections to Chengdu, Xining, Lhasa and Xi'an.

Hazards

Altitude, weather and dogs. As the lowest point on the route is still nearly 11,000ft (3353m), altitude sickness can be a serious danger, and taking time to adequately acclimatise is crucial. Travelling through the high mountains can mean serious snowstorms at any time, in any season: be prepared. And Tibet's many free-roaming dogs are famously aggressive: keep a few rocks with you at all times with which to ward them off.

Gear

Most of the route is doable on high-volume gravel tyres or similar. The backcountry section through the Si Chu Valley, however, is best suited to 2.4in or wider tyres. Excellent wet/cold weather gear is crucial for comfort and safety. Satellite navigation (GPS or mobile phone) is necessary, as is a battery brick for charging devices. Google Translate is indispensable for communication; download the Chinese language pack for offline use.

Info

Most visitors to China will require a tourist visa – check requirements and application procedures for your home country. Sichuan's mountain passes are generally open between May and October, but may be snowed in at the beginning or end of that period. Clear-flowing water is widely available, but should be purified. Accommodation is available in Ganzi, Manigango and Yushu; supplies can be purchased there and in the market town of Luoxu.

Though most people think of Tibet only as the Tibet Autonomous Region (TAR), the cultural, geographical and historical extent of Tibet is actually much larger, incorporating 25% of contemporary China's total land area. The Kham region of Tibet in particular is known as its most diverse, incorporating soaring snowcapped mountains, deep river gorges and lush valleys across large parts of Sichuan, Qinghai and Yunnan provinces. This superb route takes you through all of these environments, as well as through the incomparable Tibetan cultural surround: small villages and bustling market towns; maroon-robed monks and invitations to share butter tea; golden Buddhist temples; and more prayer flags and stupas than you can shake a stick at.

Over the Cho La Pass

The route begins in the buzzing market and monastery town of Ganzi (sometimes written Garzê or Kardze), gently climbing for 55 miles (88km) on the smooth tarmac of the G317 highway to the crossroads town of Manigango, which is the last bit of real civilisation you'll see for a few days. From Manigango the road breaks southwest past the gorgeous turquoise glacial lake of Yihun Lhatso, gradually climbing for 15 miles (24km) to a fork in the road. One way leads to a tunnel beneath the mountain; instead turn right on to the long set of dirt switchbacks climbing to the 16,000ft (4877m) Cho La Pass above.

The grade of the road isn't bad, but the weather (and heavy trucks) on the road to the pass are no joke, and it feels like quite an accomplishment to crest Cho La (right) hours later: your lungs burning, prayer flags fluttering in the wind, and a vista of sharp snowcapped mountains opening before you. Take a moment to appreciate the view, then lock in for a long, fast descent.

The Kham region

Though you've likely never heard of it, the region of Kham (known in Tibetan as Chushi Gangdruk – 'Four Rivers and Six Ranges') is one of three main areas of what is geographically, culturally and historically Tibet. Located on the eastern edge of the Tibetan Plateau, it's home to more than 35% of China's Tibetan population. Covering more than 350,000 sq miles (90,6500 sq km), it is also absolutely gigantic, encompassing not only large portions of Sichuan Province and the TAR, but significant sections of Yunnan, Qinghai and Gansu Provinces as well. Kham is known for its enormous geographical diversity, with high-altitude grasslands, sharp high mountains, dense evergreen forests and deep river gorges. Its people – the Khampa Tibetans – have also historically been known as the finest horsemen and fiercest warriors of Tibet, warring for more than a thousand years against not only various Chinese empires encroaching from the east and adventitious Tibetan rulers in Lhasa to the west, but extensively against each other as well, defending a huge patchwork of contentious independent kingdoms and chiefdoms. The region also boasts incredible cultural diversity, and is inhabited by more than a dozen culturally and linguistically distinct ethnic groups.

The Si Chu Valley

It's rumoured that the track through the Si Chu Valley is the remains of an ancient caravan route between Lhasa and Chengdu, but whatever its provenance, it now promises some of the sweetest bikepacking in Sichuan. While sparsely inhabited, much of the valley is also genuine backcountry, and you'll want a good satellite map to be sure you're on the right track. It's also worth making sure that you have adequate spares and tools in case of a mechanical issue.

From where the tarmac resumes at the bottom of the Cho La Pass it's another 20 miles (32km) of fun, easy swooping downhill through relentlessly picturesque hill country, dotted with small villages, temples and waterfalls, to the village of Khorlomdo with its gilded, ox-blood-red Sakya Buddhist monastery. A short distance later a small bridge leads across a stream and to an unmarked track leading hard north into the mouth of the Si Chu Valley. From here the dirt-track route travels north through more sparsely inhabited country. Continue for some 20 miles (32km), keeping to the western-side tracks running through the valley and crossing several streams along the way, until the track breaks northwest into a connecting valley (you'll need to have this clearly marked on your map, as the valley is nondescript and without signage). From here, the track grows extremely rough and disused, with multiple water crossings, climbing gradually before reaching a short, sharp slog to a pass at 14,700ft (4480m) roughly 5 miles (8km) later.

Chasing valley into valley

From here the route descends steeply down unprotected switchbacks into a long, narrow green valley, the land becoming inhabited once again as the road begins a more gradual descent past a handful of tiny settlements. Chasing the end of one valley into another, turn northwest on to County Rd X038 some 15 miles (24km) beyond the pass.

The route continues west by northwest on the X038, the road eventually rising to a winding track high up on a slope with spectacular views across a broad green valley below. After approximately 30 miles (48km) it descends to the busy little riverside market town of Luoxu, with restaurants and opportunities to resupply.

The River Road & onward to Yushu

From here the road closely follows the Jinsha River west on a sometimes hairy road cut directly into the cliffside above it. Almost 40 miles (64km) later it descends sharply to cross the deep river gorge on a narrow suspension bridge. Climbing past a monastery on the west bank, the track resumes, heading north for 10 miles (16km) high above the river. The road then turns west, climbing for 10 miles (16km) to a final pass at almost 14,000ft (4267m), then descends into a lovely broad valley bounded by high mountains to the north and south.

Some 15 miles (24km) later, prepare yourself for a shock as the track abruptly joins the broad, busy modern G214 highway. Twenty miles (32km) north along the highway you enter the city of Yushu (Tibetan name Gyêgu), sitting at 12,000ft (3658m) on the Tibetan Plateau's northeastern edge. With its sprawling hilltop monastery, this bustling crossroads metropolis is worthy place to explore while you rest at the end of the route.

The Border Roads

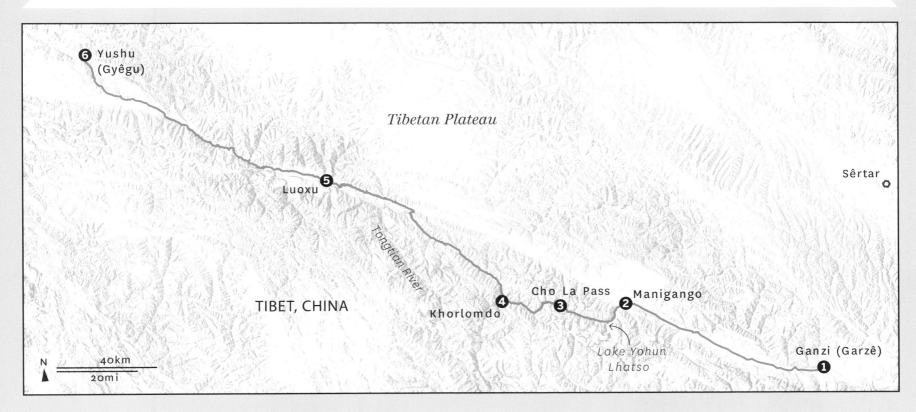

Yushu
(Gyêgu) **6**

Tibetan Plateau

Sêrtar

Luoxu **5**

Tongtian River

Cho La Pass

TIBET, CHINA

Khorlomdo **4**   **3**   Manigango **2**

*Lake Yohun
Lhatso*

Ganzi (Garzê)
1

N   40km
20mi

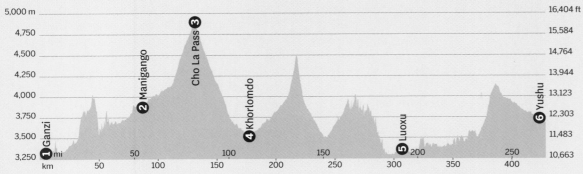

➡️ Distance: 137 miles (220km)   ➡️ Ascent: 10,873ft (3314m)   ➡️ Difficulty: 2-3

The Kazakh Corner

Kazakhstan

A superb short route in a country long overlooked, the Kazakh Corner boasts an incredibly diverse range of highlights – including high grasslands, wild river gorges, remote lakes and even its own miniature Grand Canyon – all with easy access from Almaty.

Plan and Prepare

Logistics

The route runs between Almaty in the west (with good air connections) and Charyn Canyon in the east, and can be ridden in either direction. If you're on a short schedule, take your bike in a taxi for the 3hr ride from Almaty to the start of the route at Charyn. The Kazakh Corner route also has easy overland links to other popular routes in Kyrgyzstan and China.

Hazards

Descents can be steep, loose and rough – exercise caution. Weather can change fast up on the high Assy Plateau, and there's often no shelter to be found. Good foul-weather gear is essential, but be prepared to hunker down if you get caught in a sudden storm. Traffic on the highway coming into Almaty can be hectic.

Gear

Tyres of 2in or wider will make life easier on much of the route (though you should still be prepared to walk some sections). Offline satellite maps are essential for navigation up on the Assy Plateau, where route-finding can be ambiguous.

Info

The Assy Plateau is often under heavy snow from October to April – riding the route in summer is the safest bet, though be aware that temperatures in Charyn Canyon can be scorching over this period. Accommodation is available in Almaty and Charyn Canyon, and you can provision in both of these places, as well as in the truck-stop towns of Kokpek and Turgen.

Though hardcore bikepackers could easily smash through this route in half the time, they'd only be cheating themselves. Each site here in the most diverse corner of Kazakhstan is spectacular, and time should be taken to appreciate the highlights – both on and off the bike.

The Valley of Castles

The route starts at one of Kazakhstan's best-kept secrets: the geological wonder of Charyn Canyon. It's a brutally steep descent into Valley of Castles, the most famous of Charyn's many canyons, and only 2.5 miles (4km) before the road dead-ends into the rushing white Charyn River, but you'll want to stay here at least one night.

Carved out of the surrounding clay steppe by river action over the last 12 million years, the Valley of Castles – with its towering, wind-eroded, Grand-Canyon-esque formations – punches far above its weight in terms of natural beauty. You could easily spend a full day on foot exploring its spires, ridges and side-canyons (with another day to explore nearby Temirlik, Uzunbulak and Bestamak canyons, if you have the time).

Onward to Bartogai

When you're ready, pack up and prepare for the steep climb out of the canyon and on to a mixture of gradually rising dirt and paved roads to the tiny town of Kokpek, 23 miles (37km) away. With its truck-stop restaurant and small shops it's a good place to provision for the following days.

From Kokpek, turn hard west across the open steppe for 11 miles (18km) until you reach the sky-blue waters of Bartogai Lake. A reservoir on the Chilik River, Bartogai is far from any development, as its crystal-clear waters attest. Swim, set up camp or soak in the serenity of its many small, sheltered pebble beaches.

© Matthew Crompton

The Assy Plateau

At 8500ft (2591m), the verdant upland valley of the Assy Plateau – a vast carpet of undulating green grass bounded by high snowcapped mountains – is one of the last places in Kazakhstan where the country's traditional herding lifestyles persist. While the yurt – the iconic round, felt-covered shepherds' tent – is most associated with the neighbouring nation of Kyrgyzstan, it's also a common sight on the Assy Plateau. As Kazakhstan's largest and most important *zhailau* (summer pasture), semi-nomadic herders decamp to the Assy Plateau each summer during the short grazing season, taking with them sheep, goats and horses in their thousands to fatten on the rich forage. *Kumis*, a beverage of sour, lightly fermented horse milk, is a staple that can be found anywhere that herders are – but be aware that it's an acquired taste. The Assy Plateau is also home to dozens of artefacts of the ancient Saka culture, whose occupation of the area dates back at least to the Bronze Age. Some of these petroglyphs, burial mounds and monument stones are marked on local maps, but more are regularly re-discovered.

Up, up & away

From the eastern edge of the lake the track runs for 4 miles (6km) around its margins before turning hard west on a long, hard climb of more than 3300ft (1006m) over 9 miles (14km), passing a freshwater spring as it enters a series of grassland valleys. At a junction the way turns west as it descends on a very rough track to the Assy River at Toraigyr, where petroglyphs hide among the eroded red-rock cliffs. Toraigyr makes an excellent sheltered campsite before the road resumes climbing again, high up along the valley wall above the river.

Five miles (8km) and 1640ft (500m) above Toraigyr, the track turns sharply and makes a short, sharp, rough descent onto the broad green Assy Plateau itself. Follow the crisscrossing jeep tracks west across the plateau for 20 miles (32km) to the junction with a gravel road at the Assy Pass, where a short detour leads to the colossal Soviet-era Assy-Turgen Astronomical Observatory.

What goes up...

From the pass it's 8 miles (13km) and 3000ft (914m) of rough descent, following the Assy River as it crashes steeply downward and eventually joins the Turgen River at Batan, where the road is paved once again. Follow the tarmac downhill for 15 miles (24km) alongside the roaring Turgen Gorge to the town of Turgen, with ample restaurants and resupply. After a cheeky wild-camp near Turgen, it's an easy 40-mile (64km) day on the highway to end at Almaty – Central Asia's most cosmopolitan city.

The Kazakh Corner

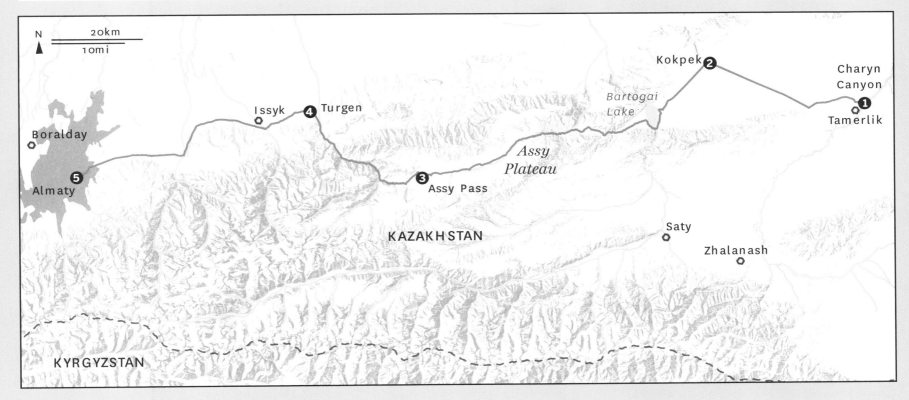

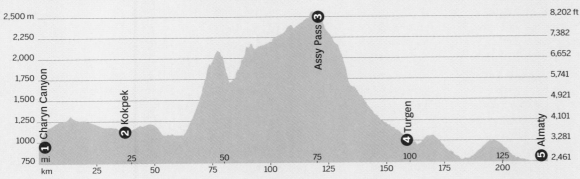

→ Distance: 217 miles (350km)   → Ascent: 13,450ft (4100m)   → Difficulty: 2

Shiretoko Loop

Japan

Explore Hokkaidō's eastern extent over a week or more on this mellow and accessible loop along the island's coast and through some of its volcanic national parks. You'll get to know some of Japan's indigenous culture and communities along the way.

Plan and Prepare

Logistics

This looping ride starts from the northeast city of Abashiri, which can be reached by direct Japan Railways Hokkaidō trains (www.jrhokkaido.co.jp) from the island's capital, Sapporo, in around 6hr. All trains in Japan will carry bikes, but you'll need to pack them compactly (by taking one or both wheels off) and cover them completely with a bike bag, box or perhaps a tarp.

Hazards

This corner of Hokkaidō has the island's highest concentration of brown bears, but you're extremely unlikely to encounter these shy animals; nonetheless, attach a bear bell to your bike as a precaution. More common hazards are giant Japanese hornets and ticks that can carry Lyme disease – take local advice on avoiding both. The climate in Hokkaidō can also be challenging, with very cold temperatures from November to April and rain at any time.

Gear

Much of the Shiretoko Loop is on tarmac, with a few gravel roads and bike paths present. A robust touring (or gravel) bike with fast-rolling tyres is ideal. Camping is an easy option on this route so if you're carrying a tent, mat and sleeping bags you'll need quite a lot of luggage capacity, using either panniers or frame bags. Water can be replenished relatively easily along the way.

Info

The route was developed by Rob and Haidee Thomson of HokkaidoWilds.org; there's more information about the loop on their website. The best time of year to ride is the peak of summer, in July and August, when temperatures in this northern region are at their warmest. Much of the route is flat so you could ride it in anything from three to nine days.

The northeastern tip of Japan's northern island of Hokkaidō is a place of forests, windswept beaches and fluffed-up red foxes. This tour is a relatively easygoing loop of the Shiretoko peninsula, taking in two national parks and some flat coastal riding. This area is one of the least-populated parts of Japan and the traditional home of the Ainu indigenous people. But that's not to say that this is an inaccessible region: the advantage of this ride is that a direct rail connection between Sapporo and Abashiri means visitors can bring their bicycle up here on Japan's famously accommodating trains (or rent a bike in the city). Most often ridden in a clockwise direction, the Shiretoko Loop could take up to seven days at a very leisurely pace, although fitter riders can do the distance in three days or thereabouts.

Towards Shiretoko

Exiting Abashiri is easy: from the train station simply keep the shore to your left as you pedal east. The road often has a cycle lane. You'll pass Lake Tōfutsu along a narrow spit of sand as the road curves around the bay. Then, as the urban landscape fades, watch out for a wild-bird sanctuary in the sand dunes and a wildflower park. Once you're on the peninsula itself, you'll enter the Shiretoko National Park (right) and the foliage grows green and thick. The road still hugs the coast, past a *kissaten* (cafe) where you can recharge with a strong coffee. A campground near Utoro offers a place to sleep, with friendly wild deer to keep you company. A long day in the saddle is soon soothed with a soak in an onsen. These hot springs are a regular fixture along the route but remember to wash yourself before sinking into one.

Hokkaidō's Ainu

The Ainu were the first people to settle on Hokkaidō or, as it is known to them, Ainu-Moshiri, 'Land of the Ainu'. For centuries they fished for salmon, hunted and foraged this formidable land, which froze solid in winter and steamed with volcanic energy. While mainland Japan went through dynasties, Hokkaidō was largely left as a trading post until more Japanese started colonising the island in the 19th century. The Ainu, as has happened to numerous indigenous peoples, were stripped of their fertile lands along the rivers and coasts and torn from their traditions, language and culture. This continued into the 20th century as researchers raided Ainu cemeteries to gather human remains that were never returned. In the 1970s, their story took another turn. Ainu people began to regain rights and finally, in April 2019, they were officially recognised as an indigenous people of Japan. The Ainu language, from which many of the place names on Hokkaidō derive, is becoming more widespread and shared. The name Shiretoko itself, means 'of the ground' – (*siri*) and 'protruding point' (*etuk*) in Ainu. The northeast region is rich in Ainu culture and the Akan-Mashū National Park has a visitor centre that hosts Ainu events.

Climbing into Shiretoko

From about the 50-mile (80km) mark the road turns away from the coast and uphill. But first you can take a short 18-mile (29km) detour to the Five Lakes area, where deer, foxes and (very elusive) bears abound. There are hiking trails around the lakes.

But the real work comes when you resume the ride up the Shiretoko Pass. From the top, you can spy Russia on a clear day but you earn the view with a steady climb (the gradient is always single digits) up a comfortably wide road through native forest and more open landscapes. The highest point, about 2445ft (745m), comes after some 9 miles (14km); to your left is Mt Rausu and you might catch the white Shiretoko violet blooming on its alpine slopes if you arrive early in summer (the show is usually over by mid-July). From here there's a fast and twisty descent to the town of Rausu on the other side of the peninsula. Here you can enjoy the free Kuma-no-yu hot spring, and there's also a campground in town

Coastline & cranes

Beyond Rausu, the ride changes pace again with a long, flat stretch along the coast towards Odaito, about 37 miles (60km) south. Fewer settlements mean fewer opportunities to stop for snacks, but you can watch the local fishing and kelp-harvesting from your saddle. There's another excellent campground in Odaito or you could carry on riding.

After checking out the Kuril Islands in the distance, it's time to ride inland from Odaito towards Nijibetsu via quiet backroads through low-lying dairy country. Among the cows, look out for tall, elegant red-crowned cranes; these iconic Hokkaidō birds frequent the fields around here, performing synchronised courtship dances during the icy months of February and March.

Nijibetsu itself is about 37 miles (60km) from Odaito. You can take a break here before heading into Akan-Mashū National Park.

Volcanic Akan

The landscape of the ride's second national park is the result of ancient tectonic turmoil, a reminder that Hokkaidō lies on the Pacific's Rim of Fire. Volcanic activity has dotted Akan-Mashū with hot-steam vents and several beautiful lakes to explore. Head first to Mashū-ko, set in a huge caldera and known to the Ainu as 'lake of the devil'. It's a stiff ascent up to the edge of its crater, from where you can look down over the lake's still waters. Formed relatively recently – about 32,000 years ago – Mashū-ko is one of Japan's deepest lakes. It's frequently shrouded in fog, so it's wise to check the weather forecast before setting off.

Your next destination is Kussharo-ko, where onsens and lakeside campgrounds make for a pleasant place to spend the night. Southwest on the shore of Akan-ko, Ainu Kotan is Hokkaidō's largest Ainu community; its theatre hosts Ainu dance performances, and restaurants serve traditional Ainu food such as venison and wild vegetables. Elsewhere in the park, explore bubbling mud pools at the Akan Kohan Eco-Museum, or climb the active volcano of Me-Akan-dake.

From Kussharo-ko it's another straightforward ride of around 40 miles (64km) back to Abashiri along roads that grow gradually busier.

Shiretoko Loop

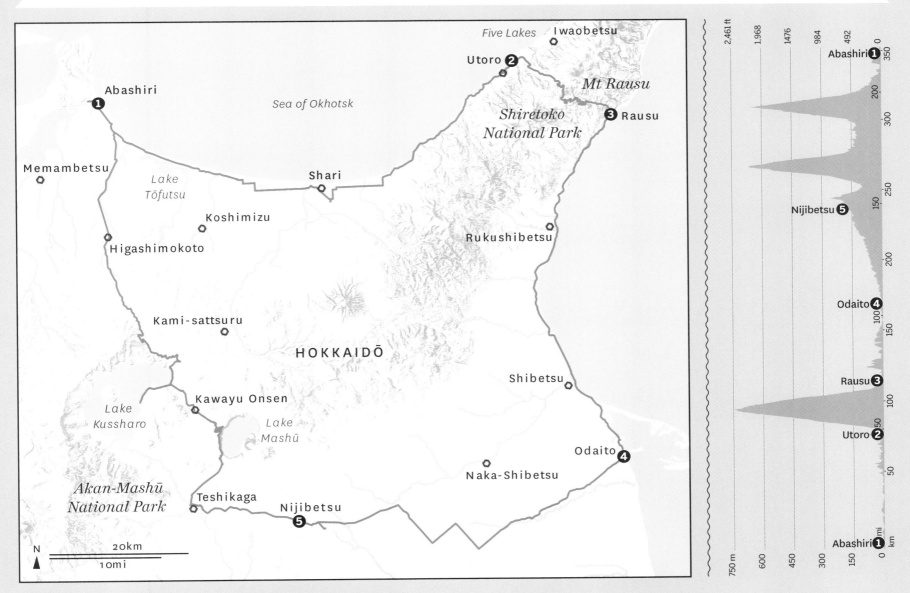

Five Lakes · Iwaobetsu

Utoro ❷

Mt Rausu

Shiretoko National Park

❸ Rausu

Sea of Okhotsk

Abashiri ❶

Memambetsu

Lake Tōfutsu

Shari

Koshimizu

Higashimokoto

Rukushibetsu

Kami-sattsuru

HOKKAIDŌ

Shibetsu

Kawayu Onsen

Lake Kussharo

Lake Mashū

Odaito ❹

Akan-Mashū National Park

Teshikaga

Nijibetsu ❺

Naka-Shibetsu

N

20km
10mi

2,461 ft · 1,968 · 1,476 · 984 · 492 · 0

Abashiri ❶ 350

300

200

Nijibetsu ❺ 250

150

Odaito ❹ 200

100

Rausu ❸ 150

Utoro ❷ 100

50

Abashiri ❶ 0 mi / 0 km

750 m · 600 · 450 · 300 · 150 · 0

→ Distance: 130 miles (210km)   → Ascent: 8250ft (2515m)   → Difficulty: 2

The Goldfields Track

Australia

Discover the legacy of Victoria's gold rush on this off-road ride that connects handsome country towns via quiet eucalypt-shaded tracks, farmland and forest. Delicious sustenance keeps you rolling.

Plan and Prepare

Logistics

The Goldfields Track runs between Ballarat and Bendigo, both easily reached from Melbourne by rail. It's usually no problem taking a bike on board the V/Line regional trains; travel at off-peak times to maximise your chances. Journey time to/from Melbourne is about 1.5hr to Ballarat and just over 2hr from Bendigo. At the end of the trail, it's worth staying another night in Bendigo to explore this regional city and its pubs before heading back to Melbourne.

Hazards

Snakes can be seen anywhere along the route, especially in spring. In some locations there are abandoned mine shafts, so take care if you're exploring off the track. The other main hazard is the sun – as always, protect yourself and carry lots of water. Bushfires are an ever-present threat during fire season so stay up-to-date on conditions.

Gear

Most of the route is on smooth dirt roads and hardpacked singletrack. A mountain bike is a safe choice, but the Goldfields is also possible on a gravel bike, ideally with wide and knobbly tyres. You can travel very light given the short distance, and the fact that food and accommodation are available on the route. A GPS unit is useful, but the maps on most smartphone apps are adequate.

Info

The two best seasons for the Goldfields are spring (September to November, when the yellow wattle is in blossom) and autumn (March onwards); both are neither too hot nor too wet. In theory the route is rideable during the summer, but be aware of overdoing it on the hottest days. Temperatures can be icy in winter on the higher stretches around Daylesford. There's lots of info and maps at goldfieldstrack.com.au.

Many of the Australian bikepacking routes presented here will appear arduous and require some experience and expertise. Not so the Goldfields Track. It's not easy but it is accessible, fun and fairly forgiving, making it an ideal route on which beginner bikepackers can practise the basics of navigation. You'll be riding between some of Victoria's biggest country towns and cities, places built upon the money generated by the gold trade. In the 1850s, gold fever hit the region west and north around Melbourne. Many people made the journey to Victoria and then trekked out to the goldfields in the hope of digging up their fortune. And, yes, many did: by 1860, Victoria's population had grown ten-fold to 540,000, and around 61 million oz (1.9 million kg) of gold had been unearthed here by 1896. Paths were formed across the goldfields and it's these tracks that we follow today. The Goldfields was initially a walking trail but there has been a push by regional government to encourage cyclists to use it too – thankfully so, because it's a great little adventure.

The full Goldfields Track is actually the sum total of four individual tracks end-to-end: the Eureka Track from Mt Buninyong to Creswick; the Wallaby Track from Creswick to Daylesford; the Dry Diggings Track from Daylesford to Castlemaine (right); and the Leanganook Track from Castlemaine to Bendigo. Most riders will break their journeys two or three times, for example at Daylesford and Castlemaine, depending on their schedule.

The Eureka section

Officially, the route starts (or ends) at Mt Buninyong, which is 12 miles (19km) outside Ballarat (but in the wrong direction). It's a famous climb up an ancient volcano for road cyclists, having hosted the national championships, but nobody would blame you for picking up the path from central Ballarat.

The story of the discovery of gold near Ballarat, in 1851, is told at the Sovereign Hill open-air museum (overleaf), a place that's probably familiar to every schoolchild in Victoria. The gold revenue and subsequent industrial growth of Ballarat (left) meant that many substantial homes and buildings were constructed in the city, most of which you can cruise around by bicycle today. In 1854, an armed rebellion against costly mining permits resulted in the Battle of Eureka Stockade, which lends its name to the first track, Eureka, on the Goldfields ride.

You'll pick up the track from train station and follow the Yarrowee River out of the northeast corner of town. Gold-tipped posts mark the route for the whole way (and are placed at almost every junction), but note that they can be hiding behind bushes or be placed out of sight lines so don't rely on them. The Eureka Track turns north and there are some stiff climbs early on, before you reach an area of plantation forest. The trails and the scenery improve as you get closer to Creswick, a small country town that has some big ambitions for becoming a mountain-biking trail hub, with the local community looking forward to the construction of many miles of purpose-built trails in the coming years. The twisty descent through open woodland into Creswick is a lot of fun.

Wallaby & Dry Diggings tracks

From Creswick, 15 miles (24km) from Ballarat, most riders will continue on (at least until the trail-building project concludes). Goldfields cyclists now switch onto the Wallaby Track, named by swagmen for the large numbers of swamp wallabies in these parts. The trail climbs up some straight gravel and bitumen roads through fertile farmland, enriched by the volcanic soils. Once you reach Wombat State Forest, there's an engaging stretch of riding en route to the spa town of Daylesford.

© Kevin Hellon / Shutterstock; Visit Victoria_Jochen Schlenker/robertharding / Getty Images

Daylesford

In a fortuitous twist of fate, Victoria's spa capital, Daylesford, and the adjoining town of Hepburn Springs, are about midway along the Goldfields Track and make for a refreshing place to stop. This is a volcanic area, about 2460ft (750m) above sea level. In fact, there could still be magma below the surface. Several million years ago, lava flows filled the valleys and where the basalt lava meets a fault, mineral springs bubble up, each with a different taste – Tipperary Spring is even fizzy. There are several bathhouses and spas in both towns and upscale hotels and restaurants have sprung up to meet demand. Daylesford is not a cheap place to stay, but there are holiday parks and campgrounds in the area.

If you missed Sailors Falls, 4 miles (6km) south of Daylesford, double back to take a look at the water tumbling over basalt columns and into a fern-filled gully. Then head on to Hepburn Springs (also a pleasant place to stay) and bear right to tackle some steep climbs before a descent to Chocolate Mill. Crossing the road, you'll pedal uphill for a bit before crossing Porcupine Ridge. The next section offers the Goldfields' most thrilling mountain biking, with rocks and roots galore. Take care on a laden bike; the echidnas (left) will scurry out of your way.

Eventually, you'll pop out at Castlemaine Diggings National Heritage Park which, as the name suggests, is an expansive mining area with several remnants of that period. It's also an opportunity to learn about the impact of the mining on the Dja Dja Wurrung Country and its Traditional Owners. Topsoil was removed, destroying ecosystems, and the mining also displaced Aboriginal people.

From the park, you'll pass historic Eureka Reef, once a mining settlement, then ride undulating tracks and roads to the Poverty Gully water race, which you follow into charming Castlemaine. This is another small town built on gold, with Australia's oldest continually operated theatre (built for the benefit of the miners), a steam railway to Maldon and, at the top end of town, botanical gardens and a creative complex that houses a brewery, cafes, shops and artisans in a former woollen mill. There are plenty of great places to eat in Castlemaine, such as Saffs Cafe, making it a good spot to spend the night.

The Leanganook to Bendingo

The last leg takes riders along the Leanganook to Bendigo (previous page), a straightforward ride of 36 miles (58km). You'll skirt Mt Alexander (the mountain-bike trails at Harcourt are fun), then meander down into Bendigo via Bendigo Regional Park, following more mining-era water channels.

The Goldfields Track

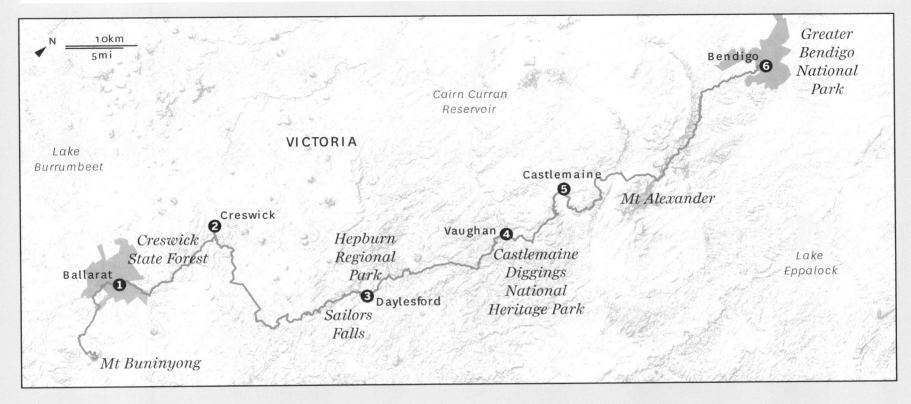

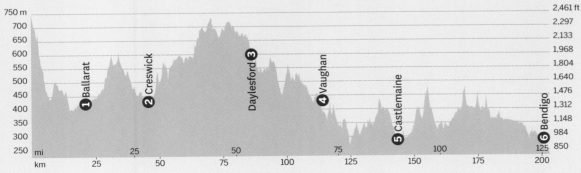

➜ **Distance: 200 miles (322km)**   ➜ **Ascent: 4650ft (1417m)**   ➜ **Difficulty: 2**

Alps 2 Ocean

New Zealand

Descend to the South Island's east coast from New Zealand's highest mountain, Aoraki/Mt Cook, on this relatively easy ride on graded gravel paths. With several settlements along the way and hot tubs to enjoy, this is a fun, beginner–friendly bikepacking trip.

Plan and Prepare

Logistics

Logically, the trail is best ridden from the high ground to the coast. This means starting at White Horse Hill Campground, just over a mile (2km) north of Aoraki/Mt Cook Village. There are usually buses to the village from Christchurch, Lake Tekapo and Queenstown, though operators such as InterCity require bikes to be dismantled. You will also need to take a helicopter across the Tasman River; starting from Lake Tekapo skips this step.

Hazards

New Zealand has no snakes or big predators – but it does have many small biting flies, so bring insect repellent. Other hazards are mainly unpredictable natural phenomena such as earthquakes or inclement weather (the latter is common on the South Island). Bring appropriate clothing for every season.

Gear

A gravel bike or mountain bike with gear-carrying capability would be ideal, but people have ridden the trail on anything from folding bikes to penny-farthings. There are plenty of accommodation options and places to eat on the route, so you don't need to carry a tent unless you prefer to camp and cook for yourself. E-bikes (up to a certain power) are also permitted and can be recharged overnight.

Info

The route's official website (alps2ocean.com) has stacks of helpful information, including food and accommodation recommendations and downloadable PDFs. Summer (December to February) and autumn (March to May) are the ideal times to ride, with wet weather a risk in spring (September to November) and snow being likely during winter (June to August). Remember that any weather can happen at any time on the South Island.

Kickstarting New Zealand's status as a cycling-touring destination, the first section of the Alps 2 Ocean cycle trail opened in 2013 and is being improved all the time. Fittingly, it runs from New Zealand's highest mountain – 12,218ft (3724m) Aoraki/Mt Cook, in the heart of New Zealand's Southern Alps – all the way to Oamaru on the east coast. It's one of the longest of New Zealand's 22 Great Rides but it's not one of the toughest, being graded either easy or intermediate. Although the Alps 2 Ocean starts in Aoraki/Mt Cook Village, the resort on the southern slope of snowcapped Aoraki/Mt Cook (right), the route takes riders mainly downhill to the coast via plentiful small towns, so you're never far from a bed or a filling breakfast. This means that it's a suitable trip for first-time bikepackers or casual cyclists; experienced riders may prefer more of a challenge.

The scenery soon compensates for the smooth-going cycling. With your back to Aoraki, which means 'cloud piercer' in Māori, you'll encounter wide, glaciated valleys peppered with the turquoise lakes that only New Zealand can deliver. The small farming towns on the route are always welcoming, and there are plenty of diversions to enjoy, including wine-tasting, stargazing, craft beer, hot tubs and penguin-watching. Helpfully, the route designers have divided the trail into nine sections and suggest taking four to six days to cover them all, depending on the time you have and your level of experience.

From the mountain

The start point is just north of Aoraki/Mt Cook Village but it's only 4 miles (6km) until you have to pack the bike on to a pre-booked helicopter for a lift over the Tasman River. Start from Lake Tekapo if you wish to give the chopper a miss.

Offbeat Oamaru

Home to some of the best-preserved Victorian architecture in the southern hemisphere, it's appropriate that Oamaru is also the world's capital of steampunk, the quirky movement that imagines how Victorians would have interpreted the modern world, blending fashion, technology and art into a vivid alternative reality. Oamaru's steampunk scene was started by Iain Clark, aka Agent Darling, who hosted an exhibition of sci-fi sculptures in 2010. The trend blossomed and there's now an annual festival, held in June. But the town itself is perhaps the most eye-opening attraction: Oamaru's Victorian Precinct has a stunning collection of buildings, dating from 1865 to 1885 and built from local limestone.

After pedalling along the eastern shore of Lake Pukaki, Twizel makes a good target for the night at around 45 miles (72km) from Aoraki/Mt Cook. The town is the hub for adventure activities in the Mackenzie Basin, as well as for stargazing. Since 2012, the region has been part of the Aoraki Mackenzie International Dark Sky Reserve (the largest such reserve in the world); guided stargazing trips are offered from Twizel and Lake Tekapo, where the University of Canterbury hosts astronomy experiences at the Mt John Observatory.

Continuing the ride, Omarama is the next major settlement, after a descent through meadows. A soak in outdoor cedar hot tubs is the reward here. The next leg takes riders into the Waitaki Valley, one of the world's most southerly wine regions. The scenery is more agricultural here, with several large lakes and dams promising a variety of watersports, including boating, fishing and swimming. Benmore is New Zealand's largest earthen dam and feeds the Waitaki hydroelectric power stations.

Wine time

Passing through tiny Otematata, continue to cheery Kurow, gateway to the Waitaki Valley Wine Region, with opportunities to taste the local Pinot Noir and Riesling at cellar doors or in town. Vines were only planted here in 2001 and, being so far south, the winemaking in Waitaki is a more precarious business than in other parts of New Zealand, but the results are fresh-tasting and interesting.

From Kurow, it's a ride of just 17 miles (27km) to Duntroon, then another 33 miles (53km) to the endpoint at Oamaru, a metropolis in comparison. The well-preserved historic town grew as a trading post thanks to its sheltered harbour. Today, it's buses that depart for Christchurch, taking about four hours. But first grab a beer at Craftwork, set in a handsome Victorian building.

Alps 2 Ocean

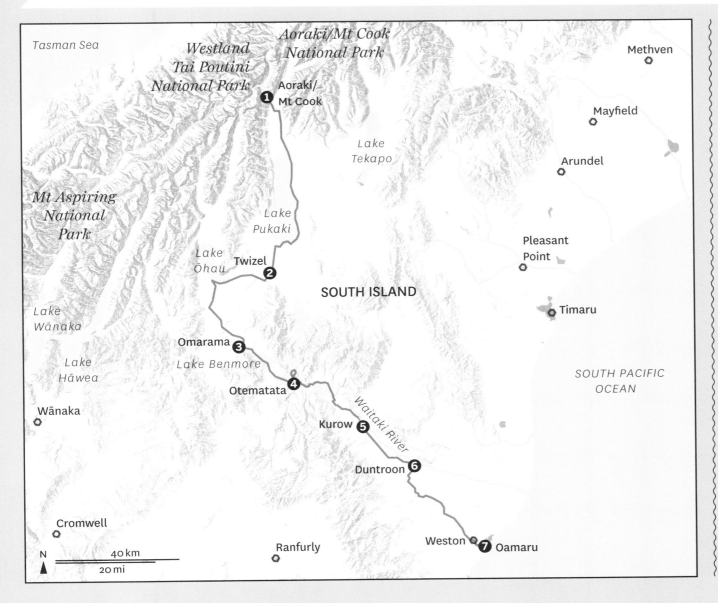

Tasman Sea

Westland
Tai Poutini
National Park

Aoraki/Mt Cook
National Park

Methven

Aoraki/
Mt Cook **1**

Mayfield

Lake
Tekapo

Arundel

Mt Aspiring
National
Park

Lake
Pukaki

Lake
Ōhau

Twizel **2**

SOUTH ISLAND

Pleasant
Point

Lake
Wānaka

Timaru

Lake
Hāwea

Omarama **3**

Lake Benmore

SOUTH PACIFIC
OCEAN

Otematata **4**

Wānaka

Waitaki River

Kurow **5**

Duntroon **6**

Cromwell

N

40 km

20 mi

Ranfurly

Weston **7** Oamaru

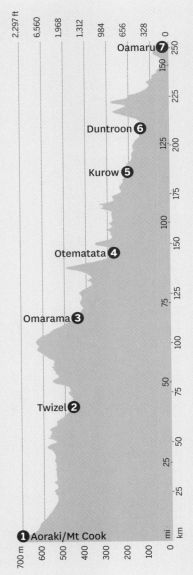

2,297 ft

6,560

1,968

1,312

984

656

328

0

Oamaru **7** 250

225

Duntroon **6** 200

175

Kurow **5** 150

Otematata **4** 125

Omarama **3** 100

75

50

Twizel **2** 25

1 Aoraki/Mt Cook mi km

700 m   600   500   400   300   200   100   0

→ Distance: 559 miles (900km)   → Ascent: 26,112ft (7959m)   → Difficulty: 4

The Mawson Trail

Australia

This dirt-track rollercoaster barrels deep into the outback from Adelaide, passing through the wine regions of Barossa and Clare before heading into the Flinders Range and South Australia's highest town, Blinman. It's a long and challenging ride but achievable with careful preparation.

Plan and Prepare

Logistics

The Mawson Trail stretches between Adelaide and Blinman. Adelaide can be reached by trains from Perth, Melbourne and Sydney (if slowly; book bicycle slots in advance) or by flights from many Australian towns and cities (check airline baggage costs). But it can make sense to start the ride from Blinman. On request, Genesis Transport provides a bus service from Adelaide to the trailhead near Parachilna; journey time is about 9hr.

Hazards

The usual Australian dangers from the sun, snakes and spiders are present. But add rain to the mix: when it hits the trail in certain places it creates deep, sticky mud that is soul-destroying and sometimes impassable. Check forecasts and ask ahead about conditions. Also check the forecast for the prevailing wind direction and decide where to start accordingly. During the Dry, the corrugations in some places can be a juddering experience.

Gear

The surface of the Mawson Trail doesn't typically require a mountain bike, although they get the job done. If it's muddy no bicycle will work. Generally, a gravel bike with tyres wider than 40mm will be fine, although select the widest and most puncture-resistant tyres possible, while retaining as much tyre clearance as you can. Don't take a pure road bike. Think about gearing – there are some steep pitches so low gears are recommended.

Info

The Australian summer from December to March is too hot. June, July and August (winter) sees the highest rainfalls (and resulting mud). So spring (September and November) or autumn (April and May) are best. Start in Gorge Rd, Athelstone, north of Adelaide, finish in Blinman – or vice versa. The trail is waymarked with posts at intersections, but GPS and a map are recommended. Maps are available from www.southaustraliantrails.com

Douglas Mawson was an Australian polar explorer best known for surviving a grim, blizzard-blighted trek on Antarctica's Cape Denison, during which dogs, team members and most of their food supply fell into a crevasse. Mawson was forced to ration out 10 days of supplies for a return journey that would take a month; they ended up eating their remaining dogs as they went. And further misfortunes struck: Mawson missed his ship back to Hobart and spent an extra year waiting on the ice for the next. Fortunately, few people suffer as much on a bike ride along the 559-mile (900km) Mawson Trail into the Flinders Ranges, but the route is a challenge for even strong cyclists. It extends north from Athelstone, a northeastern suburb of Adelaide, past Clare and Quorn, and into the Flinders. Note that the wind often blows strongly from the north here, so consider starting from Blinman and riding to Adelaide.

Surfaces throughout vary from 4WD tracks and gravel roads to a few stretches of singletrack or highways. With 559 miles (900km) to cover you can choose to break it down according to your fitness: most people aim for something between 30 miles (48km) and 60 miles (96km) per day (although the fastest known time is less than three days). There are stretches of around 50 miles (80km) between some settlements, so be aware of how much water and provisions you need to carry for each leg. Trails South Australia recommends a trip of around 13 segments (and provides maps for each), taking at least two weeks.

Wine & roads

From Athelstone, there's a rude shock to the system: a number of steep hills to climb as the trail heads up into the Adelaide Hills before turning north after 31 miles (50km) at Lobethal. You can break the journey here or continue into the Barossa Valley.

Press on from Tanunda in the Barossa towards Riverton. If it's been raining, there are plenty of roads on which to avoid the mud. The route becomes less built-up from now on as you enter farmland and pedal past beautiful gum trees. Surfaces range from potentially muddy tracks to gravel and a little bit of tarmac. You're steadily climbing towards Clare Valley (left), where some of the world's best Riesling wine is made. Riverton is a possible pitstop, or you could continue a further 28 miles (45km) into Clare itself along the Rattler Rail Trail, which offers some fast and smooth cycling. Clare is a great place to break the journey (as is Auburn), given the number of wine estates to explore, set down quiet tree-lined lanes.

Into the Outback

Continuing north out of Clare – frame bags bulging with provisions – the geology of the land starts to change and the vistas become vast. The trail switches in character every couple of hours so there's always something new to enjoy. Past Burra and Hallett, the gradient is best described as rolling, with windfarms hinting at a possible hindrance (although the route weaves around a little here so you may avoid a headwind). The Bundaleer irrigation channel is a useful navigational aid. You can pick up some more sustenance in the agricultural town of Spalding or stop in Laura, which has a range of accommodation and places to eat (Golden North ice cream is made here).

After whizzing through the Bundaleer and Wirrabara forests on either side of Laura, there are some steep climbs as the gravel track turns towards the town of Melrose, home to some of South Australia's best mountain-biking trails (and coffee). Melrose's annual Fat Tyre Festival takes place in June and there's some racing in September; you can explore trails around Mt Remarkable year-round.

Ikara-Flinders Ranges National Park

This 950-sq-km (370-sq-mile) reserve is a place of great significance to its Adnyamathanha Traditional Custodians, who co-manage the national park; their name means 'from the hills or rocks'. You can see Adnyamathanha rock paintings at Perawurtina Cultural Heritage Site; elsewhere in the park, a conservation program has seen populations of rare yellow-footed rock wallabies bounce back, for example in Brackina Gorge. The heart of the park is the rock amphitheatre of Ikara (Wilpena Pound; 'pound' was the settler name for stock enclosures, located here due to the water holes). Stroll along the Wilpena Creek, shaded by red gum trees.

Melrose makes another good base. From here, a recently restored rail trail from Melrose to Wilmington skips a less interesting stretch of the Mawson. Continuing to Quorn means covering more of the straight, flat roads that lead towards the Ranges. There are greater distances between settlements here, so plan your water and food supplies accordingly.

Flinders finally

From Hawker, the distinctive rock formations of the Flinders loom closer on the horizon before the red-dirt track begins to weave around them. The air is filled with the squawking sound of local birdlife, including more than a dozen species of parrots and cockatoos. It's a long ride (56 miles/90km) from Hawker to Rawnsley Park, but you can take a break at Rawnsley Park Station and its famous Woolshed restaurant. This is now national park country (lower left), and while there's some distance between facilities, there's a lot of tourist infrastructure.

An hour or two's ride from Rawnsley Park is Ikara/Wilpena. It's worth spending some time here (not least to take advantage of the telephone signal hereabouts). The trails en route are rougher, as they venture through scrubby pine forest and up to one of the Mawson's highlights, Razorback Lookout (opening page), which offers timeless views of dirt roads swooping beneath the ancient Flinders Ranges. Fossils discovered in these mountains, of creatures that lived in stromatolite reefs 550 million years ago, represent the earliest evidence of complex life on Earth. Since the warm seas of that period subsided, the Ranges have been steadily eroding.

This is the final push up to Blinman, where there's a pub serving cold beer. Nearby (a 20-mile/32km ride away along a wonderful dirt road), Parachilna offers more accommodation (including camping) and is the hub for transport back to Adelaide.

The Mawson Trail

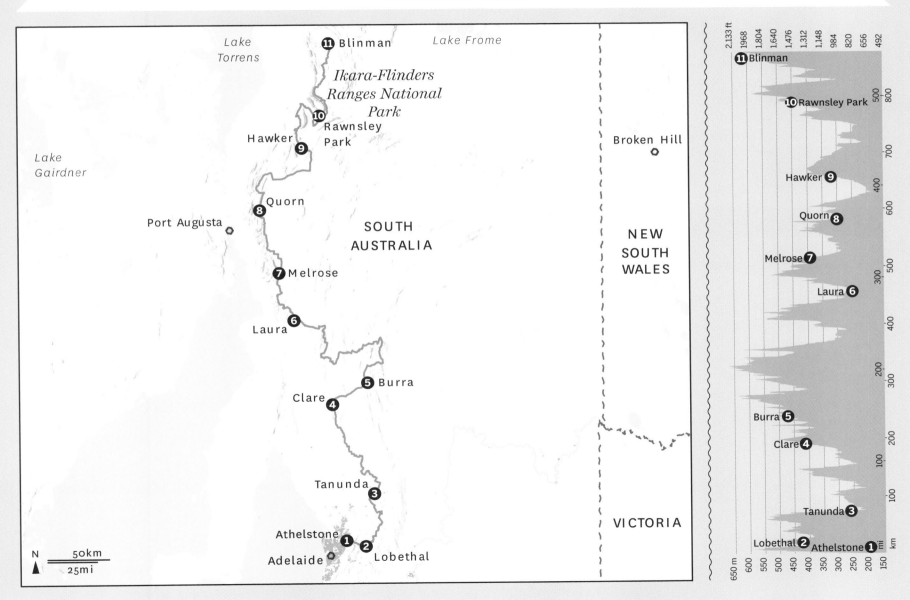

→ Distance: 200 miles (322km)   → Ascent: 15,395ft (4692m)   → Difficulty: 2

Attack of the Buns

Australia

Get back to nature for a few days in this underappreciated corner of New South Wales on the edge of Canberra. This easygoing ride takes quiet gravel tracks through enchanting forests and past the waterfalls and rock formations of the Southern Highlands.

Plan and Prepare

Logistics

The route begins from Bungendore, about 25 miles (40km) east of Canberra and reached by bus or train from Canberra's Kingston station. If using NSW TrainLink, note that bicycles must be boxed or in a bag, which could be a problem. Spaces are very limited and bikes must be booked in advance for a fee. The same is true of rail or bus links with Sydney and Canberra from the endpoint at Bundanoon.

Hazards

There's not a lot to worry about on this relatively mellow ride, aside from the typical Australian hazards of very venomous snakes and extremes of temperature. Bush fires and a couple of creek crossings are a couple of natural hazards to be aware of. Just be sure to practise your navigation skills, carry sufficient water and take note of fire warnings.

Gear

With trails that aren't especially technical and only a handful of steep hills, this route would suit gravel bikes and hardtail mountain bikes. More than half the route is off-road but typically on moderate gravel tracks. You may wish to carry camping gear, but there's plenty of accommodation along the way.

Info

Abundant camping options plus regular towns mean that the choice is yours in terms of how much camping and cooking kit to carry. The modest distance means that riders take anything from three to five days to complete the route. The most sensible months to ride are September to November (spring) and March to May (autumn). Winter can bring floods and summer dries up some water sources.

The centrepiece of the tiny Australian Capital Territory, Canberra is an unusually symmetrical city, radiating outwards from its parliament building. It's a city that was designed rather than evolved. But on its outskirts, the organic confusion of nature quickly takes over: stirring landscapes of open eucalypt woodlands, misty rainforest, rivers, waterfalls, gorges and plateaus. This is the lower edge of New South Wales, an area known as the Southern Tablelands, part of the Great Dividing Range that shapes so much of southeast Australia.

The Attack of the Buns route is a bike ride that wiggles its way north through this region from the outskirts of Canberra towards Sydney. It drops in on a number of country towns and rural cities as it passes through a couple of national parks, never gaining or losing any great elevation and never far from a comfortable campsite. That makes it an ideal trip for a long weekend of riding with buddies, away from the urban grind. But it's also a great trip for soloists and first-timers, being relatively safe.

The route was created by Adam Lee of Endless Cycle with the intention of sharing some of his beautiful backyard. It rewards those who make the effort to notice the natural world: listening out for the bird calls; watching water eddy around fallen tree trunks; meditating on the fresh green plant growth in fire-damaged landscapes.

Goodbye Canberra

From the town of Bungendore, which you may reach via alighting at its heritage-listed railway station (if so, be aware of New South Wales' famously cycle-unfriendly transport policies – see opposite), head south on Hoskinstown Rd. This takes you through agricultural land and into Tallaganda National Park, your first taste of eucalypt forest.

© Adam Lee

Morton National Park

Much of this route passes through Morton National Park, and it's a very special place to explore. It's perhaps best known for the waterfalls that plunge off its sandstone cliffs, as if sections of the landscape just dropped away; top falls to check out are Belmore and Fitzroy. Over an extra day or two, you can also explore the rivers that feed the falls by canoe or kayak. Book a very relaxing trip on the Kangaroo or Shoalhaven rivers to discover sunken forests, quiet creeks and perhaps a platypus or two. Other wildlife to watch for include swamp wallabies, potoroos and gliders. Listen out for the remarkable mimicry of the lyrebird, and look to the skies to spot yellow-tailed black cockatoos, although you can hardly miss their screeching calls.

After the huge boulders, giant ferns and shaggy eucalypts of Tallaganda, you'll pop out on the road to Braidwood, where you can pick up pastries, sausage rolls and more supplies at the Dojo Bread artisanal bakery. Then, 45 miles (72km) into the ride you return to a dirt road as you skirt Budawang National Park. There are a couple of campgrounds at the 60–70 mile (96–112km) point, at Wog Wog and Corang, and then there are plenty more as you turn east into Morton National Park. Here, the Red Ground Track is a joy to ride, with plenty of varied scenery to enjoy. Also, take the short detour to Tianjara Falls near Sassafras, which sends a delicate stream of water over a high sandstone plateau.

Around Sassafras there are lots of quiet camping options, with fresh water from the Endrick River. After Tianjara Falls (left), the trail descends gradually through the park so savour the forest with all your senses. Listen out for elusive lyrebirds and rambunctious cockatoos. Also note that this 100-mile (160km) section from Braidwood to Nowra is mostly through wilderness, so you'll need to carry adequate provisions for that distance.

Nowra to Bundanoon

Reenter civilisation at Nowra, near the Shoalhaven River estuary. This next section north and west, is much more populated, including with Southern Highland wineries. The first stop, though, is at Kangaroo Valley, a base for activities on the Kangaroo River here, including canoeing and kayaking. The town is busy with weekending Sydneysiders taking selfies on the slightly incongruous historic suspension bridge.

Continuing onward, you'll reach a very steep off-road climb before Renown Lookout and Fitzroy Falls, the latter so spectacular that they have their own visitor centre. From Fitzroy, it's just 20 miles (32km) to the ride's finish in Bundanoon.

Attack of the Buns

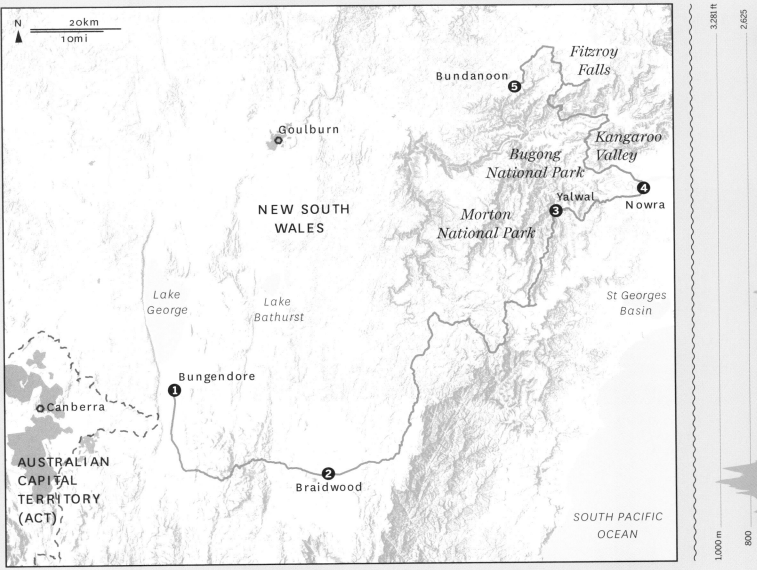

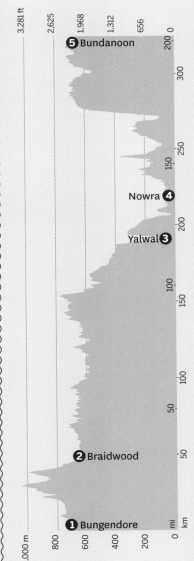

→ Distance: 322 miles (518km) → Ascent: 29,330ft (8940m) → Difficulty: 4

Kahurangi 500

New Zealand

The north of New Zealand's South Island is crammed with once-in-a-lifetime biking routes. Why not combine two of them into an epic loop around the northwest? The stellar Kahurangi 500 covers misty highland forest, pristine coast and historic mining trails.

Plan and Prepare

Logistics

The Kahurangi 500 route is a loop that you can start from anywhere, but Riwaka is a convenient point being close to Nelson, a regional hub. You can take a taxi or bus (with a dismantled bike) from Nelson to Riwaka. To get to Nelson, there are flights from across New Zealand (including Auckland, Wellington and Christchurch), or you can take a bus from Blenheim (where ferries from the North Island arrive).

Hazards

There are no dangerous predators in New Zealand (except perhaps the giant carnivorous snails on the Heaphy Track!). The main dangers come from the climate. The weather can change very quickly for the worse on the South Island, so always carry extra clothing for cold and wet conditions. Some of the trails are exposed and there are river crossings; if you're riding alone, tell someone where you're heading.

Gear

A mountain bike is best for this route due to the rough and rocky sections of the Old Ghost Road. Also, firmly attach any frame bags and baggage so they don't swing around too much and upset your balance. Carrying wet-weather kit is essential – rainfall averages 150in (380cm) per year on the Heaphy.

Info

The Heaphy Track is only open to cyclists during New Zealand's winter, from 1 May to 30 November, which will limit your options if you wish to ride it. You could always bypass it at other times of the year. Winter means cold and wet weather so pack accordingly. Check doc.govt.nz for more on riding the Heaphy, and oldghostroad.org.nz for info on that track.

Two tracks in the northwest South Island rank as must-ride destinations for mountain bikers around the world. The first is the Old Ghost Road, New Zealand's longest continuous stretch of singletrack trail. It opened in 2015 following years of construction and negotiation by a group friends, who discovered a section of road hewn by gold miners, and formed the Mokihinui-Lyell Backcountry Trust in order to develop it into a world-class trail for both bikers and hikers. The full 53-mile (85km) Old Ghost Road trail arcs north towards the west coast from Lyell to Seddonville.

Almost connecting with it is the Heaphy Track, one of New Zealand's 10 famed Great Walks. What sets this walk apart is that for half the year it is open for cyclists to ride (albeit in the colder and wetter part of the year). The Heaphy meanders through beech forest and tussock downs for 49 miles (79km) in another broad curve across the top of the South Island (right). On their own, the two trails make incredible two- or three-day rides. But the Kahurangi 500, taking its name from the national park in which the Heaphy lies, connects the two routes with little-used tracks and roads to form a challenging but safe loop that will delight all sorts of bikepackers.

The Old Ghost Road, in the southwest corner of the loop, is best ridden from south to north, meaning that the Kahurangi 500 is best tackled in a clockwise direction. From the end of the Old Ghost Road at Seddonville, you'll start the Heaphy (right) from Kōhaihai, travelling from east to west over the top of the loop. You can join at any point on the route but it makes the most sense to hop on from as close to Nelson as possible, such as from the town of Riwaka. Both trails have several huts available for overnight stays (book in advance).

The Old Ghost Road

The Old Ghost Road's story begins with the discovery of an uncompleted road between Lyell and Seddonville, which was transformed into a thrilling 53-mile (85km) trail. It opens with a climb to the Lyell Saddle bunkhouse, one of four built by the trail guardians, the Mokihinui-Lyell Backcountry Trust. From here the trail is all-new. It emerges on to the flanks of Mt Montgomery then skips up a tricky track along Rocky Tor. Ghost Lake is the next beautiful landmark, with views across the wilderness. From here, you'll tackle the Skyline Steps; Earnest Valley, with its alpine tarns; the zigzags of the Boneyard; and a descent to Goat Creek and the final hut at Specimen Point. The home stretch follows a river gorge to Seddonville.

To the Old Ghost Road

Starting from Riwaka and riding south, the first stretch of the Kahurangi lulls you into a hazy sense of security: it takes quiet roads along the Great Taste Trail, passing farms and vineyards en route to the town of Tapawera. Riders will be following the Motueka valley, where some of the sought-after, citrus-flavoured hops that lend New Zealand's craft ales their fruity notes are grown. All the while, the route is gently climbing, with a few off-road sections, until after 80 miles (129km) you reach Lake Rotoroa, at over 3000ft (914m) in Nelson Lakes National Park; there are campgrounds at Tapawera and Rotoroa. The park is punctuated by a number of glacial lakes surrounded by beech forest. In New Zealand, beech trees come in several varieties, including red, silver and, higher up, the diminutive mountain beech. As you cycle through the trees, listen for the call of the kākā, a mountain parrot that is related to its much less shy sibling, the mischievous kea.

Descending to Murchison is mostly off-road and brings you to the town known as New Zealand's 'whitewater capital', thanks to the convergence of the Matakitaki and Buller rivers here, and easy access to plenty more, including the Gowan, Mangles, Matiri, Glenroy and Maruia rivers. Given the Kiwi propensity to squeeze every drop of adrenaline out of life, jetboats shoot along the Buller through a narrow canyon; you can also try rafting, canoeing, fishing and splashing about in clean, icy Class 2 to 4 waters for moderately more sedate thrills. As an adventure town, there's plenty of food and accommodation choices here before you head west along the road towards Lyell, a fast and flat 20-mile (32km) ride. Lyell is the trailhead for the Old Ghost Road mountain-bike track, which turns immediately uphill for 14 miles (22km).

Killer snails and kiwis

Giants prowl the Heaphy Track after dark. You might hear the roroa, or great spotted kiwi, but it's extremely rare to see one. Foraging after dark, New Zealand's largest kiwi species lets out distinctive high-pitched trills, which can be an eerie experience in the bush. The kiwis currently inhabit only the higher elevations of the northern South Island but are still preyed on by non-native stoats and feral cats. Another example of New Zealand's unique evolutionary history is the Powelliphanta, or giant snail. The largest of these is found in Kahurangi National Park and measures 3.5in (9cm) across. These beautiful creatures slurp up slugs and earthworms on their nocturnal hunts but are not very fast-moving predators. Watch where you're riding!

The Heaphy Track

From Seddonville, the route turns inland along the Rte 67 road through Corbyvale, before following the west coast northwards through the town of Karamea. This is one of the wettest places in New Zealand (if not the world) so be prepared for wintry rain. But it's no less epic a setting for all the precipitation. Once through Karamea, you'll pick up the Heaphy Track at Kōhaihai. Look out for the local nīkau tree that is New Zealand's only native palm – there are nīkau forests to explore on foot around the Kōhaihai campgrounds.

The Heaphy is one of New Zealand's famed Great Walks, but it's less popular with trampers (the local lingo for hikers) than the Milford and Routeburn tracks to the south. Perhaps it doesn't have the dramatic mountain vistas of those two but, unlike those two, it is open to cyclists during the southern hemisphere winter, offering 49 miles (79km) of enjoyably testing trails to explore. Bikers can take advantage of the huts along the route. But there are a few restrictions, including not riding at night so as to protect the area's great spotted kiwi birds and giant snails as they forage for food.

The Heaphy continues along the misty coast then turns inland to climb up to 3000ft (914m) through moors of tussock grass and stunted beech forest (left). You'll be following in the footsteps of early Māori traders who sought in the rivers of Westland valuable *pounamu* (greenstone) with which to make ornaments and tools. Don't rush the riding – you can expect to spend a couple of nights in the Department of Conservation huts along the track. The Heaphy spits you out on the road to Bainham, from where you head down to Collingwood on Golden Bay, over Tākaka Hill and back to Riwaka on a mixture of quiet roads and the Rāmeka Track.

© deLoon / Shutterstock; Hot Pixels Photography / Shutterstock; LH1 / Shutterstock

Kahurungi 500

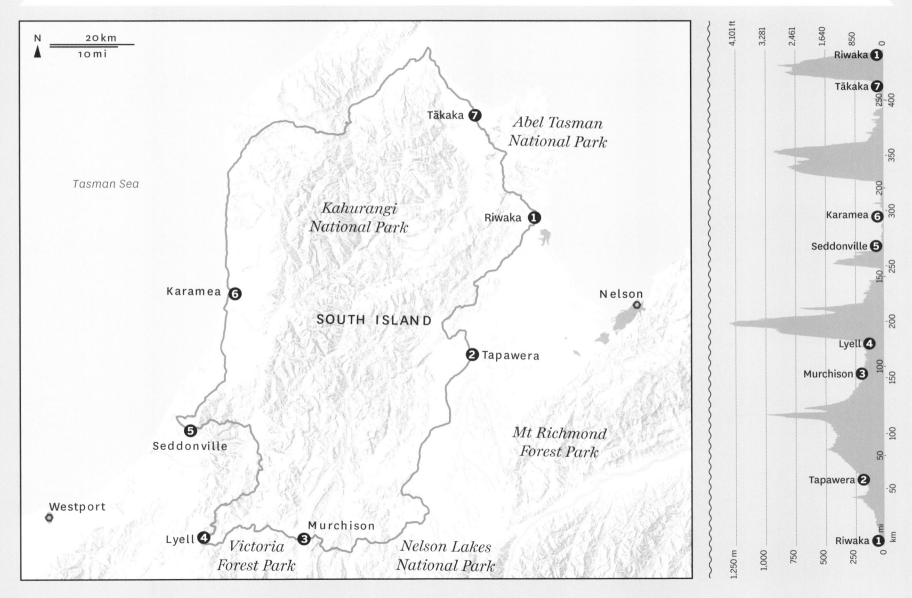

N

20km
10mi

Tasman Sea

Abel Tasman
National Park

Tākaka 7

Kahurangi
National Park

Riwaka 1

Nelson

Karamea 6

SOUTH ISLAND

2 Tapawera

Mt Richmond
Forest Park

5
Seddonville

Westport

Lyell 4   3 Murchison

Victoria
Forest Park

Nelson Lakes
National Park

4,101 ft

3,281

2,461

1,640

850

0

Riwaka 1

Tākaka 7

250
400

350

200

Karamea 6

300

Seddonville 5

150

Lyell 4

Murchison 3

100

150

Tapawera 2

100

50

50

Riwaka 1

1,250 m   1,000   750   500   250   0 mi
km

➔ Distance: 621 miles (1000km)   ➔ Ascent: 73,000ft (22,250m)   ➔ Difficulty: 5

Hunt 1000

Australia

Cross southeastern Australia between Canberra and Melbourne and experience the solitude of the Snowy Mountains, the history of the High Country and the temperate rainforest of the Yarra Ranges on this extremely challenging but beautifully rewarding ride.

Plan and Prepare

Logistics

Rideable in either direction, this huge route has international cities (Melbourne and Canberra) at both ends, each with good connections by air, rail and road. Returning to Melbourne from Canberra by train means taking a coach to Albury; not all operators accept bicycles (and Greyhound charges $49). You'll also need to coordinate with train departures (bike spaces are not guaranteed on V/Line trains). It's at least 8hr by coach/train, or 3hr by plane.

Hazards

This is the Australian wilderness: there are venomous snakes, extremes of temperature and (occasionally badly driven) utes (pick-ups). Check the weather forecast and avoid hot spells. You will also need to be a skilled navigator since there are some remote stretches in which to get lost. Intervals between food and water sources are irregular and need planning – treat any water from streams to kill giardia and parasites.

Gear

A mountain bike is best for this ride, due to the rugged terrain and the requirement to carry a lot of kit. The huge amount of ascending means that there is also a lot of descent – so carry spares such as extra brake pads. Be confident in fixing mechanical problems. You will also need to plan how to use and charge any electronic devices, such as phones and GPS units (there are various options available). Take a SPOT tracker or EPIRB beacon.

Info

This route is typically raced during late November and early December (late spring in the southern hemisphere). The organiser, Dan Hunt, recommends riding between October and March as much of the higher ground is impassable in winter. See huntbikes.com for more info. Commuter Cycles in Melbourne (commutercycles.com.au) is a good bike shop for last-minute prep; owner Huw Vellacott has completed the Hunt 1000.

The Hunt 1000 was developed in 2016 by Dan Hunt, founder of Australian bike company Hunt Bikes, as a way to cycle mainly off-road between Victoria's state capital, Melbourne, and national capital Canberra. To the surprise of many first-time visitors, Australia's southeast corner is actually quite high and cool, often with snow in winter. It's across this High Country – an extraordinarily beautiful and emotive landscape that includes the national parks of Kosciuszko and the Yarra Ranges, plus the stark Jagungal Wilderness Area – that the Hunt 1000 weaves its way, mostly via 4WD dirt tracks and the occasional township or shepherds' hut. The stats are sobering: 73,000ft (22,250m) of climbing over 621 miles (1000km). Fewer than half the race entrants usually finish the event, with most finishers taking around seven days. Do not underestimate the experience: it's a challenge that will require training, even if already fit, and the know-how to camp in the bush. But, if you're not racing, you can break the ride down into spectacular sections, such as between Melbourne and Mt Hotham, and take your time.

Toward Kosciuszko

The Hunt 1000 can be tackled in either direction, depending on what is most convenient. You'll generally gain a little descent going from Canberra to Melbourne. Leaving Canberra via Stromlo Forest Park, you're quickly in the wilds and it's only 30 miles (48km) until you cross into New South Wales. The landscape is generally open, with gentle hills and the occasional river crossing. There are few roads and any campgrounds (there are a couple at the 60 mile/96km point) are a short ride off the route. After about 100 miles (160km) you'll enter Kosciuszko National Park; shortly afterwards, on crossing the B72 main road, you'll reach one of the ride's highlights: the Jagungal Wilderness Area.

The Jagungal Wilderness Area, which is Ngarigo land, is part of the Snowy Mountains and the highest portion of the Hunt 1000 at an elevation of over 5000ft (1524m). It's a highlight of the route for several reasons. Firstly, and unusually for Australia, there are abundant tracks that are open to cyclists. There are also a number of shepherds' huts, where early cattle drovers and graziers would shelter as they moved their herds between settlements. Many of the historic huts here, such as pretty Valentine Hut (although this one was actually built in 1955), are maintained by the Kosciuszko Huts Association and offer very basic facilities, although it is preferred if visitors camp nearby. Bushfires in 2020 destroyed a number of the Jagungal's huts so check in advance if you're planning to stop at one. A good quantity of campgrounds provide alternative accommodation and there are several water sources, so the riding is relatively comfortable. Remember that your average speed will be lower here due to the gradients and rough tracks. The lowest gearing you can fit is recommended.

Into Victoria

After you pass through the Jagungal, you'll descend to the Murray River, which forms the border between New South Wales and the next state of Victoria. Note that crossing the Murray River will be impossible after heavy rains, so exercise caution here. You'll climb back up to 4500ft (1372m) through a vast, undulating landscape that seems little troubled by human presence. Raucous cockatoos call from the gum trees and you'll certainly spot kangaroos, wallabies and wombats in the early mornings. At night, the stars will seem thicker than ever imaginable in the cities. Out in the High Country, your mind will wander as readily as your wheels.

Mt Hotham

The highest point of the Hunt 1000 is a ski resort called Mt Hotham. It's also the start of a classic Australian hike, the Razorback Walk, which follows a ridge to Mt Feathertop (below) for 13 miles (22km), providing panoramic views over the High Country. The landscape here is truly ancient, which is why there are no jagged peaks – they've all been eroded over 500 million years to the round-shouldered hills you see now. If you can break your journey and spend some time in this region, there's plenty to explore off the bike, including the towns of Harrietville and Bright, about an hour northwest by bus from Mt Hotham and packed with places to eat and drink, such as Bright Brewery.

Warburton

The town of Warburton, next port of call after Woods Point, is the gateway to the Yarra Ranges, sitting at the foot of Mt Donna Buang and at the eastern end of the Lilydale Rail Trail. Big things are afoot for this former logging town, which hasn't benefited from tourism to the same extent as its neighbours. Plans to build one of Australia's largest network of mountain-bike trails, like those of Derby in Tasmania, have inched forward. The town is already a tranquil base (with an excellent motel and pizza place) and it's expected that the biking hub will prosper without negatively affecting the surrounding rainforest and rivers. Walk along the Yarra River in the evening here, and you may spot a platypus hunting in the shadows.

At around 250 miles (400km), you'll start to see signs of civilisation at the town of Omeo, where you can rest and restock. This is the edge of Victoria's ski region and you'll be climbing up to the highest point of the whole ride, Mt Hotham at 6000ft (1829m), and also sharing the tracks with more people. From Hotham, the trail follows backcountry tracks all the way down to Dargo in Gippsland, which is probably one of Victoria's most isolated communities – now that gold miners and cattle drovers no longer pass by, it's home to just 150 people.

After Dargo, you'll be on the homeward leg but there's still the steep Billy Goat Bluff Track to tackle; it's a tough hike-a-bike taking at least four hours, so carry sufficient water and delay if there's rain forecast. There are several campgrounds in the area and plenty of water. The route now bears west to Woods Point, another very remote community but one with a hotel, bar and restaurant. This is fishing and hunting country (surprisingly there are a lot of deer in the northeast of Victoria, where they're an invasive species) so expect to see a few more 4WDs and dogs in the middle of nowhere.

The Yarra Ranges

From Woods Point it's just 120 miles (193km) to Melbourne through the Yarra Ranges National Park. The terrain doesn't change much, being still up-and-down with tracks that take the steep and direct route up a hill rather than skirt around it, but the fauna and flora does change. Standing straight and graceful in the mists, forests of some of the world's tallest trees – eucalyptus regnans or mountain ash – are a delight to cycle through. You'll feel Lilliputian among their trunks and the giant ferns of the Ranges, all enjoying the cool, moist air. It's an uplifting way to finish the route, before you enter Melbourne's eastern suburbs.

Hunt 1000

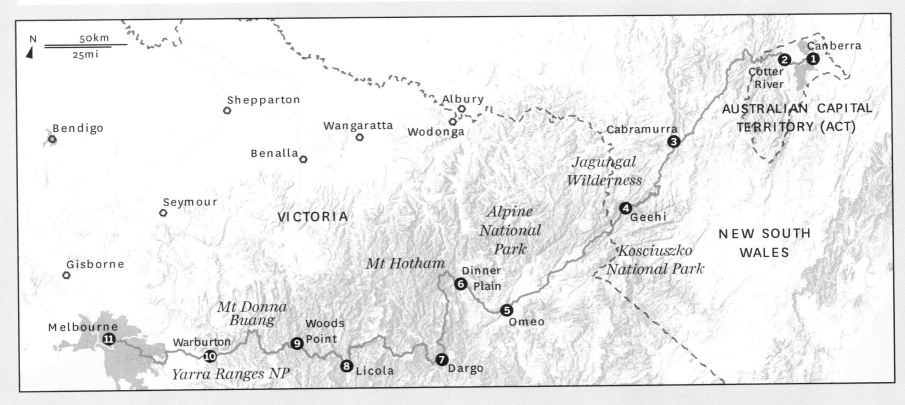

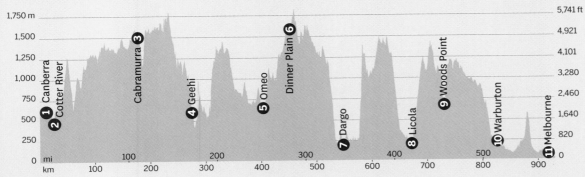

→ Distance: 1990 miles (3200km)   → Ascent: 90,000ft (27,432m)   → Difficulty: 2

Tour Aotearoa

New Zealand

Take a quest across the entire length of New Zealand (or ride half at a time) on this epic route through the North and South Islands, which connects countless bike paths and trails via fantastic sights and landscapes.

Plan and Prepare

Logistics

The route starts at Cape Reinga at New Zealand's northern tip. It's difficult to reach, with options including a series of buses via Kerikeri and Pukenui then a taxi (or a lift, if you can organise one) to the Cape. A ferry runs several times daily from Wellington to Picton on the South Island, where you can pick up the new Sounds2Sounds route. This finishes at Milford Sound; several firms provide transfers to Te Anau and Queenstown.

Hazards

There are natural hazards to note: the weather, especially, can change in an instant and become very challenging. Be prepared for the worst. Watch for flooding rivers and streams and practise safe crossing techniques; get local advice if necessary. An emergency locator beacon is useful (mobile phones won't always have a signal). Less likely are natural phenomena like earthquakes. There are no dangerous wild animals, but New Zealand's drivers can be erratic.

Gear

Terrain varies, and rough tracks tend to be avoided, but a 29er mountain bike is probably best – with or without front suspension as preferred. A robust gravel bike is also suitable for experienced riders. People riding electric bikes have also completed the North Island half of the route. When on the South Island, carry a mid-season sleeping bag and warmer layers. A water purification kit is also useful.

Info

The Tour Aotearoa began as an event, an annual brevet, which takes place through February and March. But you can follow the route at any time, bearing in mind that New Zealand's winters are wet, windy and snowy on high ground. Ideal timing would be November to April. The Kennett brothers provide a huge amount of info at kennett.co.nz and offer essential guidebooks for sale. See also touraotearoa.nz for more info.

New Zealand's Kennett brothers are to bikepacking what the Wright brothers were to aviation. Jonathan, Paul and Simon Kennett have pioneered mountain-biking routes across New Zealand since the birth of the sport in the early 1980s. In 1986, they founded New Zealand's first mountain-bike race, the Karapoti Classic, and have gone on to devise bike trails and routes throughout the country, not least as project managers on the New Zealand Cycle Trail. They've shared their wealth of information with an extensive range of guidebooks, which are essential companions for anybody exploring New Zealand by bicycle.

One of their greatest achievements is the Tour Aotearoa, which is nothing less than an impeccably mapped route from the northernmost tip of the North Island to the foot of the South Island, meandering through New Zealand's famed landscapes from the verdant wine country of the north to the epic mountains of the south. The Tour began as an event known as a brevet, a timed ride via predetermined checkpoints (but not exactly a race). The first Tour Aotearoa was held in 2016, with riders required to pass 30 checkpoints within 30 days. However, it's now a classic bikepacking route outside of the annual event, supported by a growing community that can provide up-to-date advice and information. What's more, given that New Zealand is split across equally sized islands, it's easy to focus on completing a section at a time.

From the top

New Zealand's capital lies two-thirds of the way up the North Island. North of here, the country grows ever more tropical as you travel past idyllic destinations such as the Bay of Islands. But it's hard to reach the beaches and lighthouse of Cape Reinga (right) without bagging a lift from someone (multiple bus connections are the alternative).

Reinga is the Māori name for the underworld, and a Māori belief holds that the spirits of the dead depart our world from here. Cape Reinga's lighthouse is also the departure point for your adventure. Tour Aotearoa links together a number of preexisting cycling routes, and the first beneath your wheels is the Far North Cycleway. This 100-mile (160km) route soon swerves onto Ninety Mile Beach: try to time your arrival for low tide and ride on the harder, wet sand. You'll be covering about 50 miles (80km) on the beach, but it passes swiftly with a tailwind.

Next, you'll follow quiet roads to connect with the Kauri Coast Cycleway, which continues south through quaint towns and forests of kauri trees. There are plenty of places to stop and stay when travelling at your own pace. After around 400 miles (644km), the Helensville to Mt Eden leg takes you into the suburbs of Auckland. And then you're swiftly out and onto the Hauraki Rail Trail to Auckland, which you'll pick up on the east coast as you enter the Waikato region. Significant stops along this section include the Hobbiton set (left) from *The Lord of the Rings* movies at Matamata.

The Waikato River guides you deeper into the heart of the North Island on bike paths that follow the river as it cuts through gorges (right). The Waikato River Trail connects with another of New Zealand's stellar cycling routes, the Timber Trail. Using former logging tracks and traversing 35 bridges, including some lofty suspension bridges, this 53-mile (85km) purpose-built path weaves through old-growth forests alive with birdsong from tūī and other native species. Highlights from the rest of the North Island section include exploring the backroads of the Wairarapa Wine Region and taking the stunning Remutaka Cycle Trail along the coast approaching Wellington.

The Kauri Coast

The Kauri Coast Cycleway passes through Waipoua Forest, home to the last of New Zealand's giant kauri trees. Kauri have thrived in this subtropical climate for millions of years, their trunks growing to a diameter of more than 6ft (2m) by the time they reach 1000 years old; some are known to have had trunks of 23ft (7m) or more. Human lifespans are just a flicker to a kauri tree (they can live for 2000-plus years), and they play an important part in Māori creation myths. But they're disappearing fast due to kauri dieback, a disease cause by a microscopic fungi carried into forests by humans and animals. To help stop the spread, wash down footwear, gear and tyres at forest cleaning stations.

From Blenheim, you'll cycle into the St James Conservation Area to follow the Clarence River (known to Māori as Waiau Toa) all the way to the resort of Hanmer Springs, through expansive, high-country cattle stations.

After about 310 miles (500km) you'll reach the South Island's largest city, Christchurch, passing through its historic centre, still being rebuilt after the earthquakes of 2010 and 2011. More of a twee town than a city, there's still a way to bypass Christchurch if you're not into urban areas. The route continues on past Lake Tekapo, in the shadow of Aoraki/Mt Cook, and then the conveniently located town of Twizel. After crossing into Otago, the mountains get larger and the climbs longer, with passes like the Omarama Saddle requiring a solid off-road climb then descent. A valley floor offers some respite as you pedal towards Alexandra in Central Otago, home to some of the world's southernmost wineries.

Having now covered about 680 miles (1100km), it's time to turn west up to Cromwell, which brings you to a gold-rush-era town best-known today for its fresh stone fruit. Pack some sweet supplies for the final quarter of Sounds2Sounds, because it's the most rugged. You'll skirt behind Queenstown and the Remarkables mountain range to reach Te Anau and its lake, then follow Hwy 94 for 75 miles (119km) to Milford Sound in Fiordland National Park, one of the greatest of New Zealand's natural wonders. This southwest corner of New Zealand, although small on paper, is gigantic in terms of topography and in natural history, being one of the best and last surviving examples of Gondwana, the 500-million year old continent that began to break up during the Jurassic period. Having cycled here, take some time to recuperate in Te Anau – but don't miss Mitre Peak (top left) and some of the once-in-a-lifetime walks in the region.

Into the South

On landing on the South Island, the standard Tour Aotearoa route south hugs the wet and windy west coast. But in 2022 the Kennett brothers launched an alternative way of riding north to south, which charts a more easterly course, thus avoiding the worst of the weather; they called this new route Sounds2Sounds. It starts from Ship Cove (known as Meretoto in Māori) at the fringe of Marlborough Sounds. The bay was a base for James Cook on his early visits to New Zealand and where Māori people first met Europeans. If you're landing by ferry from Wellington at Picton then you can either double back to Ship Cove or commence the route from Anakiwa, 14 miles (22km) to the west.

Similar to the North Island section, this route stitches together a number of existing trails and cycleways, albeit with greater distances between settlements and more hills to climb.

Tour Aotearoa

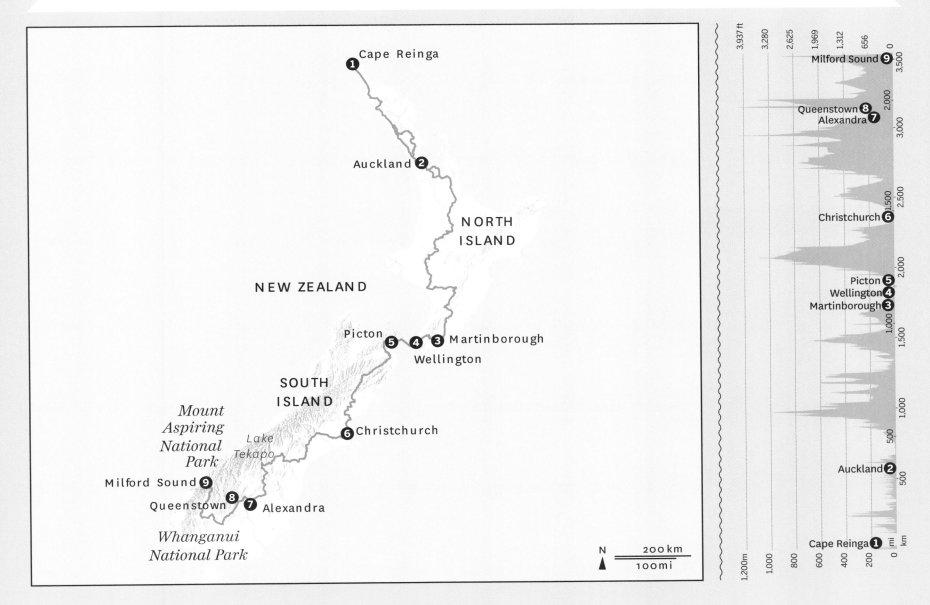

Cape Reinga ❶

Auckland ❷

NORTH
ISLAND

NEW ZEALAND

Picton ❺ ❹ ❸ Martinborough

Wellington

SOUTH
ISLAND

Mount
Aspiring
National
Park

Lake
Tekapo

❻ Christchurch

Milford Sound ❾

Queenstown ❽ ❼ Alexandra

Whanganui
National
Park

N
200 km
100 mi

Milford Sound ❾

Queenstown ❽
❼
Alexandra

Christchurch ❻

Picton ❺
Wellington ❹
Martinborough ❸

Auckland ❷

Cape Reinga ❶

3,937 ft
3,280
2,625
1,969
1,312
656
0

2,000

3,000

2,500

2,000

1,500

1,000

500

500

0 mi
km

1,200 m
1,000
800
600
400
200
0

➜ Distance: 627 miles (1010km)   ➜ Ascent: 42,000ft (12,802m)   ➜ Difficulty: 4

Munda Biddi

Australia

Linking friendly towns along a natural corridor across southwest Australia, Munda Biddi is one of the longest purpose-built bike routes in the world, and one of the first in Australia. Tackle it in stages or attempt the whole thing over a couple of weeks.

Plan and Prepare

Logistics

The trailhead is in Mundaring, just 30min east of Perth by car. The endpoint at Albany, on the south coast, is a 6hr journey on coaches from East Perth (with intermediate stops such as Bunbury) run by regional transit operator Transwa; bicycles need to be booked in advance. There are also frequent (and far quicker) flights to or from Perth.

Hazards

The usual Australian dangers apply here: biting insects, snakes and dehydration or heatstroke. The last two can be avoided by riding from March to December and being aware of water sources where bottles can be refilled. The weather can play a part at other times of the year – sections of the trail suffer after heavy rain and are best avoided. Not so much a hazard but a hindrance is the pea-sized gravel on the northern third.

Gear

Most riders who complete the Munda Biddi recommend a mountain bike, if only for comfort. The north third features notorious gravel, which is both slow and unstable, so wider tyres will help. Bikepacking bags are a good option to stay streamlined and avoid using a trailer. There are frequent towns along the way so you don't need to carry much food at a time – or even much camping equipment if you prefer to stay in huts or accommodation in towns.

Info

The Munda Biddi Trail Foundation (mundabiddi. org.au) is an excellent resource with maps and details of diversions and of the best towns at which to stop. You can become a Foundation member for further benefits. Avoid the baking heat of summer. Spring is wildflower season, which reaches the southwest of Western Australia in October and November and is a beautiful time to ride. Autumn and winter are also possible.

n the indigenous Noongar language of Australia's southwest, 'munda biddi' means 'the path through the forest'. This is a little of an understatement. This 627-mile (1010km) trail connects an almost continuous line of reserves and parks all the way from Perth's outskirts to the searingly bright seaside of Albany on Western Australia's south coast (right). Along the way it passes through stands of fragrant jarrah and marri eucalypt forest, or pale ghost gums growing on sandy ground strewn with scrolls of bark. Tingle trees and spiky grass trees fill out the lower levels of the forests. And towering above in certain places are karri trees, the arboreal kings of Western Australia. Flitting between the boughs are Australia's bright and noisy birds, an endlessly entertaining spectacle.

The completed Munda Biddi was opened in 2013, and is Australia's longest off-road multi-use trail (though its signposts are not to be relied upon). It was designed to connect inland communities in this very sparsely populated corner of Australia and also to enable visitors to experience some of the Indigenous and natural history of the region. On all fronts it has been a success. But although the trails are not too technically difficult and there are no major mountain ranges in the way, the challenge of the whole route is certainly not to be underestimated. Not only is the distance daunting, but some of the hills are very steep and some of the surfaces, such as the pea-gravel in the northern section, are slow going. But that is where the clever route plotting counts: hopping short distances from town to town means that riders never get too demoralised and can recharge their batteries (perhaps literally) easily. Plus it's also simple to ride the route in sections and skip bits: Transwa's GS3 coach service stops at Boyanup, Balingup, Pemberton and more on its way to Albany.

Heading south

The first leg from Mundaring tips up and down as you follow the yellow posts past ghost gums under a blue sky. An unwanted penalty is that the trail surface in places is deep, pea-sized gravel, which makes pedalling a bicycle quite frustrating. Official guidance says to allow for between 25 miles (40km) and 45 miles (72km) per day over a three-week period; however this is very conservative and many fit or experienced riders will be managing much more, even at a leisurely pace. In 2020, two-time Albany sportsperson of the year Craig Wiggins rode the whole route in less than three days. 'Obviously, I'm really shattered,' he said afterwards. 'It was a big couple of days on the bike.'

On this opening third, which is predominantly off-road, there are some rutted slopes to watch out for – less confident cyclists can easily navigate on to a road to avoid some climbs. The trail is designed so that there's a town or a purpose-built hut every 25 miles (40km), such as the hut at Dandalup on top of the Darling Range, which has views along the northern portion of the trail.

Trailside pursuits

Stopping and exploring the towns along Munda Biddi is part of its appeal. From the north, you'll first pass the former logging settlement of Jarrahdale and then, after about 110 miles (177km), Dwellingup, deep in jarrah forest. It's an adventure hub with canoeing, hiking, fishing and an annual mountain-bike race. Indigenous Noongar people, whose presence in the region dates back more than 30,000 years, would visit the valleys and coast here to fish.

The charming country town of Boyanup on the Preston River (with a coach service to and from Perth) is an ideal place to fuel up on fresh local produce from the farmers' market.

Pemberton's karri trees

In the 1940s in Pemberton, which the trail passes, pegs were embedded in eight local karri trees to create nature's own fire-lookout towers. Karri trees were selected because they're the world's third-tallest tree species and also very straight, comparable to a redwood. The tallest top out at about 262ft (80m), though some say there are even bigger karri that are yet to be measured. Some of the fire-lookout trees can still be visited and climbed, such as the Gloucester Tree and the Dave Evans Bicentennial Tree; the latter reaches the dizzying height of 246ft (75m) with 165 pegs spiralling up the trunk, and was made a fire lookout in the 1980s. The 250-year-old Diamond Tree in nearby Manjimup was closed to climbers in 2019.

Victoria's mountain ash forests, which you can ride through on the Hunt 1000 route – see p78). The natural wonders are not just giant around here – the area is also known for its rare orchids.

The next town is Pemberton, which is the capital of karri tree country. Nearby in Gloucester National Park, on the outskirts of town, you can climb the huge Gloucester karri and survey the forest from its viewing platform. There are lots of forest walks and drives to do here, so it's worth taking time to appreciate nature and just sit still watching wrens, robins and fantails in the undergrowth.

The trail continues south towards the ocean on mainly dirt roads of varying degrees of interest. You'll start to sense the ocean as you approach Walpole, which is within the gorgeous Walpole and Nornalup Inlets National Marine Park. If you feel like you're almost alone on the edge of continent here, that's because you are. Back on the trail, the Valley of the Giants tree-top walk (which is exactly what it says) is just east of Walpole. Explore the karri canopy on newly refurbished walkway, but don't miss the 400-year-old tingle trees too, which only grow in this area.

A final WOW

From Denmark, the next stop and about 30 miles (48km) from the Valley of the Giants, you're approaching the end of the trail. But there's one more marvel to enjoy: a new extension to Munda Biddi along the Wilderness Ocean Walk (WOW) Trail, which curves around the coast of Wilson Head and provides majestic views of the Southern Ocean. It's about another day's cycling from Denmark to Albany, where you can reflect on your epic ride. And if you're there from late May to early October you might like to witness another amazing journey: the migration of humpback and southern right whales.

The Karri trees

The town of Donnelly River is roughly the halfway point of the Munda Biddi, and if you're heading south you're about to enter the tall trees and perhaps the most awe-inspiring half of the route. Look out for a rare subspecies of red-tailed black cockatoo in these forests, which favour jarrah, marri and blackbutt trees. Donnelly River is pleasant place to relax, with a swimming hole, a general store and a large number of friendly kangaroos and emus. From here, there's an enjoyable stretch of trail with switchbacks before the next stop at Manjimup, the regional centre. If any maintenance is required, head to the bike shop in town.

The trail is easy between Manjimup and Quinninup, which is beautifully set amid karri trees, one of the world's tallest species (although generally thought to be beaten in height by

Munda Biddi

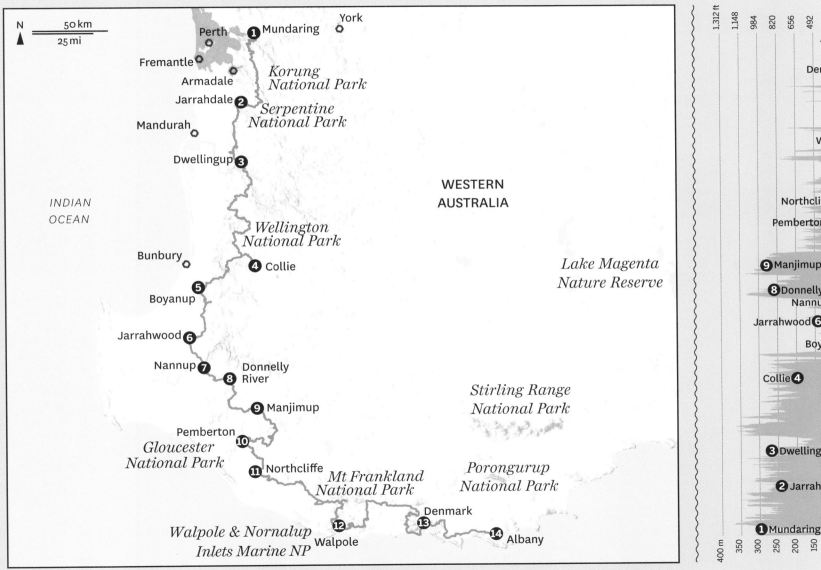

N
50 km
25 mi

Perth
Mundaring ❶
York

Fremantle
Armadale
Jarrahdale ❷

Korung National Park

Serpentine National Park

Mandurah

Dwellingup ❸

INDIAN OCEAN

WESTERN AUSTRALIA

Wellington National Park

Bunbury

Collie ❹

Lake Magenta Nature Reserve

Boyanup ❺

Jarrahwood ❻

Nannup ❼
Donnelly River ❽

Manjimup ❾

Stirling Range National Park

Pemberton ❿

Gloucester National Park

Northcliffe ⓫

Mt Frankland National Park

Porongurup National Park

Denmark

⓬

⓭

Walpole & Nornalup Inlets Marine NP

Walpole

Albany ⓮

Elevation profile (right):

1,312 ft · 1,148 · 984 · 820 · 656 · 492 · 328 · 164 · 0

Albany ⓮
Denmark ⓭
Walpole ⓬
Northcliffe ⓫
Pemberton ❿
Manjimup ❾
Donnelly River ❽
Nannup ❼
Jarrahwood ❻
Boyanup ❺
Collie ❹
Dwellingup ❸
Jarrahdale ❷
Mundaring ❶

400 m · 350 · 300 · 250 · 200 · 150 · 100 · 50 · 0
km

→ Distance: 72 miles (116km)   → Ascent: 5085ft (1550m)   → Difficulty: 1

Murray to the Mountains

Australia

Australia's most popular rail trail makes for a gentle introduction to bikepacking and offers opportunities to explore food, wine and adventure along its mostly car–free route through Northeast Victoria.

Plan and Prepare

Logistics

The route's terminals are Wangaratta, which is on the Melbourne to Albury train line; and the High Country town of Bright, connected to Wangaratta by a V/Line coach service. Bicycles can generally be carried on trains from Melbourne to Wangaratta and back, on a first-come-first-served basis. The coach from Bright to Wangaratta also carries bicycles at no cost, space permitting.

Hazards

There are few hazards to be wary of here, aside from the heat and sun during the summer months. Most of the route is on paved or gravel surfaces and away from the road. The only gruelling gradient is going up and down from Beechworth. Even if you run out of water, there are plenty of places along the way where you can refill.

Gear

Any sort of bicycle will be suitable for this rail trail, but a road or gravel bike will be most efficient; you don't need a mountain bike. You can travel quite minimally too, given that there are towns offering fantastic food and accommodation along the way. At the very least, a puncture repair kit, a pump and a credit card will suffice.

Info

You can get some background about the region alongside specifics on the Murray to the Mountains route at ridehighcountry.com.au; discover more of Australia's excellent rail trails at railtrails.org.au. There's lots of accommodation (typically at the higher end of the budget) in Beechworth and Bright, including a caravan park, but limited legal camping without heading out of town to a handful of designated areas.

More than 170 rail trails in Australia offer a brilliant taste of cycle touring to those with less bike-riding experience. Their appeal lies in providing largely traffic-free trails that are typically surfaced and signposted; and because they're also often built along one-time railway routes, they tend to be fairly level and without steep gradients. One of Australia's best rail trails is the Murray to the Mountains route in northeast Victoria.

This trail travels east from Wangaratta, near the Murray River, to the mountain town of Bright (right) on the edge of the Australian Alps. Along the way, like the river, Murray to the Mountains offers several out-and-back diversions, but the core of the ride is the 60-mile (97km) section between Wangaratta and Bright, via Beechworth and along the Ovens Valley. The former railway line once ferried tourists to the resorts of Bright and Mt Buffalo, but was closed bit by bit in the 1980s. In the '90s the route was reborn as the rail trail, with most of the station platforms still intact.

Choosing your route

Although there is a short section of trail around the wine-producing region of Rutherglen, we'd suggest skipping that and embarking on your adventure from the regional hub of Wangaratta. Here, the signposted trail sets off straight from outside the train station.

The first choice you need to make is whether you wish to ride via the gourmet region of Milawa to the south or continue direct to Beechworth in the northerly direction. We'd recommend riding via Oxley and Milawa, on what is known as the Heritage Section, and perhaps popping into the Milawa Providore for a coffee. Milawa lies at the top of King Valley, home to numerous wineries and food producers.

Gourmet trails

For anybody who enjoys finishing a day of cycling with wine or beer made down the road and a plate of locally grown food, the Murray is not only the best route in Australia – it's probably one of the best in the world. After WWII, Italian migrants arrived in King Valley to the south of Milawa and began planting vines and growing ingredients from the Old Country; since then, the region has developed an enviable food and drink culture. Beechworth is surrounded by wineries creating great vintages at the town's higher elevation, while breweries in Beechworth and Bright make beer using hops and water from the Ovens Valley. Favourite post-ride meals include pizzas from Bridge Road Brewers (below) in Beechworth, and burgers from Tomahawks in Bright.

On the trail to Beechworth

From Milawa, you can rejoin the Murray to the Mountains at Everton after a short ride along the Tarrawingee Rd. At the former Everton station, head uphill and north to Beechworth, along a sustained but gradual climb through dry eucalypt forest. Scrolls of bark decorate the gravel track and you'll likely spot wallabies or other Aussie wildlife, and plenty of squawking birds. The 10-mile (16km) climb levels out at the edge of Beechworth, one of Victoria's most handsome country towns. It's worth staying overnight here and exploring: there's a lake for swimming, some natural mountain-bike trails, a selection of very high-quality restaurants and a lot of gold-rush history (including a courthouse and the Old Gaol where bushranger Ned Kelly was tried and imprisoned). And many of Beechworth's wineries, such as Pennyweight, merit a visit for a tasting. Also note that the trail is being extended here around the equally appealing town of Yackandandah.

Along the Ovens Valley

From Beechworth, head back down to Everton and turn left along the Ovens Valley towards Myrtleford. This undulating section covers 16 miles (26km). From Myrtleford, it's another 18 miles (30km) to Bright, mostly in a straight line along the floor of the Ovens Valley, passing through lush farmland. There are no further diversions but Bright itself is a treasure and again worth exploring over a few days. There's some extremely good cycling around here for more experienced riders: the long road-climbs up Mt Buffalo or Mt Beauty, passing through scenic forests, are rites of passage for Victorian cyclists. Off-road riders may prefer the trails of Bright's Mystic Mountain Bike Park. But a simple pleasure for anybody is sitting beside the Ovens River with a cold beer in the evening, watching for platypus playing and hunting in the water.

Murray to the Mountains

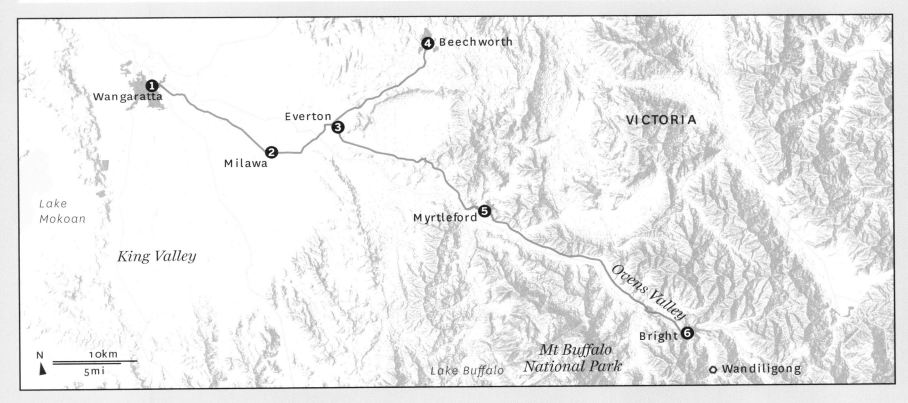

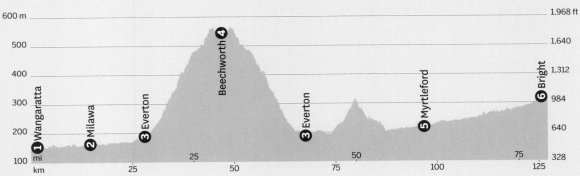

→ Distance: 58 miles (93km)   → Ascent: 4466ft (1361m)   → Difficulty: 2

St James Trail

New Zealand

This short loop around the Canterbury region, in the northern part of the South Island, takes in wild landscapes, New Zealand farming heritage and Māori trading routes. It's an easy two-day trip on which to spend time with pleated hills, icy rivers and big skies.

Plan and Prepare

Logistics

Many riders start the St James Trail from Maling Pass car park, at the northeast corner of the loop near Lake Tennyson. There's little public transport in the area, so you'll need to arrange a lift or drive – either via Rainbow Rd, which runs alongside the Wairau River off State Hwy 63 from Blenheim; or on Hwy 7 from Christchurch. Whichever route you take, the gravel-road driving is slow; expect a 4-6hr journey time.

Hazards

Although this is a short ride in a country with no dangerous animals, nature can still pose a threat. Be very careful around rivers, which can flood. Some bridges may be damaged; keep in mind that most backcountry accidents occur when crossing rivers – exercise caution. Avalanches can also be a hazard. Bear in mind too that this is a sparsely populated region, so help may not be easily available.

Gear

A robust gravel bike or a mountain bike will be ideal. With just one night out and the option of hut accommodation, you don't need to carry a tent. But do carry a stove, some food and water purification equipment, as you'll need to refill along the way.

Info

It's best to ride the loop from November to April. Some riders can manage it in a day but it's more fun to stay overnight at one of the huts along the route: Scotties, Lake Guyon or Pool. For more info, visit nzcycletrail.com, which also has details of the Huruni Heartland ride, the Molesworth Muster and the Rainbow Trail, all linking with the St James route.

The northeast of New Zealand's South Island has a number of attractions, including its largest city, Christchurch, and the region's whale-watching hub, Kaikoura (both still recovering from earthquakes in the 2000s). But when you tire of gigantic sperm whales and genteel Victorian architecture, it's easy to escape inland to the St James Conservation Area. This vast swathe of high country, not quite as intimidating the snowcapped Alps to the south, covers what was once one of New Zealand's largest sheep stations, St James, and is now managed by the Department of Conservation. Following the huge glacial valleys of the Waiau and Clarence rivers, the St James Trail is a relatively short route that is sufficiently remote to allow a sense of riding through the wilderness, while being only a few miles from the bustle of Hanmer Springs ski and spa resort. The elevation along the route tops out at 4300ft (1310m), so the trail is best attempted from November to April for anybody not experienced with New Zealand's climate.

Onto the trail at Maling

Starting from the trail's northeast corner at Maling Pass car park maximises the downhills if you head anti-clockwise. The car park is just to the south of beautiful, glacial Lake Tennyson (right), where there's a campground too. You'll begin by climbing a steep gradient of up to 10% up to Maling Pass itself, the high point of the route. From here the trail turns downhill through gnarled beech forest and mountain meadows as you enter the Waiau Valley. Once you reach the main river, you'll turn south towards Saddle Spur Bridge on a purpose-built bike trail. About 10 miles (16km) from the start there's a turn-off to Lake Guyon, where there's a small four-bunk hut, often used by people fishing for trout in the lake.

After crossing the Saddle Spur Bridge, the next huts are Pool and Scotties; both small and basic, they're around halfway along the route, so make good options for overnighting. Note that there are several stream and river crossings along the trail and that floods can wash bridges away (the McArthur swing bridge was removed in 2021); you may need to follow a diversion. The rocky trail from Saddle Spur Bridge is the most challenging stretch, with steep climbs and descents and a degree of exposure, complicated by plenty of thorny matagouri bushes. You'll cross Charlies Saddle, where you'll pick up the Edwards River as you turn east.

From Scotties Hut, the riding surface becomes easier but you'll be climbing gradually for 8 miles (13km) to Peters Pass before a descent to historic St James Homestead. You can leave the trail here for Hanmer Springs, or close the loop on a gentle upward gradient along the Clarence River for about 16 miles (26km) to Maling car park.

St James Trail extensions

If you want to extend your St James ride over more nights, try the Rainbow Trail, which starts from St Arnaud to the northwest and ends at Hanmer Springs (above). There's also the Molesworth Muster route south from coastal Blenheim to Hanmer Springs, adjacent to the Clarence valley. Should you wish to ride all the way to the regional capital, plump for the Huruni Heartland route, connecting Kaikoura with Christchurch via 160 miles (257km) of quiet county rides.

Sheep stats

Like much of the northern South Island, today's St James Conservation Area lies amid farming country. The first sheep to set hoof on the South Island were a ram and an ewe released from Captain James Cook's ship on his second visit to the islands in 1773. They didn't survive more than a few days. But within a century, sheep farming had become a major earner for New Zealand, with wool and meat being exported by the 1880s. By the 1980s the country was home to more than 70 million sheep, mainly of the resilient Romney variety. (The human population was around 3 million then; it's now 5 million). Countless sheep would have roamed the landscape covered on this ride because, from 1862, the area was one of the country's largest sheep stations. Several homesteads were grouped together and there are many remnants to discover. At the St James Station, a woolshed and cookhouse are still standing, while at Lake Guyon Homestead, the orchards, yards and sheep-dips have remained largely unchanged over the decades. The Stanley Vale Homestead, a timber-clad hut dating from the 1860s, was restored in 1988.

© SannePhoto / Shutterstock; Pete Seaward / Lonely Planet

St James Trail

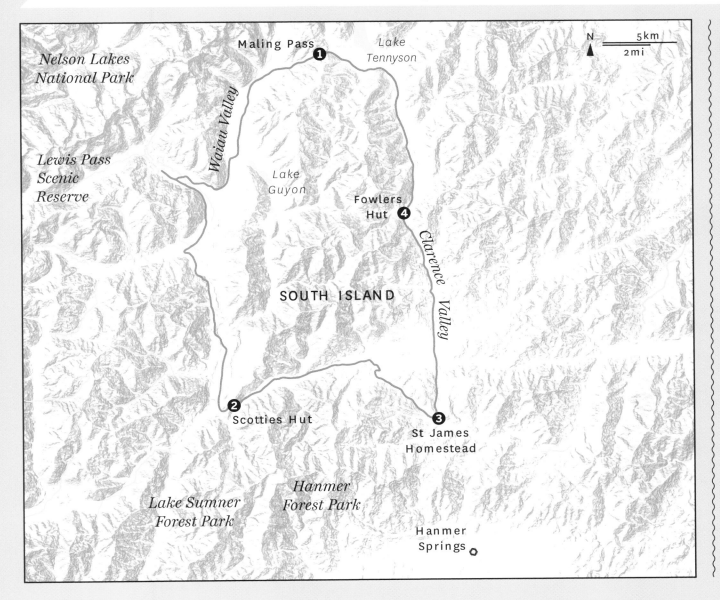

Nelson Lakes
National Park

Lewis Pass
Scenic
Reserve

Waiau Valley

Maling Pass ❶

Lake
Tennyson

Lake
Guyon

Fowlers
Hut ❹

Clarence Valley

SOUTH ISLAND

❷
Scotties Hut

❸
St James
Homestead

Lake Sumner
Forest Park

Hanmer
Forest Park

Hanmer
Springs ⊙

N
▲

5km
2mi

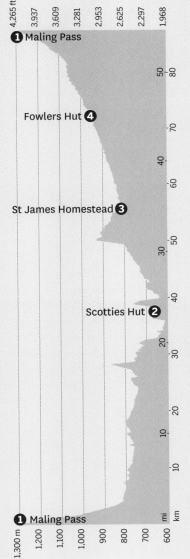

4,265 ft   3,937   3,609   3,281   2,953   2,625   2,297   1,968

❶ Maling Pass

Fowlers Hut ❹

St James Homestead ❸

Scotties Hut ❷

❶ Maling Pass

mi   km

1,300 m   1,200   1,100   1,000   900   800   700   600

→ Distance: 298 miles (480km)   → Ascent: 28,850ft (8793m)   → Difficulty: 3

Tasmanian Trail

Australia

Cross the island state of Tasmania on this relatively well-maintained trail and sample some of the highlights of this natural haven: great food and wine, beautiful wilderness and a (mostly) cool climate.

Plan and Prepare

Logistics

The trail bisects Tasmania between Dover on the south coast and Devonport on the north coast. It can be ridden in either direction: Dover is close to Hobart, the state capital, while a ferry connects Devonport with Melbourne (10hr). But for a tailwind, riding south to north is the best bet. It's possible to ride the 46 miles (75km) between Hobart and Dover in half a day; there's also a direct bus (but bicycles must be booked in advance).

Hazards

The weather can change in an instant in Tasmania: prepare for all four seasons in one day. Bushfires are a serious summer menace so keep up to date on fire warnings. Tasmania has three varieties of snake – tiger, copperhead and white-lipped – with the first two being the most venomous. Carry filters with which to purify water. And be wary of riding on roads after dark.

Gear

The Tasmanian Trail can be ridden on a gravel bike with tyres that are as wide and robust as possible. A hardtail mountain bike is also a good choice. Carry plenty of puncture repair kit as well as tools to repair a broken chain and spoke, as there are no bike shops on the route. A water filter is also recommended, as is warm and waterproof clothing.

Info

The Tasmanian Trail Association website (tasmaniantrail.com.au) has maps, updates on trail conditions and changes, advice and recent reports, and also offers local contacts. Most people ride the trail during the summer months (typically November to March). There are some locked gates on the route; if you prefer not to lift a laden bike over them you can hire a key (you'll need to return it).

Fall in love with this heart-shaped island on a week-long ride from south to north (or vice versa if need be) along the Tasmanian Trail. Although two-thirds unpaved, the route doesn't require as much bush-bashing as other trips, using instead farm and forestry tracks where possible (and avoiding national parks). It also passes through a number of small towns and hamlets, deliberately connecting visitors with local communities and enabling you to overnight in a bed if you prefer not to use any of the many campgrounds along the way. The trail is mostly waymarked and multi-use, meaning that you may encounter hikers and horse-riders. But, although accessible and relatively easygoing for experienced cyclists, it's not without challenges. These include the daily distances and big climbs; the lack of support services (such as bike shops) if anything goes wrong; and sometimes the weather.

North from Dover

Most people start from Dover, although the prevailing wind direction is westerly so it probably doesn't really matter (wind speeds are highest in spring). Some ride light and rely on stopping at hotels; others carry a tent and stove, and pitch up at the numerous campgrounds. Just remember that the further you travel from the coast, the more sparsely populated Tasmania becomes. The first township after Dover is the former logging town of Geeveston, 20 miles (32km) into the ride and an interesting place to explore. Check out the chainsaw-carved sculptures of local figures, and the local walks through temperate rainforest.

From Geeveston, the route passes through farmland and then the forest of the beautiful Huon Valley. The area is noted for its fruit farms (cherries, peaches, pears and berries), so you should be able to pick up some snacks.

© Matty Waudby

Into the Central Highlands

After around 56 miles (90km) you'll reach the town of New Norfolk, home to the award-winning Agrarian Kitchen Cooking School & Kitchen Garden and its associated restaurant, where seasonal, local produce is prepared and served with Tasmanian wines. Note that a lot of the accommodation options in the area are of the boutique variety, but there's campground in town for $20 per tent.

Continuing on, you'll cross the Derwent River, which flows on towards Hobart (famed art gallery MONA sits on its shores there), and arrive at the town of Ouse at around the 115 mile (185km) mark. From here the terrain tilts sharply upward, on a dirt track that takes you up to about 2500ft (760m) and to the geographical centre of Tasmania on the edge of Bronte Lagoon, complete with a modest monument. Plenty of fishers, angling to catch some of the wily local brown trout, make a trip here; the Bronte Park Village pub on the Marlborough Hwy adjacent to Lake Big Jim is great place to stop for a meal and a chat about the one that got away.

The trail keeps climbing up into the Central Plateau Conservation Area, a subalpine plateau speckled with tarns that is appealing unpeopled. To your west is the Walls of Jerusalem National Park, a remarkable glaciated highland region with very limited road access. Up here the weather can become severe even in summer, but this gorgeous wilderness rewards with wildlife-watching opportunities when wallabies, wombats and spotted quolls come out at dusk.

Tassie wildlife

The wildlife that everybody thinks of when visiting Tasmania is the island's own devil: a growly, grumpy marsupial with bone-cracking jaws and an odd, stiff gait that makes you realise how ancient a creature it is. The terrier-sized Tasmanian devil is the island's top predator but it's really more of a scavenger, cleaning up carcasses. This is bad news for its survival as it's drawn to roadkill and therefore can be hit by cars. Also, the species suffers from a facial cancer that is easily transmitted by the creatures biting and grappling with each other. There is some promising work going on with conserving the species so they may become a less rare sight in the wild. But they're not the only carnivores to watch for here: two species of quoll, the eastern and spotted varieties, live on the island. These are smaller than a housecat and far more agile than the devils. They too are increasingly rare but are exceptionally exciting to spy at night – and also very elusive, as they're shy and camouflaged with spots. Fear not if you don't get lucky: you're certain to see ambling wombats and bouncing wallabies throughout.

Derby biking

In recent years, Tasmania has become an immensely appealing destination for mountain bikers thanks to development in the town of Derby, at the northeast of the island. Best reached via the pleasant hub of Launceston, the Blue Derby mountain-bike network here is truly world-class, with a range of trails for all abilities and some longer out-and-back routes to St Helens on the coast. You can rent mountain bikes and book shuttles with several operators, such as Vertigo MTB. Now rejuvenated after decades in the doldrums, Derby is gaining more food and accommodation options each year, but you will still need to book ahead. Buses are infrequent so you might prefer to try and snag a lift (or ride there).

The north section

The trail tops out at 3500ft (1067m) before a steep off-road descent down to Blackwood Creek. For the final 100 miles (160km) the route covers undulating terrain through agricultural land and eucalypt-shaded tracks. In this northern quarter of Tasmania, more local food producers make for very tempting stops. Some of Australia's finest food and drink hails from these parts, such as wine from the Tamar valley to the east. Just outside the handsome town of Deloraine, with its Victorian and Georgian architecture, quiet backroads hold several food producers: try the excellent smoked fish from the salmon farm or head out on a dog-led hunt in search of fabulous fungi from the truffle farm.

After these delicious diversions, the Tasmanian Trail turns on to a dirt track and enters the Alum Cliffs State Reserve, where the cliffs – Tulampanga to their Traditional Owners – were an important source of ochre for local Aboriginal groups. However, you'll be riding along the north side of the ridge so you'll miss the viewpoint over the Mersey River to the south. Once you pop out of the forest and back on to the road, you'll be among more farms and small towns, never more than a short pedal from somewhere to overnight, whether a campground or boutique B&B. The next notable town is Railton, where you can camp in the pub garden, sample beers at Seven Sheds brewery or just admire the town's terrific topiary.

The surroundings become more built up as you approach endpoint Devonport, following the Mersey River to its mouth and the *Spirit of the Sea* sculpture. Like so many places in Tasmania, Devonport takes its name from the UK (a naval shipyard in this instance), and is the jumping-off point for ferries across the straits to Melbourne, onward travel to Launceston or flights to Hobart.

Tasmanian Trail

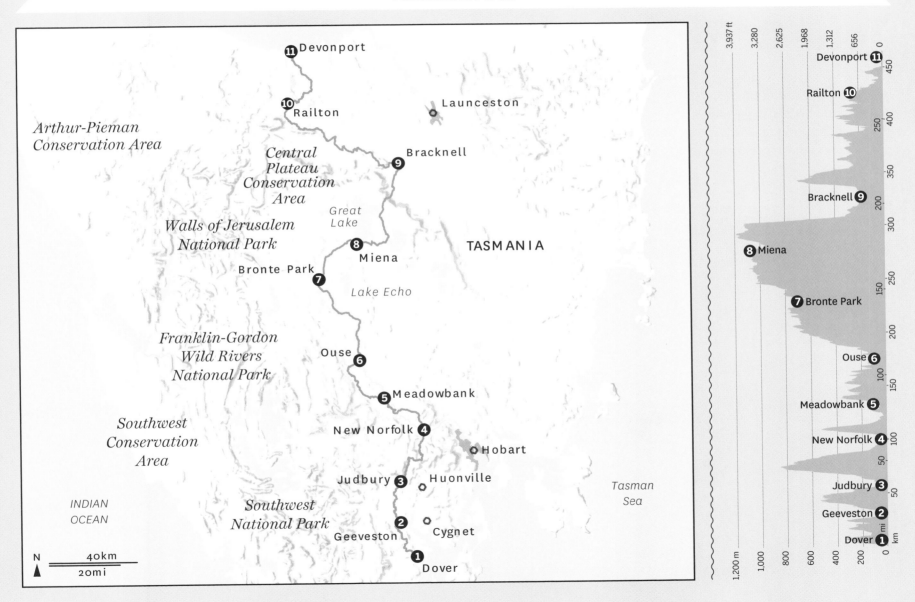

Devonport 🅫

🔟 Railton

Launceston

Bracknell
🅈

*Arthur-Pieman
Conservation Area*

*Central
Plateau
Conservation
Area*

*Walls of Jerusalem
National Park*

*Great
Lake*

🅇 Miena

TASMANIA

Bronte Park ⑦

Lake Echo

*Franklin-Gordon
Wild Rivers
National Park*

Ouse ⑥

*Southwest
Conservation
Area*

⑤ Meadowbank

New Norfolk ④

○ Hobart

Judbury ③ ○ Huonville

*Tasman
Sea*

*Southwest
National Park*

②
Geeveston ○ Cygnet

*INDIAN
OCEAN*

①
Dover

N
40km
20mi

Devonport 🅫
450

Railton 🔟
400

Bracknell 🅈
350

🅇 Miena
300

⑦ Bronte Park
250

Ouse ⑥
200

Meadowbank ⑤
150

New Norfolk ④
100

Judbury ③
50

Geeveston ②

Dover ①
0 km

→ Distance: 390 miles (628km)　　→ Ascent: 10,828ft (3300m)　　→ Difficulty: 3

Tour D'Top End

Australia

This adventurous route in Northern Territory's tropical Top End offers some of the best of Australia: the primeval landscapes, waterfalls and gorges of Kakadu and Litchfield National Parks; colourful outback culture; and a connection to the country's Aboriginal heritage, past and present.

Plan and Prepare

Logistics

Access to the route is from the city of Darwin, which has good domestic and international flight connections and a wide variety of shops for provisioning. It ends at Ubirr in Kakadu National Park, 180 miles (290km) west of Darwin via the Arnhem Hwy. There's a Greyhound bus service from Jabiru back to Darwin (bicycles are $49 extra); you could also try to organise a lift.

Hazards

The dangers are best summed up in two words: crocs and heat. Crocodiles can be present in almost any body of water in the Top End. Heed local advice and any signs before swimming, and err on the side of caution at river crossings. As for heat, it's best to cycle early/late in the day when temperatures are cool, and to carry more water than you think you'll need.

Gear

The rocky, sandy tracks in Litchfield and Kakadu national parks are best suited to a tyre 2.4in wide or greater (though you'll do fine on narrower rubber in most places). Bugs and the scorching sun are both an issue – make sure you've got a mesh barrier for sleeping and full lightweight sun coverage for riding. A minimum of 8 litres of carrying capacity for water is desirable, plus purification tabs.

Info

The dry season (May to October) is the best time to visit, as much of the route is underwater at other times – always check the latest road conditions. SeaLink NT operates the short ferry ride from Darwin to the start of the route at Mandorah, with frequent services. Water can be scarce along the route; fill up when you can. Hotel accommodation is available in Darwin, Pine Creek and Jabiru.

The Top End of the Northern Territory is Australia's 'wild north', which for generations defeated British colonisers' attempts to establish a settlement in an environment marked by extreme heat, floods and ever-present crocodiles. The land's Traditional Owners, however – the Top End's Aboriginal peoples – have thrived in this harsh and beautiful environment for more than 40,000 years, and it is their country through which guests are privileged to ride. The Tour d'Top End is a mixed bikepacking route that can be done in as little as a week, but it's best to give yourself 10 days or more to explore the many highlights of Litchfield and Kakadu National Parks.

The Reynolds River Track

The route begins with a short ferry trip from Darwin across to Mandorah on Cox's Peninsula, from where a long day's ride on a mix of quiet pavement and dirt leads south into Litchfield National Park, with its profusion of spectacular waterfalls and rock pools. It's worth taking an extra day here just to explore, swim and soak up the ambience.

When you're ready, gird yourself to tackle the crux of the route: the Reynolds River Track. Running 27 miles (43km) south on a rough, remote, sandy 4WD track, it passes through savannah dotted with towering magnetic termite mounds, crossing several croc-infested rivers before hitting pavement again. If in doubt at a dodgy water crossing, wait for a jeep to ferry you across.

From that point it's a long day's push 60 miles (96km) east to the ghost town of Grove Hill, and then a further 37 miles (60km) on quiet dirt roads to the relative metropolis of Pine Creek (population 328!), with resupply options and a superb outback pub.

© Matthew Crompton

Waterfalls and rock holes

Litchfield and Kakadu national parks boast an embarrassment of superb waterfalls, swimming holes and rock pools, and exploring these spots (with a plunge to beat the heat) is one of the true joys of the route. In Litchfield, check out the high twin cascades at Wangi Falls; the spectacular segmented Florence Falls; and the plunge pools at Buley Rockhole and Surprise Creek. In Kakadu, seek out unmarked locals' swimming spot, the Rock Hole; and once you've admired the crashing cascades at Gunlom and Maguk Gorge, hike up onto the Arnhem Land plateau above them, enjoying a croc-free dip in the pools at the mouth of the falls with great landscape views unfolding below.

Kakadu south: rock holes & waterfalls

Once you've recharged and resupplied in Pine Creek, head northeast up the Kakadu Hwy and into the enormous Kakadu National Park (at nearly half the size of Switzerland, it's Australia's largest national park). Kakadu is Unesco-listed for both its natural and cultural significance, with outstanding environmental and biological diversity, and some of the world's richest Aboriginal cave paintings, rock carvings and archaeological sites.

From here, the route's main roads are mostly flat and well paved, but side-trips – like the one to unmarked Rock Hole, 40 miles (64km) from Pine Creek and 4 miles (6km) from the park's entrance – are often on dirt that can vary from smooth to brutally rough and corrugated. Thirty miles (48km) north up the highway, a dirt spur leads 6 miles (10km) east to the waterfall at Maguk Gorge; the campsite here makes a great spot to overnight.

Kakadu north: cultural sites

Another 45 miles (72km) up the highway lies the turnoff to the astonishing Aboriginal rock art sites at Burrunggui (Nourlangie): Dreamtime paintings of animals, spirits and human forms among the rock shelters and outcrops are a vivid reminder of the region's many millennia of Indigenous history. En route to Burrunggui, detour to the wetlands and billabongs at Yellow Water and Muirella to see some of Kakadu's vibrant birdlife.

From Burrunggui, it's an 20 easy miles (32km) north to the park's main settlement, Jabiru, built in the 1980s to support the now-defunct Ranger Uranium Mine and formally handed over to its Mirarr Traditional Owners in 2021. With hotels, campgrounds, restaurants and the best supermarket on the route outside of Darwin, it's a great place to relax and recharge.

Kakadu's Aboriginal heritage

The Northern Territory is a region rightly synonymous with Aboriginal Australia: 30% of the Territory's population identifies as Indigenous, compared to just 3% nationally. And while mixing with the Top End's diverse contemporary population is one of the true pleasures of the route, the region also offers some of the country's richest expressions of Australia's ancient Aboriginal history and heritage. Nowhere is this more present than in Kakadu's two main rock-art sites: Burrunggui and Ubirr. The three clustered rock-art sites at Burrunggui (Nourlangie) show how the Traditional Owners of the land have lived over millennia. They contain powerful depictions of Creation ancestors like Namarrkon, the Lightning Man, as well as animals and food sources endemic to the area. Ubirr contains hundreds of outstanding individual paintings, serving not only a spiritual function, but providing a historical and cultural record stretching back more than 20,000 years. In an evolving range of styles and often rendered in red ochre pigment, the works depict human handprints, Dreamtime spirit figures and animals (many of them long extinct), as well as European first contact with Indigenous people here.

Pedalling north out of Jabiru, the road winds 30 miles (48km) toward the top corner of the park, with the wild stone country of the Arnhem Land escarpment rising in towering rock formations to the east.

Nearing the northeastern edge of the park, the road approaches a trio of highlights. The first of these is Cahills Crossing (above), a causeway across the East Alligator River, which is completely submerged at high tide, the waterway teeming with huge saltwater crocodiles. Keep your distance.

Turning south from the crossing, a network of sandy backcountry trails (the Bardedjilidji walk) winds through a wild landscape of sandstone outcrops, caves, billabongs and dry riverbeds, all set amongst scrubby tropical savannah. Animals cluster around the waterholes, and you run a good chance of spotting birds like sulphur-crested cockatoos along the route, or mammals like the short-beaked echidna or black wallaroo.

The crown in the jewel of the area, and a fitting finish to the route, however, is the sprawling rock-art site at Ubirr, which boasts some world's most outstanding examples of traditional Australian Aboriginal painting.

The art at Ubirr is spectacular at any time of day, but sunset is the ideal time to visit the site. Climb the towering rock outcrop for an incredible golden-hour view over the green floodplains to west, then turn around to regard the Mordor-like formations of the Stone Country rising out of Arnhem Land to the east.

Tour D'Top End

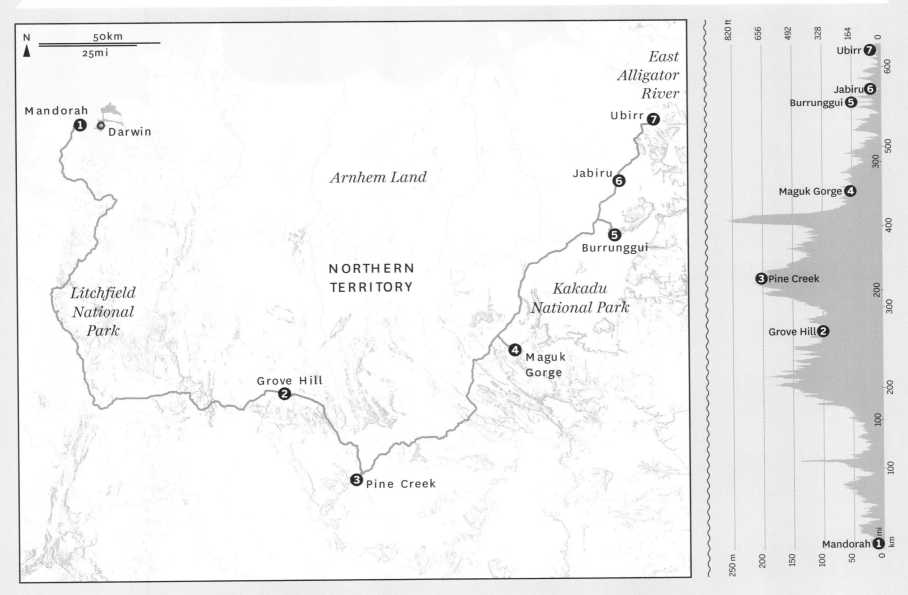

N

50km
25mi

Mandorah **1**

Darwin

East Alligator River

Ubirr **7**

Jabiru **6**

Arnhem Land

Burrunggui **5**

NORTHERN TERRITORY

Litchfield National Park

Kakadu National Park

4 Maguk Gorge

Grove Hill **2**

3 Pine Creek

820 ft
656
492
328
164
0

Ubirr **7**

Jabiru **6**

Burrunggui **5**

Maguk Gorge **4**

3 Pine Creek

Grove Hill **2**

Mandorah **1**

600

500

400

300

200

100

250 m
200
150
100
50
0 km
0 mi

More to ride

Six more superb routes in Africa, Asia and Oceania

Cycle Route 1
Taiwan

Distance 600 miles (965km)
Difficulty: 3

The island of Taiwan is one of the world's best cycling destinations but also one of its most unsung. Taiwan's signature tour is Cycle Route 1, which circles the coast of the island and is typically started from Taipei. It was developed by the Taiwanese government and opened in 2015. Using mostly traffic-free bike paths, Route 1 is usually billed as a beginner-friendly challenge to be attempted over 10 days, but the heat and humidity do add difficulty. Highlights include ocean views, hot springs, tropical plants and plenty of temples, such as Lukang's Longshan Temple. The terrain is mostly easygoing, since riders skirt Taiwan's extremely beautiful and mountainous interior, where gruelling ascents such as the 50-mile (80km) climb up Taroko Gorge attract hardcore cyclists.

Mae Hong Son Loop
Thailand

Distance: 400 miles (644km)
Difficulty: 3

Starting from Chiang Mai in mountainous northern Thailand, the Mae Hong Son route (below) is a well-known circuit around this fascinating region on surfaced roads. It's most often done on motorbikes but is also a popular and straightforward cycling route, offering easy navigation, swooping roads through misty jungle and plenty of places to explore along the way. The amount of steep ascent (more than 42,650ft/13,000m) means that even fit riders might want to take a week or more to complete it. Stopping at towns such as Pai allows for rest and refuelling. For a more difficult off-road alternative out of Chiang Mai, take on the 1500-mile (2415km) Bamboo Byway, a long-distance, work-in-progress route through northern Thailand, Laos and Vietnam.

Jordan Bike Trail
Jordan

Distance: 453 miles (730km)
Difficulty: 4

Jordan's epic desert drama is on show throughout this top-to-bottom ride through the Middle Eastern kingdom. The route was developed by various private enterprises (and later supported by USAID) and is designed to be ridden from north to south, starting in Umm Qais and ending in Aqaba after crossing the widescreen wonder of Wadi Rum. Riders also take in the Dead Sea and the ruins of Petra (above). The route is split into three sections – Northern, Central and Southern – so it's possible to break it down bit by bit. And the terrain becomes drier and more rugged the further south you go (mountain bikes are recommended). Local business may be able to offer shuttles and bike rentals as required; jordanbiketrail.com has detailed information.

The Otway Rip
Australia

Distance: 160 miles (257km)
Difficulty: 1

The giant, shaggy mountain ash trees of Australia's southeast are your tall companions on this easygoing and accessible spin through the Otways. West of Melbourne, this temperate, forested region of Victoria is bordered by the Great Ocean Road, but you don't spend much time on tarmac, instead taking to shady dirt roads littered with great scrolls of bark. Rowdy Australian birds provide the soundtrack. The route starts from Camperdown, which can be reached by train from Melbourne and Geelong, and heads east via lakes, waterfalls and a bit of ocean swimming in Port Campbell Bay. The Great Otway National Park is a beautiful place to explore, and the tiny town of Forrest toward the end of the route has some fun mountain-bike trails to try if you have time to linger a day.

Twin Coast Mega Loop
New Zealand

Distance: 265 miles (426km)
Difficulty: 1

It's less than 60 miles (100km) from the beautiful Bay of Islands on the east coast of New Zealand's North Island to the west coast, meaning that cyclists can ride coast-to-coast in a day, mostly along the Twin Coast Cycle Trail. But if you add sections of the Kauri Coast Cycleway you can turn the trip into an easygoing multi-day loop and see much more of New Zealand's tropical north. Hard as it is to ride away from the Bay of Islands, tranquil Hokianga Harbour on the west coast is equally pretty. The route then turns south through a forest of kauri trees (above), stout giants that play an important role in Māori creation tales, and ends with a loop back to the start via Whangārei. Check nzcycletrail. com for detailed information.

Mountains to Sea
New Zealand

Distance: 143 miles (230km)
Difficulty: 2

New Zealand's 22 Great Rides vary from family-friendly rail trails to long-distance epics, and this route from the Tongariro National Park's volcanic peaks to the Whanganui River as it meets the Tasman Sea is definitely at the latter end of the spectrum. That's not because of the distance but the terrain and tracks used, which may be washed out after wet or severe weather – and there's a compulsory jet-boat ride along a 20-mile (32km) stretch of river. This southwest corner of the North Island is relatively little-visited and feels somewhat isolated. The route takes in a descent from Mt Ruapehu towards Okahune's Old Coach Road, through Tongariro National Park and along Hāpuawhenua Viaduct. Riders then traverse rural landscapes and Whanganui National Park on dirt tracks.

Contents

Europe

Adriatic Crest (Croatia)	120
Burrally (Spain)	124
Caucasus Crossing (Georgia)	128
Danube Cycle Path	
(Germany, Austria, Slovakia & Hungary)	132
The Hebridean Way (Scotland)	138
Hope 1000 (Switzerland)	142
Isar Cycle Route (Germany)	148
Jura Traverse (France)	152
Bikepacking Kjölur (Iceland)	156
The Meuse Cycle Route	
(France, Belgium & the Netherlands)	160
Mjølkevegen (Norway)	166
Trans-Cambrian Way (Wales)	170
Trans-Dolomiti (Italy)	174
West Kernow Way (England)	178
Wild Atlantic Way (Ireland)	184
The Wolf's Lair (Italy)	188
King Alfred's Way (England)	194
Montañas Vacias (Spain)	200
Tuscany Trail (Italy)	204
La Vélodyssée (France)	210
John Muir Way (Scotland)	216
Vuelta de Vasco (Spain)	220
More to ride	224

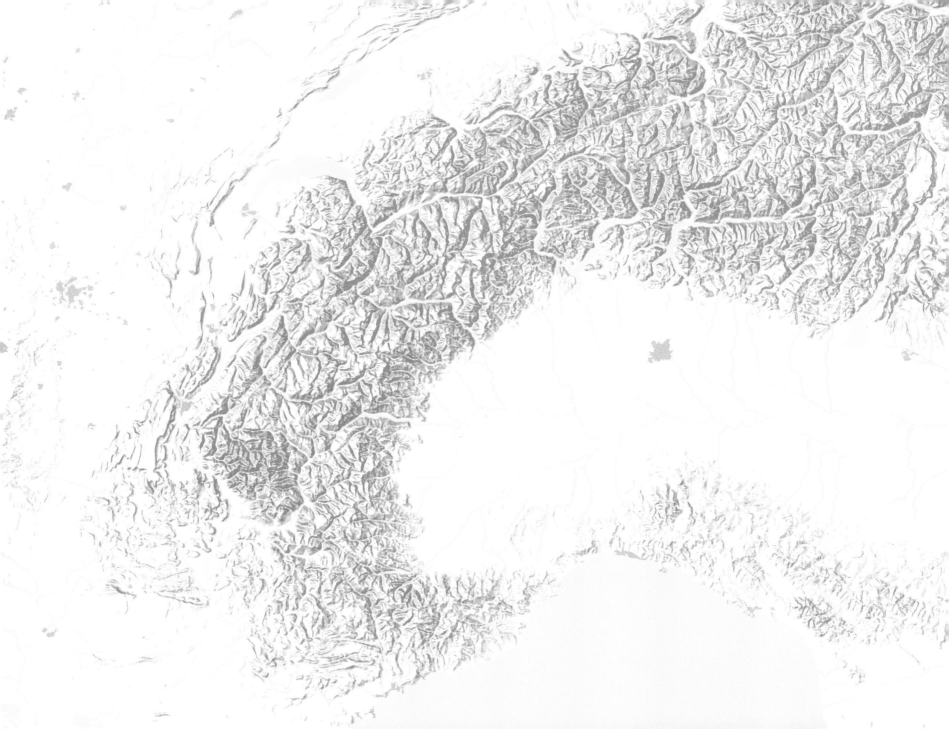

→ Distance: 380 miles (612km)   → Ascent: 35,728ft (10,890m)   → Difficulty: 4

The Adriatic Crest

Croatia

Discover Croatian culture away from the tourist trail on this challenging ride on gravel tracks over islands and across mountain ranges, finishing in the city of Split. There's history here, from the ancient Greeks to the recent Balkan wars, and plenty of warm hospitality too.

Plan and Prepare

Logistics

The ride's start-point, the Slovenian village of Ilirska Bistrica, can be reached by direct train from the Croatian coastal city of Rijeka or Ljubljana in Slovenia (on the same line) in under 2hr; from Trieste in Italy by train in under 3hr (with one change) and from Zagreb in under 5hr by train (with a couple of changes). The route ends in Split, which is well connected by domestic and international trains and flights.

Hazards

As well as a prevalence of tyre-shredding thorns, the main hazard is landmines, strewn across the landscape along some stretches of the ride in a deadly reminder of the Balkan conflicts. However, risky areas are carefully signposted and you'll be safe if you stay on the road. Water shortages are more likely to be an issue.

Gear

A mountain bike is essential: there are some rough, rocky and remote sections as well as stretches on surfaced roads. Hardtails would be ideal; and as thorns are common along much of the route, tubeless tyres may mean fewer problems. The route contains some rugged trails where hike-a-bike might be required. Be sure to have copious water-carrying capacity. The remote middle stretch can require camping kit or at least sleeping gear.

Info

Summers are seriously hot here, particularly in July and August. Storms are also quite common in the mountains in spring and autumn, so be prepared to ride to lower ground. May to June and September would be ideal. For accommodation, there are guesthouses along the way, useful if you need a break from the travel mattress. For more info, check bikepacking.com

Croatia's Adriatic coast is an irresistible draw for millions of visitors, which is great news for bikepackers because it means there is a huge hinterland of rural highlands to explore, punctuated by pleasantly untouristed towns and villages. This route runs southeast down almost the entire length of this sliver of a country to Split; and from time to time it descends to the rocky coast so riders can get their refreshing fix of the warm turquoise sea. The route even starts with a bit of island-hopping via a couple of ferry rides.

From hills to islands

The starting point is the Slovenian town of Ilirska Bistrica. Echoes of wars old and new still reverberate in these parts: here, atop Freedom Hill, you'll find the first of the route's Spomeniks, Brutalist military monuments scattered across the landscape. Heading south out of Ilirska Bistrica, you'll cross into Croatia after about 10 miles (16km), although you could start from the Croatian town of Šapjane, which is just across the border and on the same train line as Rijeka. The tracks climb into some quite rugged hills, up to about 4000ft (1220m), and then meander south towards the coast. This region of northern Croatia is thinly populated so plan ahead for provisions, water and overnighting. Wild camping is not officially permitted but in these quieter parts there's no reason not to ask permission to pitch a tent. You'll soon be skirting the crags and peaks of Učka Nature Park before reaching the ferry port of Brestova after about 50 miles (80km). Here, catch a 20-minute ferry to the island of Cres, one of the largest of Croatia's 718 islands but one that remains under the radar. Watch for griffon vultures soaring above quiet coves and groves of olive, apple and chestnut trees.

Spomeniks

In the 1960s and 1970s, nations of the former Yugoslavia began building Brutalist monuments to WWII battles and other military milestones. These concrete commemorations, often in unlikely locations – at the tops of hills, on the edges of villages, deep in forests – were usually of futuristic design: alien shapes and structures, often angular or sinuous and beautiful. Known collectively as Spomeniks (monuments), and once venerated and visited, many are now remembered only by Spomenik hunters. Find your first in Ilirska Bistrica at the start of the ride; others include *Monument to the Revolution* in Podgarić and Platak's *Monument to Victims of Fascism*.

After riding along spine of Cres, take another ferry from Merag to the island of Krk, which is just as large but far more developed. You'll cross this busy holiday isle via Vrbnik, one of its most charming villages and a good place to replenish food supplies; and then jump on another ferry to the mainland, where you'll arrive at Šmrika. From here, it doesn't take long to exit civilisation, heading southeast on forest trails and singletrack, including some steep climbs. You'll hit the ride's halfway point high in the mountains of the Northern Velebit National Park, which is the country's wildest spot and home to bears, wolves and lynx. The forested park is packed with streams, hiking trails and some mountain huts, such as the one at Zavizan-Senj. For more background, read novelist Edo Popović's Velebit travelogue, *Priručnik za hodače*. 'In the mountains,' he writes, 'nothing reminds you of the passage of time, no trams and buses with timetables, no clocks in the squares, no church bells, no radio and television program, nothing but the sun and the moon in their primordial rhythm.'

The home stretch to Split

A handful of towns to the east of the mountain range, such as Gospić and Sveti Rok, offer accommodation, food and friendly welcomes – bikepackers are a rare sight here. Just remember that some minefields still lie between those two towns, although they are well signposted. After enjoying the views of the Adriatic, sparkling in the distance, you'll start descending from the Velebit to Obrovac, where the Zrmanja River offers some swimming spots. With about 100 miles (160km) to go, the run-in to Split is relatively low-lying. Take a break at the beautiful coastal town (and Unesco World Heritage Site) of Trogir, before letting your hair down in dynamic Split.

The Adriatic Crest route map

Ilirska Bistrica ❶
SLOVENIA
❷ Šapjane
❸
Rijeka
❻ Šmrika
Brestova
❹
Vrbnik
❺
Krk
Pazin
Rovinj
Pula
Cres
Učka Nature Park

Northern Velebit National Park

Plitvice Lakes National Park
Bihać
Otočac

Bosanski Petrovac

Jajce

BOSNIA AND HERCEGOVINA

CROATIA

Gospić ❼
Gračac
Knin
Livno

Paklenica National Park
❽ Obrovac
Sinj

Zadar

Krka National Park

Šibenik
Trogir ❾
❿ Split

Adriatic Sea

N

50 km
25 mi

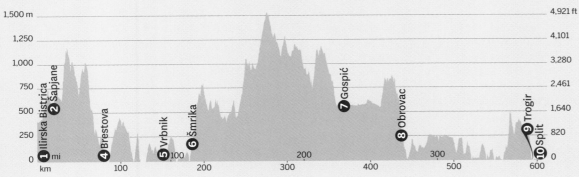

Distance: 432 miles (695km) ● Ascent: 47,230ft (14,395m) ● Difficulty: 3

Burrally

Spain

For a winter escape, this accessible exploratory arc through València's hinterland offers gravel roads, solitude, warmth and a taste of rural Spanish life away from the Costas. Based on a bikepacking race-route, it's better appreciated at a more relaxed pace.

Plan and Prepare

Logistics

The route starts from Vinaròs, a coastal town 93 miles (150km) north of València. Trains between the two cities take about 2hr. Generally, it's easy to take bicycles on Spain's trains, but be aware that some services limit the number of bikes per train. The route finishes in Xàtiva, southwest of València and just under 1hr from the city by train.

Hazards

Summer's heat can be brutal and most people ride in spring, autumn or winter to avoid it. Whenever you ride the Burrally, ensure you can carry plenty of water. It's technically illegal to wild-camp in Spain but it's often possible to ask permission. Wildfires are a perennial hazard in the drier months and camp fires are not advisable.

Gear

With quite a high proportion of tarmacked roads, a gravel bike with moderately chunky tyres will be fine for the Burrally. There are some gravel tracks and rougher rocky sections on which to take care. A mountain bike will be slower on most of the route. The means to carry plenty of water is an important consideration, as it's a dry landscape. If riding over winter, take an insulated jacket and a good sleeping bag for cold nights.

Info

The Burrally race sets off in March or April; you can ride the route at any time but summer, from June to September, is very hot here. The best months tend to be March to June and September to November, but people also ride over the winter when the days can be relatively warm. Consider your accommodation options: wild camping isn't permitted in Spain but discrete campers who leave no trace rarely have problems. Get more info at burrally.wordpress.com

One of the best things about bikepacking in the 2020s is the community that has grown up around exploring places on bicycles. Sometimes these like-minded people get together for a group ride that is more of a rally than a race, and one such event was the Torino–Nice Rally, founded by James Olsen. That meandering ride through the southern Alps inspired Luis Cordon in the Spanish city of València to create a route that wound through the arid backcountry behind the coastal city. He wanted to show off the little-frequented landscapes and the down-to-earth local culture, naming the Burrally route in a portmanteau of the Valèncian slang for crazy or extraordinary – *burrà* – and rally.

Cordon's route sets off from the town of Vinaròs, which is easily reached by one of Spain's very user-friendly trains. It then swings into the hills and stays there for around 400 miles (644km) as you pedal south. At a brisk pace, locals typically knock off the full route in around six days. The annual rally is only open to about 30 riders and takes place in March or April, but bikepackers are encouraged to visit and ride at any time of the year (just skip the summer heat).

Into the hills

There's a lot of climbing on this route, and the uphills commence straight out of the gate. Riding west out of Vinaròs you'll enter the foothills of the Sistema Ibérico, the eastern fringe of a mountain range that extends across the north of Spain as far as La Rioja. After the town of Rossell, about 20 miles (32km) in, you'll be at an elevation of 1500ft (457m) and it only gets higher from here on. Staying on a tarmacked road makes the climbing a little smoother, as you zigzag through forest and past the 15th-century Ermita Santo Domingo in Vallibona.

Chulilla

One of the most interesting towns that you'll pass through on the Burrally is Chulilla. The settlement here dates from the first millennium BCE but its main buildings, including the fortress, are mostly medieval, built during the 15th and 16th centuries. As was common in Spain, mosques and churches were constructed on top of each other, according to the whims of the various rulers; there are ruins of an earlier Moorish castle in the town. Outside Chulilla, the River Turia has carved gorges and canyons as it flows from the mountains to València. These rock walls attract climbers from autumn to spring, offering an excellent range of quality climbing routes at all grades (though mostly hard).

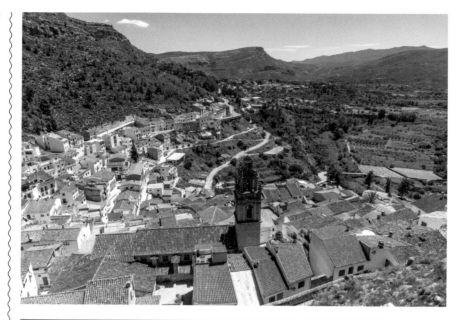

Beyond Vallibona, the tarmac morphs into dirt tracks and the landscape becomes a bit wilder as you ride into the Parc Natural de la Tinença de Benifassà. The gravelly track weaves through pine trees and rocky spires, where Spanish ibex and wild boar roam. If you look up you might spot vultures and the wide wingspan of a Bonelli's eagle.

After about 50 miles (80km), you'll pass the town of Morella, its hilltop castle giving the terrain a whiff of Don Quixote and his meandering quest (though he was from La Mancha, further inland). The climbing continues on mix of dirt and paved roads, topping out at 5000ft (1524m) as you circle the 5948ft (1813m) Penyagolosa, centrepiece of the Parc Natural del Penyagolosa. There are hiking trails to the top of the second-highest mountain in the València region, although once a year ultra-runners race for 68 miles (110km) up to the top.

The route descends and dips in and out of tiny whitewashed hamlets such as Castillo de Villamalefa, but don't count on shops being open. If they are, grab some figs, cheese and bread to replenish your stores.

Rock and roll

After Penyagolosa, the next landmark to aim for is the town of Chulilla (top left), some 207 miles (333km) in and roughly the route's halfway mark. With a little government investment to help things along, Chulilla has become one of the world's top winter retreats for rock climbers. It's an enchanting place, a cluster of red-tiled whitewashed buildings set between rock promontories. Cafes and hostels are a reminder of creature comforts, but when the crowds get too much you can jump on your bike and continue into the Spanish hinterland. From here the route, mostly paved, loops around the spectacular El Júcar gorge before descending on dirt roads to the endpoint at Xàtiva.

Burrally

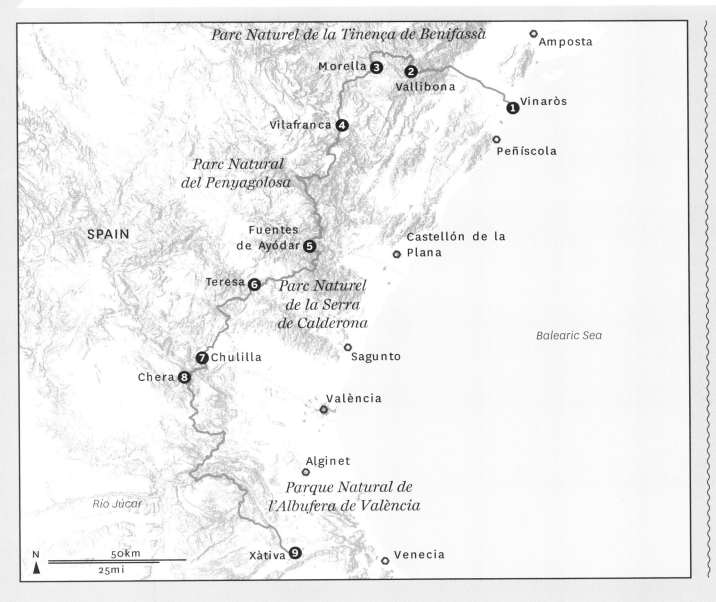

Parc Naturel de la Tinença de Benifassà

Amposta

Morella **3**

Vallibona **2**

Vinaròs **1**

Vilafranca **4**

Peñíscola

Parc Natural
del Penyagolosa

SPAIN

Fuentes
de Ayódar **5**

Castellón de la
Plana

Teresa **6**

Parc Naturel
de la Serra
de Calderona

Balearic Sea

Chulilla **7**

Sagunto

Chera **8**

València

Alginet

Parque Natural de
l'Albufera de València

Río Júcar

Xàtiva **9**

Venecia

N

50km

25mi

4,921ft
4,101
3,280
2,461
1,640
820
0

Xàtiva **9**

Chera **8**
Chulilla **7**

Teresa **6**

Fuentes de Ayódar **5**

4 Vilafranca

Morella **3**

Vallibona **2**

Vinaròs **1**

1,500 m
1,250
1,000
750
500
250
0

→ Distance: 795 miles (1280km) → Ascent: 103,625ft (31,585m) → Difficulty: 4

Caucasus Crossing

Georgia

Explore Georgia on this very challenging adventure into the Caucasus, a mountain range between worlds: you'll find wine, age-old villages, vast and empty vistas and a historic and very hospitable people.

Plan and Prepare

Logistics

The route starts in the western town of Zugdidi, which is a 6hr train ride from Tbilisi with Georgian Railway. You may need to book a space for your bike and collect a receipt to show the train's conductor. You can end at Tbilisi or, if you have extensive bikepacking experience, ride on to the finish at Telavi, from where you'll need to take a minibus for the 2hr-plus drive back to Tbilisi (and negotiate a price for your bike as baggage).

Hazards

The number one hazard in Georgia will be the sheepdogs that guard flocks in the mountains. They are aggressive and you will need to come up with a plan for them, which may include turning around and taking an alternative route. They're not to be taken lightly. Aside from the dogs, be aware that there are political tensions in certain areas. And keep an eye on the weather in the mountains, too.

Gear

A robust mountain bike is preferred for this trip; given the lack of bike shops on the route you ought to be comfortable fixing common problems such as broken spokes and chains (and carry some spares). You will likely prefer to carry camping and cooking kit too, plus equipment for water purification.

Info

The most up-to-date info, including any route changes, is likely to be on the bikepacking.com page for the Caucasus Crossing. The best time of year to ride is between mid-June and early September, especially if you're riding beyond Tbilisi to take on the challenging section around Tusheti in the Higher Caucasus. You can also take the train for stages or book a local cycling guide.

The Georgia section of the Caucasus Crossing is a great example of how exploring a place by bicycle enables far more personal and engaging experiences than by vehicle. Riding across this fascinating country will mean meeting many local people and getting to know their culture and customs, as you stay and eat where they do. It also means that money spent on the trip stays in the local economy, which is also very welcome.

The Caucasus mountain range dominates the sinew of land between the Caspian Sea and the Black Sea, connecting the land masses of Asia (the Middle East) and Europe and running through Georgia, Armenia and Azerbaijan. As you'd expect, this corridor has been hugely strategically significant over the past few millennia and it remains so today, with Russia to the north and Iran to the south. It's a fascinating place, and as bikepacking is relatively uncommon here your presence will pique people's curiosity.

Aside from the geopolitics, this is also a very challenging place in topographic terms. The Caucasus range is higher than the European Alps: the elevation of its highest peak, the 18,510ft (5642m) Mt Elbrus, is some 2737ft (835m) greater than that of the Alps' Mont Blanc. This route focuses on only the post-Soviet republic of Georgia, and although it doesn't actually climb these snowcapped peaks, they're in the background and the route as a whole is very mountainous. It takes in huge lakes, cliffside monasteries and fortified villages that are a reminder of Georgia's history, but it skirts South Ossetia, a contested region to the north (hence the U-shaped diversion).

Setting off
Kicking off in Zugdidi, 18 miles (29km) from the Black Sea, the route heads northeast on roads towards the popular hiking region of Svaneti.

Winemaking

The Georgian wine experience is like no other. This is widely recognised as the land where people first learned to tame the grapevine, around 6000 BCE. In some places here, winemaking has changed little since then. Grapes are still harvested by hand, and foot-pressed in the hollowed-out trunks of ancient trees. The juice flows into underground clay amphoras, known as qvevri, where it ferments and matures without additives. When the sealed qvevri is opened in the spring of the following year, its wine is clear and bright. There are enough artisans keeping this natural method alive. Nearly two-thirds of Georgia's wine originates in the eastern hills of Kakheti and some of its greatest wines are actually buried in villagers' backyards, awaiting release.

After about 90 miles (145km), gravel tracks take over and you'll be climbing up to about 8000ft (2438m), high enough that you'll feel breathless. In winter there's skiing; spring sees the rhododendrons in bloom and in autumn the weather is often still warm and dry. The regional hub is Mestia, where there are good transport links and food shops, but elsewhere in the region you'll be riding deeper into the valleys from village to village. From the Svaneti region the route descends down to lower levels and the city of Kutaisi, from where those completing just a third of the route can take a train to Tbilisi (left).

To Tbilisi & beyond

In the centre of the country, the next mountainous stretch covers about 200 miles (322km), passing the cave monastery at Vardzia, built in the late 12th century by Queen Tamar, Georgia's first female ruler, as protection from the Mongol warriors attacking Europe. About 300 of the original 6000 dwellings are open to visitors; the church still sports ancient frescoes. Also on this central section is Lake Paravani, about halfway along the route, where Turkish shepherds rest their flocks on a high-altitude steppe. From here the trail gradually descends again through an extremely unpopulated region (be prepared with supplies) towards the medium-sized city of Gori, where the Soviet dictator Joseph Stalin was born.

About 60 miles (95km) later is Tbilisi, Georgia's engaging capital, which displays both a timelessness and a very contemporary coolness. You'll want to explore the nightlife here. Back on the bike and the road heads north again, into the second of Georgia's adventure hotspots, Tusheti, which has tracks at 10,000ft (3048m). However, this corner of Georgia, on the border with Chechnya, is far more challenging; it can (and should) be bypassed by those without expert bikepacking experience.

Caucasus Crossing

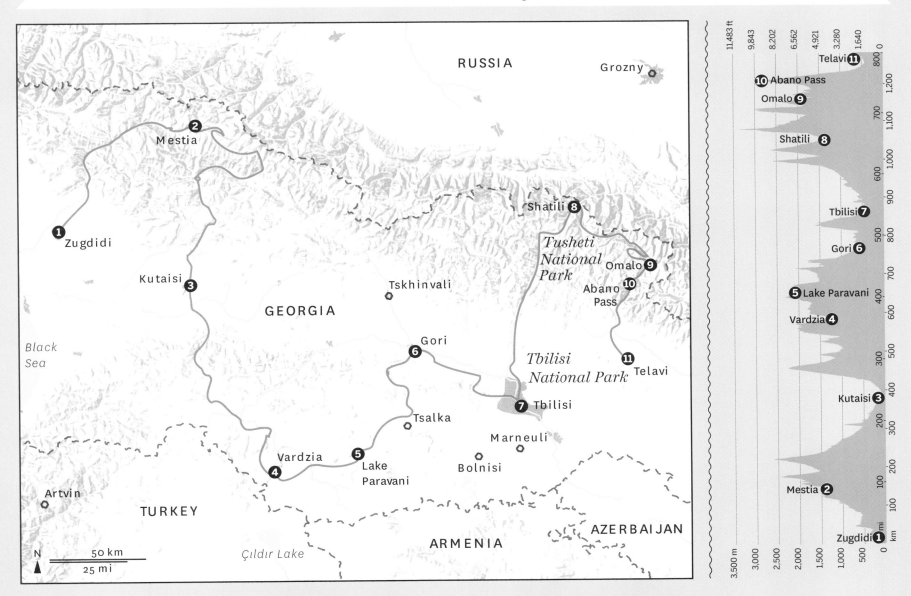

➡ Distance: 795 miles (1280km)   ➡ Ascent: 18,125ft (5525m)   ➡ Difficulty: 1

Danube Cycle Path

Germany, Austria, Slovakia & Hungary

Europe's most popular cycle-touring route follows the path of the Danube River from Germany's Black Forest to Budapest in Hungary, visiting some of Europe's most interesting cities and exploring history and culture along the way.

Plan and Prepare

Logistics

The Danube flows southeast so it makes sense to follow its direction downhill. Riding the full route means starting in Germany at the river's source in Donaueschingen and ending in Budapest, Hungary. However, most people will only cycle sections of the path at a time, for example from Germany's Passau to Vienna in Austria, so getting to and from each end will vary accordingly. Europe's excellent regional public transport makes for easy connections.

Hazards

There's not a lot to worry about on the Danube Cycle Path, except perhaps crashing into another cyclist or pedestrian. Some stretches of road are shared with people driving vehicles, who are always the greatest threat to those on bicycles. It's worth practising navigation if this is your first cycling trip, although most of the route is well signposted.

Gear

Almost any bicycle will suffice on this cycle path. There's very little elevation gain and it's all on surfaced paths and roads. You just need to be able to carry as much luggage as you require; that might mean using a bike with pannier mounts, although modern bikepacking bags can attach to most bikes. Electric bikes would also work well, and can be recharged easily overnight.

Info

Given the length of the route, few people will ride the whole distance in one attempt and can therefore avoid the cold of winter and the heat of midsummer. Accommodation options range from campsites (or unofficial bivouacs) to hostels, guesthouses and hotels. The official website for the Danube Cycle Path (donau-radweg.info) has a lot of descriptive information about the route, but not much practical assistance.

In Germany's Black Forest, just east of the small, sedate town of Donaueschingen, several headwaters start to flow into one stream – and that stream builds into Europe's second-longest river, the Danube. The unhurried river broadens as it passes through southern Germany and crosses the border into Austria, where it bisects Vienna diagonally. It shoulders the role of border between Slovakia and Hungary, connecting Bratislava and Budapest as an aquatic thoroughfare, then continues on through Croatia, Serbia, Romania, Bulgaria, Moldova and Ukraine before emptying into the Black Sea. For some 795 miles (1280km) of its length, from the Black Forest to Budapest, the Danube is accompanied by a bicycle path that is arguably the most popular cycle-touring route in Europe.

There are several reasons for its popularity but an important factor is that rivers tend to flow downhill and skirt high ground, so there's only a modest of amount of uphill pedalling required over its full extent. Secondly, it offers a varied range of experiences, from rural landscapes and natural wonders to some of the most enthralling cities in central Europe. Whether you're interested in vineyards or wetlands, classical concerts or nightclubs, there's a section of the path that will suit you. And that's the other important factor: given the route's length and the number of countries through which it passes, most people will tour just a section of it at a time. That could be the bucolic, castle-bristled German part; or the most popular stretch from Passau to Vienna in Austria; or the open riparian spaces of Slovakia and Hungary. Wherever you chose to start and end your ride along the Danube Cycle Path, there a couple of constants to consider: you will never be far from a place to sleep at night, or from the prospect of delicious food and drink.

Cultural capitals

Although the Danube Cycle Path passes through many natural parks and quiet rural stretches, it's the cities that may be most memorable, promising intense bursts of cultural discovery amid the freewheeling relaxation. There are five significant stops along the route, each shaped by its proximity to the Danube and offering something distinctive. From west to east, the German city of Passau arrives first. It stands at the confluence of three rivers, meaning that trade was profitable: the money flowed in and built an architecturally impressive Altstadt (Old Town). Next is Linz in Austria, which combines contemporary venues such as 'museum of the future' Ars Electronica and the modern Musiktheater opera house with a historic Old Town; don't miss the huge harbourside street-art murals, either. Vienna also mixes imperial grandeur, palaces and masterpiece-filled museums with a hip electronic music scene and fashionable shopping. The city's most famous resident was Wolfgang Amadeus Mozart; catch one of his operas at the superlative Staatsoper concert hall (below), then enjoy sampling wines made from grapes grown in the city at Vienna's Vinotheks (wine bars). In Slovakia's Bratislava, the cultural calendar centres on Hlavné Námestie, the city's stately main square.

The path through Germany

From Donaueschingen, about three hours' by train from Strasbourg (France), Stuttgart (Germany) and Basel (Switzerland), paved paths lead you to Mühlheim and on to Sigmaringen via a couple of spectacular castles. Sigmaringen's clifftop Burg Hohenzollern was a former royal residence, and the family now welcome the public into their ancestral home. Another castle awaits at Zwiefaltendorf, but for a sense of the region's prehistory, stop at the Heuneburg Celtic Museum, which displays excavated items traded millennia ago from what are now the Baltics, Greece, Slovenia and France.

After about 120 miles (1953km), or one tenth of the total distance, Ulm (above) is a pleasant place to stay and is home to the world's tallest cathedral steeple.

Continuing onward, the next notable town is historic Donauwörth, also a stop on Germany's Romantic Road. The path passes grassy wetland meadows, with the river flowing slowly beside you. More castles appear on the way to Ingolstadt, and the landscape becomes forested once more. Between Ingolstadt and Kelheim, riders can admire limestone gorges and sample beer brewed at Weltenburg Abbey. At the monastery of Metten, a few miles later, the monks preferred books to beer and a guided tour of the extraordinary Baroque Library is essential. The next significant stop is Passau, the final city before you leave Germany for Austria. The 'Three Rivers City', at the confluence of the Danube, Inn and Ilz, is another enjoyable place to take a break from the bike.

battles. After about 70 miles (112km) you'll come to Melk. On one side of the river lies the quirky 18th-century castle of Luberegg, now a huge hotel, and on the south bank is Melk Abbey, one of the world's greatest examples of Baroque architecture, overlooking the Wachau valley. The library of the Benedictine monastery inspired Umberto Eco's novel *The Name of the Rose*.

Beyond Melk, you'll enter the wine-producing part of the Wachau valley around the town of Krems, a good place to stay for a night. From Krems it's 45 miles (72km) to Vienna (left), another richly rewarding place to explore over a few days. In addition to its pomp and palaces, Vienna offers contemporary attractions such as the Albertina modern art museum, with works by Andy Warhol, Damien Hirst and the Austrian artist Maria Lassnig. The city's cafes are also recognised by Unesco, and there's an exciting nightlife scene centred along the Gürtel, an outer ring road below an elevated U-Bahn track. But, as Mozart once wrote to his father: 'Just to be in Vienna is entertainment enough.'

Bratislava and Budapest

En route to the Slovakian capital of Bratislava you'll glide through the Donau-Auen National Park, a floodplain of alluvial forest and meadows alive with birds. Slovakia may only have gained its independence in 1993, but Bratislava is a captivating combination of a Gothic and medieval Old Town, Baroque palaces and a Renaissance castle, plus brutal, communist-era architecture and a futuristic bridge. It's another fascinating place to stay.

Between Bratislava and Budapest, the Danube Cycle Path gets a little less polished, but there's no shortage of sights or diversions to take. The last stretch of 50 miles (80km) is from Hungary's oldest town, Esztergom, to its capital, Budapest. The river flows onward but the bike path stops here.

Into Austria

The Danube Cycle Path between Passau and Vienna in Austria is as the most popular section. It's about 186 miles (300km) in length and, over its first 25 miles (40km), starts with a bit more ascent than is usual. But soon the river's lazy rhythms take over and you can settle down to an easy pace, pedalling past the Trappist monastery of Engelhartszell and the castle at Aschach. There are frequent towns or just places to camp if you prefer. Austria's third-largest city, Linz, is the halfway goal and it's another beautiful spot to linger. Beaches on the banks of the Danube draw every age group, from promenading pensioners to young couples sharing pizza.

Continuing from Linz, the river meanders past meadows and the gorgeous town of Grein, weaving through forests into one of the most scenic sections of the whole route. The valley is punctuated by palatial castles, which look more suited to balls than

Danube Cycle Path

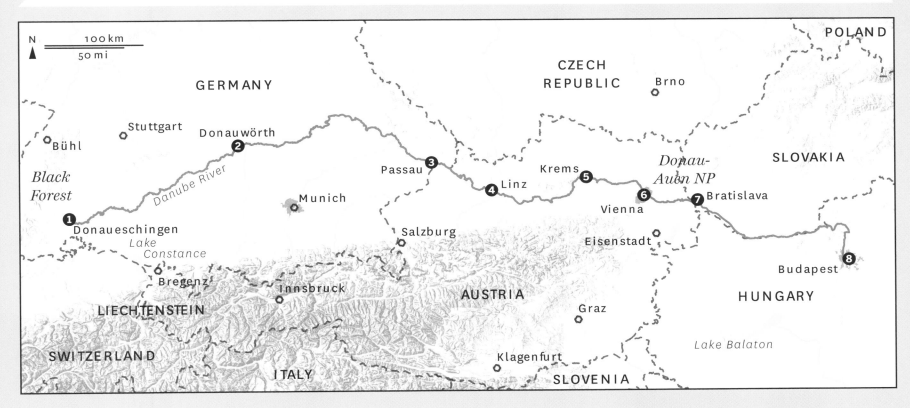

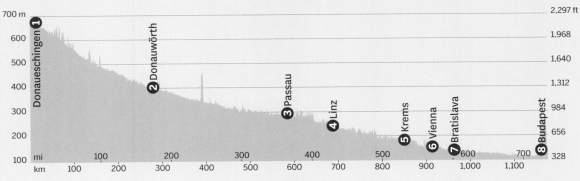

➡ Distance: 262 miles (422km)   ➡ Ascent: 9667ft (2947m)   ➡ Difficulty: 2

The Hebridean Way

Scotland

The Hebridean Way has it all: stunning white-sand beaches, dramatic mountain landscapes, great and bad weather, otters, standing stones to rival Stonehenge, and of course Harris Tweed. It's a great, accessible adventure for those beginning their bikepacking exploits.

Plan and Prepare

Logistics

The best way to the Outer Hebrides is by sea. Calmac run a daily ferry from Oban (reachable by regular trains from Glasgow) on the Scottish mainland's west coast to Castlebay on Barra (4hr 45min). Returning, depart from Stornoway on Lewis to Ullapool (2 daily; 2hr 45min). The nearest main train station is in Inverness; you can ride there along the A835 (57 miles/92km), or take the bus (bikes must be bagged) or a special bike taxi (£160 for two).

Hazards

The two big risks are the weather – and running out of supplies on a Sunday. There's no land barrier between the Outer Hebrides America, so the winds can be fierce; given the prevailing southwesterly, it's a plus that the route runs south to north. Be prepared to stop if winds make cycling unsafe and the ferries halt services. Supply posts are not regular, and outside of main towns like Stornoway, these are often closed on Sunday.

Gear

Touring or gravel bikes with semi-slick tyres are fine for this largely road-based ride. If camping, take a three- or four-season tent due to the weather's vagaries, and bring a powerbank that will last several days. Good waterproofs and warm clothes for overnights (even in summer) are essential, but don't forget the sun cream either. Credit-card tourers are well served by B&Bs and other accommodation.

Info

From late April to early June the Outer Hebrides are midge-free, but don't let their arrival put you off, as there's good riding up till October. Wild camping is allowed in Scotland (see outdooraccess-scotland. scot), and there are infrequent campsites too. Bike repairs are on South Uist, Lewis and Harris so come prepared. Calmac runs the ferry crossings between Barra and Eriskay, and Benbecula and Harris. Info and route file: cyclinguk.org/route/gpx-file-hebridean-way

For the regular cyclist looking to stretch their legs on a multi-day tour, travelling the length of the Outer Hebrides offers an ideal introduction to bikepacking. Equally, if you're racing fit and looking for a challenge, riding the length of 10 islands with two ferry crossings will test your ability to plan to the minute as well as your physical fitness.

But what's the rush? There's plenty to enjoy, especially when the winds still and the sun shines. White sandy beaches will lull you into thinking of Caribbean destinations – even if the water's temperature will not! Nature is bountiful, and as the islands are home to the largest population of otters in the UK, your chances of seeing this elusive beastie are high.

Navigation is simple: head north and follow the road. Depending on conditions, the entire route should take about five to six days.

Turn left off the ferry...

If you're planning on camping en route, then to truly complete the Hebridean Way, you'll want to turn left and ride south to Vatersay as you roll off the ferry's gangplank in Castlebay. Cattle used to swim the sound between Barra and Vatersay, but following the unfortunate drowning of Bernie the prizewinning bull, locals mounted a campaign for a causeway to be built; its construction in 1986 allows you to ride from Barra to your destination, Vatersay's south coast. Six miles (10km) from the start, head past the island's small graveyard and pitch camp as evening descends above the beach of Bagh a'Deas. If you're lucky, you'll wake to the sight of a white-sand beach and the isolated isle of Sandray, inhabited only by seabirds.

Your trip truly begins with crossing back over the causeway and riding across the hilly paradise of Barra.

© Daria Taddei

Harris Tweed

Before the arrival of synthetics, Harris Tweed was the sportsmans' fabric of choice, famous throughout the world for its hardwearing and semi-waterproof qualities. Despite the name, it can be made anywhere on the Outer Hebrides – not just Harris. To earn the famous trademark Orb and Maltese Cross stamp, it must be hand-woven by islanders, made from pure wool spun and dyed on the Outer Hebrides. Once upon the time the islands would have rattled with the clatter of looms making the Western Isles' most famous export, with Lewis alone reported to have housed 900 weavers at the industry's peak: a true cottage industry. Today, there are fewer than a hundred weavers, most based in Harris and Lewis.

Barra's Ardmhor ferry terminal (also a great otter-spotting location) is your initial destination. If you miss your ferry of choice, all is not lost. Pop along to Britain's only airport with a beach for a landing strip, and take advantage of the cafe while you wait.

The climb off the ferry from Barra in Eriskay is the most climbing you'll likely do for the next day, as you roll north through the moors of South Uist, Benbecula, North Uist and Berneray. The flat landscape has its charm, but more memorable are the causeways linking these islands; you'll feel like you're riding on water.

Over to Harris & Lewis

The ferry from Berneray to Harris is a feast for eyes starved of contours, and you'll soon head into a dramatic landscape, with mountains and gleaming sandy beaches stretching for miles. The road to the north of the white-sand Luskentyre beach houses the workshop of Donald John Mackay, one of the island's most famous weavers of Harris Tweed.

The mountain pass between Harris and Lewis is the only significant climb you'll encounter, more than made up for by the swooping descent into the valley beyond, with the potential for spotting golden eagles hovering on thermals. Head for the western edge of Lewis to visit the standing stones of Callanish. Erected between 3800 and 5000 years ago, the 13 stones of beautifully banded gneiss are arranged around a 4.5m-tall (15ft) central monolith. If you're here in early summer you'll be riding through the machair (shell meadow), a carpet of wildflowers for which the island is famous.

The last rolling moorland miles conclude with the dramatic cliffs at the Butt of Lewis, topped by a lighthouse built in the 1860s by the family of Robert Louis Stevenson (of *Treasure Island* fame). They're a fitting conclusion to the ride before heading back south to civilisation in Stornoway, the journey's end.

The Hebridean Way

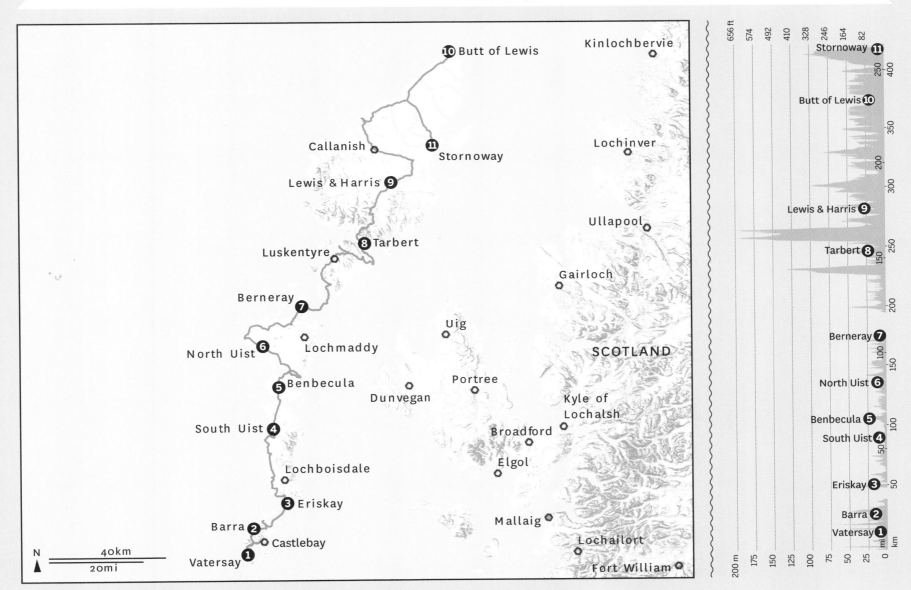

➡ Distance: 632 miles (1017km)   ➡ Ascent: 96,218ft (29,327m)   ➡ Difficulty: 4

Hope 1000

Switzerland

Ride from Lake Constance to Lake Geneva across much of Switzerland via villages, alpine meadows and many, many mountains. The Hope 1000 is certainly a physical challenge, but with cowbells chiming and the Swiss scenery surrounding you, it's easy to ignore aching muscles.

Plan and Prepare

Logistics

The route's start is at Romanshorn, on the shore Lake Constance and about 1hr from Zürich on SBB's direct InterCity trains. The endpoint is Montreux on Lake Geneva, just over 1hr from Geneva by train (sometimes with a change in Lausanne). InterCity trains require a reservation for bicycles; you can buy annual bike passes online (at sbb.ch). The country's yellow PostBuses typically have racks for bikes during the summer months.

Hazards

Switzerland is one of the safest countries in the world. The greatest hazards are probably the high prices and perhaps overzealous shepherds' dogs in mountain meadows. The latter can sometimes be calmed by dismounting, but a change of direction may be required. The cost of a trip through Switzerland can be reduced by camping and preparing your own food. Bear in mind, too, that weather conditions can change quickly in the mountains.

Gear

A lightweight mountain bike with low gearing (and luggage-carrying capacity for camping and cooking gear if needed) is best, although people have completed the route on gravel bikes. Generally, the climbs are on smoother, surfaced roads and the descents are off-road, so they will be more enjoyable on a mountain bike. Carry spare brake pads for the descents (although there are bike shops on the route).

Info

The snow melts at the higher elevations around the end of May, so the summer months and into September are the best time to ride this mountainous route. Wild camping is generally illegal unless above the treeline, and then for single nights only or with the landowner's permission. Each canton also potentially has different rules. More information on the race can be found at hope1000.ch and bikepacking.com

One glance at the serrated profile of this route tells you everything: it's up and down and up again the whole way. And this being Switzerland – where there are more than 250 summits at over 12,000ft (3658m) – the force of gravity will play a large role in the ride. The Hope 1000 itself is an annual bikepacking race plotted by Willi Felix that's typically staged in June, with the quickest riders taking four to five days to complete it. In the 2021 race, Lael Wilcox, the first woman across the line, finished in four days, 13 hours and 26 minutes. 'Riding in Switzerland is like a dream', she told the bikepacking.com team afterwards. 'New wildflowers had sprung up. So many farmers, young and old, were out. I saw cows with sunflowers tied to their heads. At first, I thought it was just grass and then realised they were carefully arranged bouquets. It was pretty unreal.'

But although being fit and prepared will help, if there's no clock ticking for your ride you can take as long as you like to complete and savour the alpine experience. There's no lack of water or delicious sustenance, so you can travel relatively lightly (even more so if you decide to stay in hostels or B&Bs). And with superb Swiss infrastructure available, it's also possible to take shortcuts by train or bus if needed.

A path to mountains

For the first 70 miles (112km) or so, the route is fairly benign, wending its way on wide bike paths on an arc towards Sirnach, where the real mountains and more testing trails begin; hotels and restaurants offer a break before you attempt them. The next day the hills remain green (in summer) as you pedal between two peaks, 3717ft (1133m) Hörnli and Hohgrat; the latter is the Thurgau canton's highest point at 3268ft (996m).

Mercury in Montreux

It seems like an unlikely match: the party-loving frontman of the rock band Queen and the serene Swiss town of Montreux. We don't know if it was love at first sight or the appeal of Switzerland's low income tax rates, but Montreux certainly captivated Freddie Mercury. Queen recorded their album *Jazz* at the Montreux Jazz Festival in 1978; the band bought a studio in Montreux the following year where they recorded most of their subsequent songs, including Mercury's final album with Queen, *Made in Heaven*. Mercury's time in Montreux is commemorated by a 10ft tall (3m) bronze statue at the lake's edge, sculpted by Czech artist Irena Sedlecká and unveiled by Brian May in 1996.

Skirting hillsides and sweeping through forest, it doesn't take long for snow-tipped peaks to appear in the distance. After crossing a valley at Wattwil, at 100 miles (160km), the trail starts to tilt up and down with frightening regularity. By the time you reach Walensee, one of Switzerland's largest lakes, and the village of Weesen (after another 30 miles/48km), you'll be glad of a rest. Ski runs overlooking the lake are busy in winter but in the summer attention switches to the water, where you can try water-skiing, diving (sky or scuba) or go further afield to the Rombach gorge for canyoning. Or just relax in a spa hotel.

Cities, lakes...and more mountains

Back on the saddle, the route now hops from lake to lake, via quiet paths, before skirting the cities of Zug and then Lucerne. Here, the elevation levels off a little as you ride through some more urban scenery. Both Zug and Lucerne make for appealing diversions if you're interested in a change of pace. Zug sits on the shore of pristine Lake Zug, in which you can swim freely in summer. It's also a good spot in which to stock up on the city's speciality, *kirschtorte*, an indulgent cherry-brandy-laced layer cake.

After a dip in Lake Sempach and a snack in Sursee at around the 260-mile mark (418km), get ready to get into the big mountains for the first time. An early climb is to the summit of Napf, a minnow at 4612ft (1406m) but still with views across to the Jura in the north, the Bernese Oberland to the south and the distant Alps of central Switzerland. You're now entering the Unesco Biosphere Reserve of Entlebuch, Switzerland's first natural reserve and noted for the sustainable relationship between the local human population and the delicate landscape of bogs and moorlands, now so rare in Europe.

statue. He guided numerous Victorian visitors to first ascents of the surrounding Bernese Alps, among them Lucy Walker, the first woman to climb the Matterhorn. The town also impressed another notable Briton: Sir Arthur Conan Doyle, who stopped here during a tour of Switzerland in 1893. Conan Doyle was inspired by the dramatic landscape to make the Reichenbach Falls, just outside town and on the route, the setting for Sherlock Holmes' shock demise at the hands of Moriarty. There's a (summer-only) funicular up to the falls from Meiringen if you want to take it easy.

Up, up and down to Montreux

The next 200 miles (322km) offer little respite from seriously huge climbs and descents. The first is the Grosse Scheidegg mountain pass, immediately west of Meiringen. It's a 10-mile (16km) slog up to 6500ft (1981m), so you'll feel short of breath. But fortunately, Willi Felix has planned the route so that most ascents (such as this one) are on paved surfaces and most descents are off-road, so as to maximise the fun factor.

There are at least another 10 passes of similar magnitude before the finish, with the rock-and-ice Nordwand, the north face of the 13,015ft (3967m) Eiger, visible off to the left for some of the way (since December 2020, the Eiger can now be summited by the Eiger Express cable car). Another notable peak is the Rinderberg, near Gstaad, surrounded by ski slopes and hiking trails. But take the passes at your own pace and they can all be conquered. Just remember that weather conditions change quickly at altitude, so bring appropriate clothing and be prepared to divert to shelter should there be a summer thunderstorm.

The final descent hugs contour lines down to Montreux, where the traditional finish is at the feet of Freddie Mercury's statue on the lakeshore.

Most of the riding in Entlebuch is between 3000-4000ft (914-1219m), along off-road alpine slopes and through coniferous forests. There are fewer places to stay up here and, as you can't wild-camp in in Swiss nature reserves like Entlebuch, you might need to research a suitable stopping point (such as Camping Thorbach in Flühli). The next landmark is Hohgant mountain, which you'll loop around, enjoying lake views to the south and west, before passing the ski slopes of Sörenberg, where beds for the night are more widespread. Rest well, because the tallest challenges of the route loom after 400 miles (644km) and the town of Meiringen, at the east end of Lake Brienz.

Meiringen has long welcomed adventurous visitors: one of the first Swiss alpine guides, Melchior Anderegg, who shepherded 19th-century British gentlemen climbers into the mountains, lived in the town and is celebrated here with a

Hope 1000

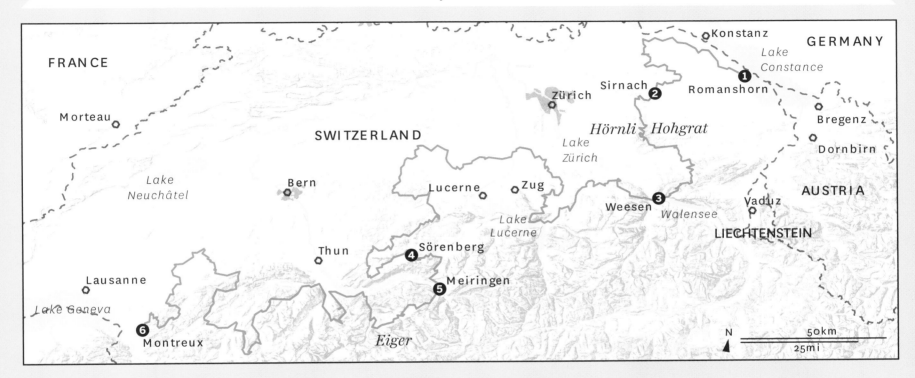

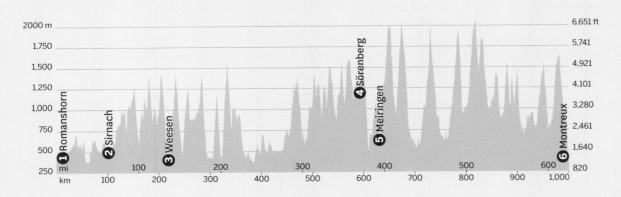

→ Distance: 185 miles (299km)   → Ascent: 4750ft (1448m)   → Difficulty: 1

Isar Cycle Route

Germany

From its source in the hills of Austria's Tyrol, the Isar River flows east into Bavaria via the city of Munich. Pedal quiet, forest-shaded paths following the river's mostly downhill course on this easygoing route.

Plan and Prepare

Logistics

The route follows the Isar River from its source in Austria's Karwendel Alpine Park. The closest towns to the start-point are Scharnitz in Austria, reached by direct trains from Innsbruck and Munich; and Germany's Mittenwald, also easily reached by train from Munich in less than 2hr. Most Deutsche Bahn regional trains will carry bikes without problem. From the route's end at Deggendorf, it's about 3hr by train back to Munich (with one change).

Hazards

There's very little to worry about on this ride through southern Germany: the terrain is relatively flat and the climate is typically mild. The Isar has flooded in the past after torrential rain but it's not a regular occurrence. Perhaps the most likely cause of a bad day on the bike is overindulging in Bavarian beer the night before.

Gear

Any bike will cope with the cycle paths, roads and tracks along this route. Puncture-resistant tyres might offer more peace of mind. It's preferable to carry luggage on the bike rather than your back, so ensure your bicycle has rack mounts or space for frame bags. With plenty of places to eat and sleep along the way, you don't necessarily need to carry cooking or sleeping kit.

Info

There's a wide weather window for riding along the Isar, but May to October are the pick of the months. Note that the paths will be much busier with tourists during the summer-holiday months of July and August. There's route info and accommodation recommendations on the official website, isarradweg.de

Rides beside rivers are some of the most enjoyable experiences you can have on a bicycle. It's difficult to get lost when you have a river to follow, and since rivers don't flow uphill you generally won't have to pedal too hard. Plus, rivers attract settlements – so you're never usually far from a town or village, whether you're following the Danube (see p132) or the Allegheny (see p270). The Isar is just such a river: it weaves its way across southern Germany from its source in Austria's Tyrol region and has numerous handsome Bavarian towns along its banks, as well as one powerhouse of a city. The landscape may not have the drama of the Dolomites but it is consistently appealing, with shady forests, shingled shores and an air of peace and quiet. Given the modest total distance and elevation, it's up to the rider how long they allow to complete the route. You could speed through it in a couple of days, or take five or six at a leisurely pace.

Riding the river

The actual start of the Isar's gravel bike path is the source of the river, Isarursprung, in the revitalising alpine setting of Austria's Tyrol. Here the river is at its most vigorous as it rushes over rapids and waterfalls. The closest access point by car or train is Scharnitz, from where you'll need to cycle 12.5 miles (20km) upriver to the source in Karwendel Alpine Park before turning around and setting off for real through the park's serene landscape. The river has a milky-blue colour here thanks to the minerals it collects coursing over rocks, but as you approach the German town of Mittenwald the valley is already broadening out, with islands appearing in the river. Mittenwald is a pleasant place to stay, but for a big day on the bike, you could continue for about 70 miles (112km) to the Baroque town of Bad Tölz (right).

Munich

For a city that is so devoted to commerce and industry, Munich offers a surprising range of activities for when work is over and it's time for play. The rivers and waterways are the focus of watersports, with canoeing and rafting popular on the Isar. You can hire a canoe to paddle from Bad Tölz all the way back to Munich in a day (if you don't linger but campsites are available if you wish to take your time). Surfers rule the waves on the Eisbach river, with the entrance of the Englischer Gardens being a good spot to watch them on the standing wave. For climbers, there are several artificial walls in the city or take a climbing tour of the roof of the stadium at Olympic Park, also home to one of Europe's longest Flying Foxes.

Bad Tölz is named for its natural springs ('bad' means bath or spa), so take the opportunity to relax in the waters in this traditional Bavarian town. If you're passing on a Friday, stock up on provisions from a farmers' market on the riverbank. The next stage of the ride takes you into the Bavarian capital, Munich. Although this is Germany's third-largest city, it's a very liveable location with lots of bike paths, parks and lakes. Spend some time exploring and perhaps visiting a beer hall or two before continuing.

After the big-city bustle, you'll return to bucolic Bavaria once you've navigated out of Munich's suburbs. The Isar meanders across a floodplain towards the town of Freising, about 25 miles (40km) east. You'll spy the cathedral tower of the Freisinger Mariendom before entering the town's outskirts. Again, it's a pleasant place to explore, either over a lunch break or for longer: the Staatsbrauerei Weihenstephan here is one of the world's oldest working breweries, having produced beer since it was part of a Benedictine monastery. You can take a tour or just taste beers like their refreshing Helles.

From Freising, the path continues alongside the Isar as the river becomes more modified by humans, feeding reservoirs, canals and hydroelectric plants. But you're never far from history in Bavaria and next comes the town of Landshut, where Trausnitz Castle has an interesting collection of art and curiosities amassed by the Wittelsbach dukes over the centuries. Also, if time is short, note that there's a fast train service back to Munich from Landshut.

The final 50 miles (80km) or so cover more traffic-free gravel paths, passing villages with beer gardens beckoning thirsty cyclists and larger towns like Dingolfing en route to Deggendorf – and the mouth of the Isar as it empties into the Danube.

Isar Cycle Route

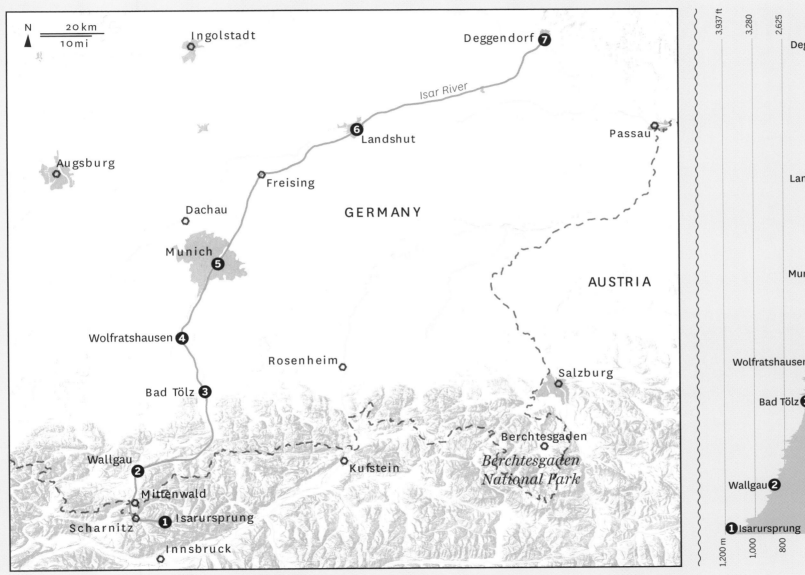

→ Distance: 260 miles (420km)   → Ascent: 34,750ft (10,592m)   → Difficulty: 3

Jura Traverse

France

The Jura mountains in eastern France see fewer visitors than other ranges but offer some unique experiences – from fabulous food to history and nature – for anyone taking a two-wheel traverse through their forests, along their rivers and past little-changed villages.

Plan and Prepare

Logistics

The route's terminals are Mandeure in the north and Culoz to the south. Riding from north to south is generally preferred. Mandeure is just outside Montbéliard, which can be reached by TGV from Paris or Strasbourg. TGV inOui services require bookings for bicycles; TGV Lyria trains require bicycles to be fully dismantled (so are best avoided). To return, take a 1hr local (TER) train from Culoz to Lyon, from where there are good onward connections.

Hazards

This is a mountainous route so fitness will be a factor. Prepare for adverse weather (you'll need warm and waterproof gear) and be aware that you might be far from help in a rugged landscape should you fall or suffer an equipment failure. Hunting season in this part of France usually starts in late September, so wear bright clothing if you're on the trails then.

Gear

A mountain bike is recommended, as the trails are steep and rough in places. There are regular places to stay overnight, from dormitories in locally owned gites d'étape (communal guesthouses) to hotels and B&Bs, so you might not want to carry full camping kit (although a bivvy bag is useful).

Info

Locals recommend riding the Jura Traverse between June and September. There will be snow in winter and much mud at other times of the year. The route is based on the Grande Traversée du Jura; you'll find maps, guidebooks, accommodation info and details of interesting sights at gtj.asso.fr

The Jura mountain range of eastern France is often overlooked by people racing to reach the Alps, but it appeals to cyclists for a number of reasons. The first is that it is off the beaten track – even for French tourists – so there's less traffic and lower prices. Secondly, its landscape is slightly less extreme than some of France's more famous mountain ranges, although these subalpine hills still pack a punch. And thirdly, there's a very distinctive and delicious local cuisine revolving around cheeses such as Comté and Morbier, as well as sausages and some very unusual wines. The geology is also interesting: the limestone strata has formed plateaus that suddenly drop off to one side, giving great views of the countryside. Forests of oak and beech cloak the lower slopes (the word 'jura' comes from the Gaulish for forest, *jor* or *juria*), and they're home to wildlife such as boar. And in recent years packs of wolves have returned to the Jura, though they remain extremely elusive. While the wolves might not be a problem for cyclists, do be aware that the forests are filled with hunters at certain times of year, so wear something bright: somehow people on bikes have been mistaken for game by shooters in the past.

Down the Doubs

On leaving Mandeure, you'll head directly south, following the direction of the Doubs River that lends this *department* of the Bourgogne-Franche-Comté region its name. There's a viewpoint over France's tenth-longest river after a few minutes' ride. After about 20 miles (32km), you'll arrive in Saint-Hippolyte, a very pretty, traditional town where the Doubs meets the Dessoubre River. There's camping as well as river activities such as rafting and canoeing. The trail then climbs up to Trévilliers, where a *fromagerie* offers an early opportunity to sample Comté cheese.

Beyond Saint-Hippolyte, the route swerves east then south, hugging the Swiss border (and crossing it at times), with the river a gentle companion for the next 10 or so miles (16km). There are lots of places to stay or eat along these lanes.

About 68 miles (110km) into the ride, you'll come to Morteau, a town that gave the world the Morteau sausage, a weighty, smoked thing of joy that is typically cooked up with potatoes for a delicious and belly-filling meal. After this point you'll split from the river and pedal higher into a rolling landscape of farms and forests. The trees change to firs as you gain elevation, with the route frequently switching from gravel tracks to surfaced lanes.

Into the wild
The next major settlement is Pontarlier (capital of the Haut-Doubs and an age-old producer of absinthe); beyond lie the route's highest areas around Mont d'Or and ski resort Métabief, which opens its lifts to mountain-bikers in summer; many trails are suitable for learners. You're now in the vast Parc Naturel Régional du Haut-Jura; despite the overwhelming sense of seclusion here, you're never far from a campground, although it might be worth carrying a bit more food and water for this half of the ride. You can restock on cheese and beer at Les Rousses before pausing at a museum of polar lands dedicated to explorer Paul-Emile Victor. Your Jura explorations come to an end 100 miles (160km) later in Culoz.

The Jura's Vin Jaune

As you ride south you'll be travelling just east of one of France's most interesting wine regions. It may not be as familiar as Champagne or Bordeaux, but the Jura produces one of France's most distinctive wines. The region, being quite cool, relies on some unusual grape varieties, including Trousseau, Poulsard and Savagnin. It is the last of these that creates the Jura's Vin Jaune ('yellow wine'). Savagnin grapes are left on the vines and harvested late. The wine is aged in barrels for six years but with a pocket of air left open, meaning that oxidisation occurs. However, a film of yeast, known as *voile*, protects the wine and adds a distinctive, dry flavour. The process is the same production method used for Spanish sherry and the results are quite similar, although Vin Jaune is not a fortified wine. It's a pale, straw-coloured white wine with a unique, mouth-puckering flavour that has notes of nuts like walnut and hazelnut, but is also spicy. It's a love-or-hate experience but one you should seek out on your trip. Vin Jaune is a great ingredient in local dishes, such as chicken with morel mushrooms, and a perfect companion to Comté cheese.

© Antoine Pouillard / Shutterstock; barmalini / Shutterstock

Jura Traverse

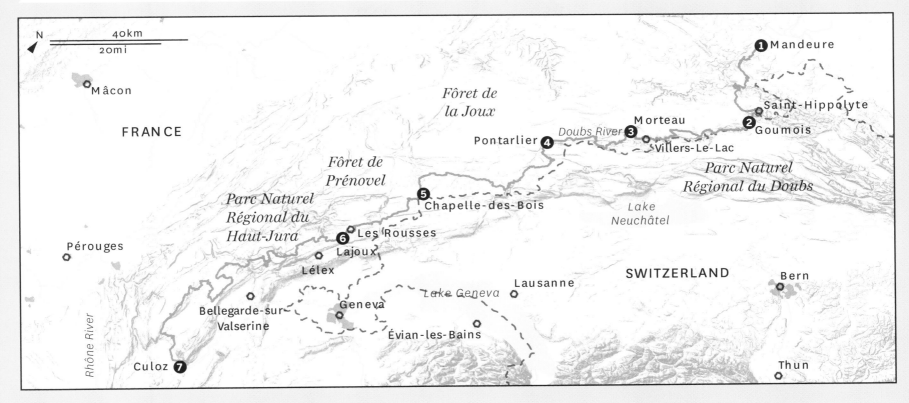

N
40km
20mi

Mâcon

FRANCE

Fôret de
la Joux

① Mandeure

Saint-Hippolyte

Morteau
Doubs River ③
Pontarlier ④

② Goumois

Villers-Le-Lac

Fôret de
Prénovel

Parc Naturel
Régional du Doubs

Lake
Neuchâtel

Parc Naturel
Régional du
Haut-Jura

⑤
Chapelle-des-Bois

Pérouges

⑥ Les Rousses
Lajoux

SWITZERLAND

Bern

Lélex

Lausanne

Bellegarde-sur-
Valserine

Lake Geneva

Geneva

Rhône River

Évian-les-Bains

Thun

Culoz ⑦

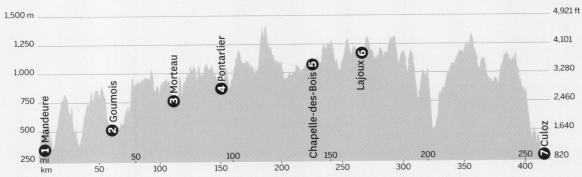

→ Distance: 192 miles (309km) → Ascent: 10,809ft (3295m) → Difficulty: 2

Bikepacking Kjölur

Iceland

Travel through Europe's largest 'desert', a landscape rich in natural wonder, and soak weary bones at natural hot springs in Iceland's highlands. This route is ideal for fledgling bikepackers looking for accessible adventure, and who don't mind a bit of serious weather.

Plan and Prepare

Logistics

If you fly into Keflavik, Iceland's main international airport, you've two options: take a bus to Iceland's capital, Reykjavík; or use the airport's specially designed Bike Pit to assemble your bike and ride from there (storing your box is tricky, though). Iceland's cycle-friendly (if costly) bus service runs regularly from the endpoint at Blönduós back to the capital (4hr); alternatively, you can ride the famous Ring Road for 156 miles (251km).

Hazards

Unsurprisingly, given Iceland's close proximity to the Arctic, it's the weather you need to watch out for. The headwinds are brutal so consider adjusting your trip to enjoy the predominant southerly winds, and factoring extra weather days into your planning just in case. Resupply points are nonexistent on the F35 itself but refreshments are available at the oasis of Hveravellir. Water sources are plentiful; you shouldn't need to use filters or purification kit.

Gear

The route is a mixture between metalled and gravel roads, but it isn't technical. A hardtail with touring tread is probably the most comfortable steed, though a gravel/touring bike with tyres as wide as possible will do. A low-profile storm resistant three- or four-season tent is money well spent, as is a ground sheet to protect the base from the hard volcanic sand. Good waterproofs are essential.

Info

You've a short window of opportunity for the 'summer' in Iceland: mid-June to mid-August. The sun will barely set (pack an eye mask), average temperatures hover at 50-59°F (10-15°C), and there's a greater opportunity for warmer, dryer days. Unless you're on a fatbike and used to travelling and camping in freezing conditions, give winter and its shoulder seasons a miss. There's further info and maps at cyclinguk.org/kjolur

Iceland is a land of extremes. This tough, unforgiving landscape is like no other – it's a place filled with natural phenomena that will stay with you till your end of days, just as its weather can conjure horror stories few will believe.

You might be forgiven for thinking that Iceland is a country only for the extreme adventure cyclist, but you'd be wrong. The Bikepacking Kjölur route follows the F35 (F stands for 'Fjal' in Icelandic, which means mountain), one of two roads to cross the island's highlands; it was originally a vital trade route to allow northerners to reach Þingvellir, where Iceland's Alþingi (parliament; Þingvellir translates as 'Assembly Plains') met annually from 930 CE to the mid-19th century.

The F35 is also one of Iceland's easier and more accessible routes through the highlands – but that 'easier' is comparative. Much of the route is rough going and requires reasonable fitness, but ultimately the biggest barrier is the weather. To make the most of this ride, you'll need to be properly equipped and prepared for the elements. At the same time you can rest assured that if you do need to bail, even at the route's most remote points, you will have options.

Keep the wind at your back

Leaving Reykjavík through its suburbs, along well designed and well-paved cycle tracks, is little preparation for the route ahead. But while the surface you ride along might be misleading, the landscape soon begins to open up. Blunt mountains rise to your right and left, giving a good taste of what's to come. After 30 miles (48km) of riding, you'll enter Þingvellir National Park, which lies in a rift valley that marks meeting point of the Mid-Atlantic Ridge; Þingvellir's steep cliffs are evidence of shifts in the Earth's crust.

Golden Circle glories

Iceland's Golden Circle promises three areas of natural beauty: Þingvellir National Park, Geysir and Gulfoss. The Viking parliament of Þingvellir is where matters of state were decided, out in the open air. Geysir is home to the famous waterspout (now dormant) from which all geysirs are named. Its neighbour, Strokkur, still shoots out blasts of boiling water up to 131ft (40m) high. Gulfoss is one of Iceland's most powerful and beautiful waterfalls. In the early 20th century, these two spectacular tiers, plummeting 105ft (32m) over the rocks, were almost destroyed by a British developer's plan to build a hydroelectric dam – thank campaigning farmer's daughter Sigríður Tómasdóttir for making sure they remain.

Þingvellir is also the site of Iceland's open-air parliament, where Icelanders gathered annually for more than 800 years, and is the first point of the Golden Circle route. The undulating road is easy to follow with clear lines of sight, but it's a popular area and traffic can be busy, as it's the main tourist route to Geysir and Gulfoss waterfall.

Leaving Gulfoss, the traffic disappears as you head into the highlands. You'll soon see why, as 10 miles (16km) from the famous falls, the metalled road ends and the F35 begins. This gravel-lined scar rising into the undulating Kjölur Plateau cuts between Iceland's two largest glaciers, the Langjökull to the west and the Hofsjökull to the east. Pockmarked with potholes that would sink a car, it's traversed by rugged superjeeps, Iceland's off-road buses and, of course, cyclists.

Around the 94-mile (151km) mark, you'll arrive at the hot springs of Hveravellir. Cabins, camping and (expensive) beer are all on offer. Beyond here, you're riding through vast plains surrounded by misty mountains, with homely houses serving hot food and drinks rare and far between: the only options are at Gljásteinn (120 miles/193km) and Áfangi (150 miles/241km). Fortunately, though, these aren't the only shelters en route. The bright-orange unmanned refuge at Arnarbæli (140 miles/225km) stands out from the stark plateau (left), offering a break from the elements or a place to stay if it's too windy for camping.

Descending from the Kjölur Plateau, the gravel plains grow greener and typical Icelandic dwellings with their steeply sloped roofs begin appearing. Thanks to the late spring that Iceland enjoys, you're likely to encounter recently born lambs and their mothers on your way, too.

The gravel track peters out as you reach Blönduós, where you can return to Reykjavík by bus or ride there along the Ring Road.

Bikepacking Kjölur

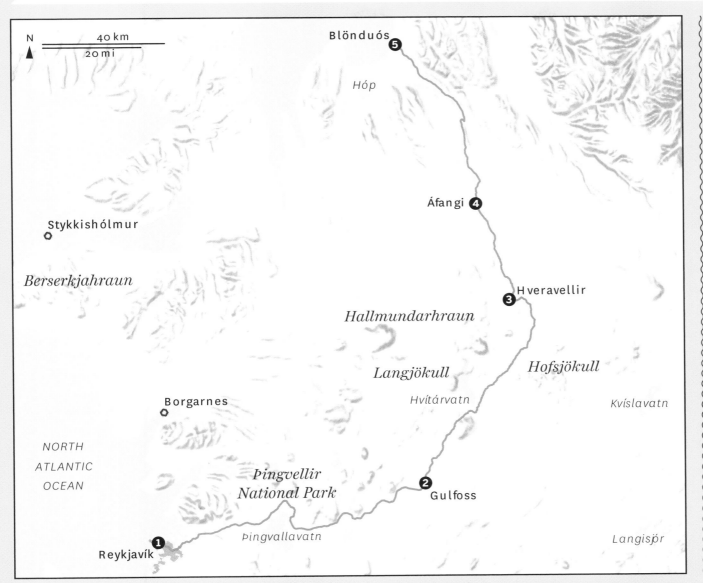

N

40 km
20 mi

Blönduós **5**

Hóp

Áfangi **4**

Stykkishólmur

Berserkjahraun

Hveravellir **3**

Hallmundarhraun

Langjökull

Hofsjökull

Hvítárvatn

Kvíslavatn

Borgarnes

NORTH
ATLANTIC
OCEAN

*Þingvellir
National Park*

Gulfoss **2**

Þingvallavatn

Langisjór

Reykjavík **1**

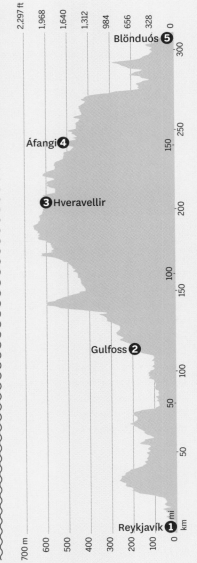

2,297 ft   1,968   1,640   1,312   984   656   328   0

Blönduós **5**

Áfangi **4**

3 Hveravellir

Gulfoss **2**

Reykjavík **1**

700 m   600   500   400   300   200   100   0

➡ Distance: 652 miles (1050km) ➡ Ascent: 8200ft (2500m) ➡ Difficulty: 1

The Meuse Cycle Route

France, Belgium & the Netherlands

As an easygoing introduction to long-distance cycling, the Meuse Cycle Route, aka EuroVelo 19, is ideal: it follows the Meuse River downhill from its French source to the North Sea at Rotterdam, passing through the Vosges, Wallonia, Limburg and plenty of WWI history.

Plan and Prepare

Logistics

Langres is the start of this route, and is reached by a direct train ride (minimum 3hr) southeast from Paris' Gare de l'Est station. At the other end, Rotterdam is well connected by trains (and planes) to northern Europe, including Paris' Gare du Nord station, which is about 3hr away by Thalys train.

Hazards

There's very little to worry about on this route. Some sections pass through large towns and cities and cross major roads, so vehicular traffic is statistically the biggest concern.

Gear

EuroVelo 19 largely follows bike paths and quiet roads, so a road-going touring bicycle that can hold panniers or bikepacking bags is probably the best bet. Take the usual precautions with punctures and carry tools to relink chains and make other common repairs. Northern European weather is often wet, so mudguards and waterproofs are recommended.

Info

Early spring to late autumn are the best months to ride, with summers likely to be mild. The official website eurovelo.com has more info – including maps and guides – on all the EuroVelo routes, including the Meuse journey.

EuroVelo is one of those initiatives that makes Europe the envy of the cycling world. This network of long-distance cycle routes extends across the whole continent, from the very north of Norway to Europe's southern edge in Spain, Italy and Greece. The routes are developed by the European Cyclists' Federation; all are mapped and many are signposted. And some of them are very long: the Atlantic Coast Route covers 6835 miles (11,000km).

In May 2021, EuroVelo published the first audit of its 17 routes. Each one (and sections within) falls into different categories, ranging from 'planning' and 'under development' to 'signposted' and 'certified'. Of the 17 trails, a few are signposted from start to finish; the shortest of these is the Meuse Cycle Route, which shadows the path of the enonymous river from its source in the Grand Est region of northeast France to the Meuse's mouth near Rotterdam in the Netherlands. Since the trail follows a river, it is predominantly downhill if ridden south to north. And because settlements tend to develop along rivers, it never strays far from places to sleep or eat, or just take a break or a shortcut. This ensures that the Meuse is one of the most straightforward and sedate of cycle-touring experiences, and also has enough variety to entertain more experienced cyclists.

Riding through France

Starting from the town of Langres, about 50 miles (80km) north of Dijon in the Bourgogne-Franche-Comté region, gives an opportunity to sample some distinctive Burgundy wines and cheeses, and also explore the surrounding lakes. Langres is on the ancient Via Francigena pilgrimage route, from Canterbury in England to Rome in Italy – there are plenty of hiking trails here to dip into before you get on your bike.

From Langres, the route skirts lakes and passes through such small, historic towns such as Bourmont and then, after some 62 miles (100km), Domrémy-la-Pucelle, the birthplace of Joan of Arc. After a look into the museum dedicated to the French heroine, head back onto the path, which continues to crisscross the river through the verdant landscape of Lorraine. As along the whole route, overnight options here are wide, from camping to a bed in a B&B or hotel.

The next major stage starts from Verdun (left), after just over 140 miles (225km). Verdun is where WWI's longest battle took place; around 300,000 soldiers died here during 10 months of fighting between French and German troops. You can reflect on the lives lost during a visit to the town's subterranean citadel, a vast network of tunnels used by French soldiers.

Shortly after Verdun, cyclists can jump onto the new traffic-free greenway between Mouzon and Remilly-Aillicourt, which meanders through meadows. More greenways, part of the Trans-Ardennes cycle route, link Givet (right) and Charleville-Mézières, and you'll pass through the city of Sedan along the way, at about 205 miles (330km) from the start. This is another great spot to linger, exploring Europe's largest fortified medieval castle. The story goes that the vast and spectacular redoubt was purchased by the city of Sedan from the French army in 1962. A council ballot was held to decide the fate of the new property, and it was saved from being knocked down by one vote.

Into Belgium

The route skirts the border with Belgium before crossing at Givet, where there's another fort overlooking the river. There's also a train station in town, useful if you wish to conquer only the French part of the ride at this stage.

Wallonia

The Meuse is broad and placid as it enters the French-speaking Belgian province of Wallonia, a forested landscape of limestone outcrops, caves and diverting riverside towns like Hastière-par-Delà. From here it's about 25 miles (40km) to Wallonia's capital, Namur (below), once you've passed below the watchful gaze of Dinant's citadel. Namur also has a historic fortress guarding the river, first built in the Middle Ages on a spot that's served as a strategic vantage point since prehistoric times. During the 17th century, the Thirty Years' War with Spain saw increasingly extensive fortifications added. Of equal interest to some cyclists will be the local Trappist beers, such as Rochefort, brewed in an abbey nearby but served in Namur's pubs.

An award-winning brewery is found in the next major city along the Meuse, Liège; stop to sample Brasserie C's refreshing blonde Curtius beer. Before you reach Liège, pause to explore the in-depth archaeological displays (plus pottery classes, spear-throwing and cave visits) at Ramioul's Préhistomuseum, set in parkland. Liège itself is a good place to take a break, and there's also some cycling history to discover: the city is the home of Europe's oldest classic bike race, the springtime Liège-Bastogne-Liège (top left), first held in 1892 and coursing through the surrounding area for some 155 miles (250km). Leaving Liège, the handsome Dutch city of Maastricht is about 20 miles (32km) north, set on both sides of the Meuse.

To Rotterdam

The Netherlands is the third country of the ride and, in addition to another language, it brings a rich artistic tradition to the trip. View interesting and unusual Dutch art at Maastricht's Bonnefantenmuseum, from little-known Old Masters to contemporary artists alongside a collection of graphic work by architect Aldo Rossi, who designed the museum's distinctive building.

The Meuse now arcs around northern Limburg province, through an increasingly waterlogged landscape. This can be flat, fast cycling if you choose, or just follow the pace of the river. The RivierPark Maasvallei project aims to restore the natural landscape here, and in the beautiful tidal wetland reserve of Biesbosch National Park, you might spot beavers and profuse birdlife, from waders to ospreys.

One last place to explore before Rotterdam is historic Brielle, which has been occupied by both the English and the Spanish. From here you'll double back on yourself to enter industrial Rotterdam (left), one of the world's busiest seaports.

The Meuse Cycle Route

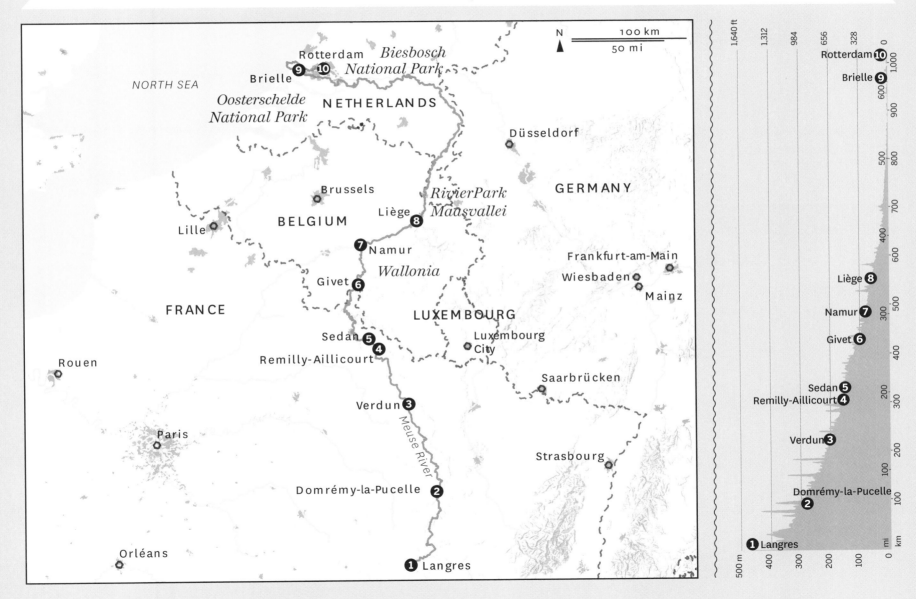

➡️ Distance: 155 miles (250km)   ➡️ Ascent: 16,404ft (5000m)   ➡️ Difficulty: 2

Mjølkevegen

Norway

Norway's most popular cycling tour reveals the high-country plateau of Stølsvidda, sprinkled with family-run farms and sparkling lakes. With several settlements on the way and excellent rail access at either end, this route is an easy win for beginner bikepackers.

Plan and Prepare

Logistics

The ride's start-point, Vinstra, is reachable via direct trains from Oslo in just over 3hr. You should be able to bring a bike on board, but check beforehand whether paid reservations are required. The Oslo to Lillehammer train has space for about 20 bikes. From the end of the ride at Gol, there's a direct train back to Oslo via the beautiful Bergensbanen line (bike reservations required).

Hazards

This is Norway: aside from the weather there are no significant hazards to worry about on this ride, except perhaps some high prices and abundant biting insects in summer (bring bug repellent). Regarding the weather, summer is usually a mild time of year and the elevation isn't excessive. That said, do check the weather forecast and bring appropriate clothing.

Gear

You can ride this route on almost any bicycle. The surface is mostly gravel or tarmac so fast-rolling tyres are fine. You can even charge an electric bike at intervals, such as Tyinkrysset (if you take the ferry option from Bygdin). Luggage can also be kept to a minimum for riding the Mjølkevegen in summer, when a bivvy bag should suffice; there's also plenty of accommodation along the route.

Info

The best time of year to ride is certainly summer, from the end of June to early September, with lovely weather and the advantage of long days. During winter the route is snowbound, and the conditions are very unstable during spring and autumn. Norway's tourist board (visitnorway.com) has useful information on accommodation options.

Have you seen the price of petrol in Norway? Once you've picked your jaw off the floor, you'll realise that it makes more sense to see this staggeringly beautiful county by bicycle and train. Norway has also realised this and encourages joined-up travel, so bikes are welcome on most trains – and there are also 10 national long-distance cycle routes that take in themes such as fjords, canals, industry and pilgrimages, plus many shorter scenic rides around the country. One such scenic bike ride is the Mjølkevegen, one of Norway's most popular cycling routes.

Its popularity is in part due to its accessibility: it's a three-hour train ride from the capital, Oslo, and can form an easy loop of three or four days away. Although the route's total distance is fairly modest, there is a substantial amount of elevation gain, as you'll be crossing highland passes and pastures. The name of the ride translates as the 'milky way', which is nothing to do with the stars above (which may not be very visible during Norway's short summer nights) but instead refers to the wild grazing enjoyed by roaming cows and goats. The livestock spend the summer making the most of the green mountain pastures, and smallholders produce cheeses sold in their farms (delicious with flatbread pancakes and sour cream), a form of agriculture known as *stølsliv*, the 'støl' being the meadows. Appreciating local culture in person is part of the appeal of cycle touring. Oh, and the cost savings on fuel, too.

On the Milky Way

Vinstra lies on a broad river, which you'll cross as you head south out of town towards Skåbu. You'll reach a traditional Norwegian mountain lodge, Ruten Fjellstue, which also makes for a bike-friendly base, not least thanks to the homemade food and in-house brewery.

From Ruten, you'll climb up to the mountain plateau via several sublimely beautiful lakes; at Vinstre a mountain lodge on the shore provides food and accommodation, and you can also take a boat out or go fishing. A summer-only toll road, the Jotunheimvegen, takes you through Norwegian pastoral country, a place that appears immune to the modern world.

The town of Beitostølen signals a return to reality, with its range of restaurants and hotels. But it's temporary. The route now embarks on the most challenging stretch, with several sustained climbs, including a schlepp to the top of Slettefjellet, the Mjølkevegen's highest point at 4314ft (1315m). The descents may be more enjoyable. At Høre, you'll also see a stave church, one of Norway's atmospheric wooden churches, many dating from the medieval ages and mostly built before 1350. Ostensibly Christian churches, they also absorbed some of the preexisting pagan Norse traditions and decorations.

To boat or not to boat

After a stop in Syndinstøga, you can cruise along Lake Bygdin from Bygdin to Eidsbugarden aboard the historic *M/B Bitihorn* during the summer months (look up an online timetable). If so, you can continue around Lake Tyin via Tyinkrysset (where you can recharge e-bikes) to rejoin the main route. You'll continue to Vaset, over more watery terrain, where there are several accommodation options. From Vaset, it's 19 miles (30km) to Storefjell and another 15 miles (24km) to reach your Gol.

The Bergensbanen

The Mjølkevegen terminates in the town of Gol – but rather than the end of the adventure, Gol could be the start of another. The town lies on the Bergensbanen, one of the world's most scenic railways and one of Europe's top train trips. The line runs from Oslo to Bergen over the Hardangervidda plateau, covering 308 miles (495km) in just over 20 stops. Gol lies about one third of the distance from Oslo – so if you take a train west rather than east, you'll continue all the way to the Norwegian coast and the handsome port of Bergen, all the while passing a landscape of lakes and hillsides barely touched by human interference. The journey takes you via Finse, a station sitting at 4010ft (1222m) on the edge of a national park; and the town of Voss, best known as the adventure-sports capital of Norway as well as the jumping-off point for a boat to Flåm and its mountain railway. But if you continue on to Bergen, Norway's second-largest city, the fabulous fjord country opens up: there are countless hikes, bike rides or boat trips on which to embark.

© Gertjan Hooijer / Shutterstock; Pete Seaward / Lonely Planet

Mjølkevegen

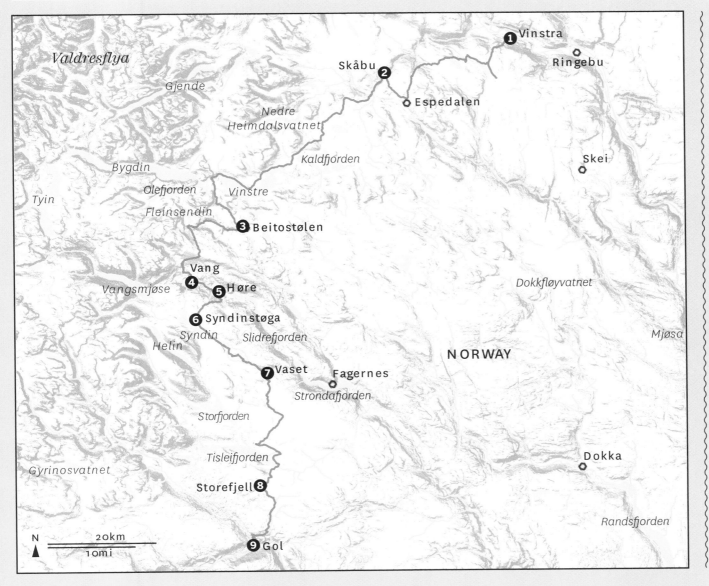

Valdresflya

Gjende

Nedre
Heimdalsvatnet

Kaldfjorden

Bygdin

Olefjorden

Vinstre

Tyin

Fleinsendin

Vinstra ①

Skåbu ②

Espedalen

Ringebu

Skei

③ Beitostølen

Vang

④ Høre ⑤

⑥ Syndinstøga

Syndin

Slidrefjorden

Helin

Vangsmjøse

Dokkfløyvatnet

Mjøsa

NORWAY

⑦ Vaset

Fagernes

Strondafjorden

Storfjorden

Tisleifjorden

Dokka

Gyrinosvatnet

Storefjell ⑧

Randsfjorden

N

20km

10mi

⑨ Gol

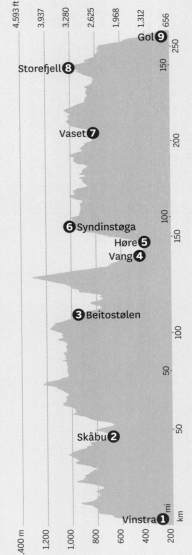

4,593 ft
3,937
3,280
2,625
1,968
1,312
656

Gol ⑨
250

Storefjell ⑧
150

Vaset ⑦
200

⑥ Syndinstøga
100
150
Høre ⑤
Vang ④

③ Beitostølen
100

50

Skåbu ②
50

Vinstra ①
200
km
mi

1,400 m
1,200
1,000
800
600
400
200

➡ Distance: 103 miles (165km)   ➡ Ascent: 10,660ft (3250m)   ➡ Difficulty: 2

Trans-Cambrian Way

Wales

Ride from the Welsh border with England to the Irish Sea on this well-established and relatively easygoing route that touches on some great mountain-biking spots in wet and windy Wales. Hospitable towns mean kit can be kept a minimum.

Plan and Prepare

Logistics

The start point of Knighton, straddling the Wales/England border, is on a direct train line from Swansea in Wales (3hr), and can also be reached from the English city of Birmingham, changing at Shrewsbury. To return from Dovey Junction at the route's end, there are trains back to Birmingham with changes at Machynlleth and Shrewsbury (or you can just ride on for 20min to Machynlleth). Leaving a car at Machynlleth is another option.

Hazards

There are few natural hazards on this ride, except perhaps the changeable Welsh climate and the likelihood of some rain. There are five ford crossings that may require extra care. Reasonable fitness is required for the climbing but an electric bike would assist riders with mobility issues.

Gear

A mountain bike is best on this route, enabling you to explore the Elan Valley further. You don't need to carry much luggage since there are towns with shops, pubs and accommodation along the route; alternatively, carry a bivvy bag and look after yourself.

Info

Wales is at its best when the evenings are lighter for longer, so plan to ride the route between April and October. There's accommodation at either end, as well as in the middle; Rhayader makes a good base for exploring the Elan Valley if you can extend the trip. There's more info on the route at transcambrianway.org.uk and you can visit ridedyfi.co.uk for more on the mountain-biking trails around Machynlleth.

There are more than 600 castles in Wales, which is the greatest density of defensive fortifications anywhere in the world. Many of these line Wales' border with England and were intended to subjugate the surrounding populace; some have been inhabited for more than a millennium. Today, of course, tensions have cooled sufficiently that it's possible to not only the cross the border on a bicycle but also ride across the whole country, via the Trans-Cambrian Way through Mid-Wales. One end is on the Welsh border, west of Birmingham and just below the Shropshire Hills Area of Outstanding Natural Beauty; the other end is on the Welsh coast (right), just north of the university town of Aberystwyth. In between lie some 100 miles (160km) of windswept Welsh moors and hills and a number of grey-stone villages and towns, often overlooked by sightseers but richly rewarding for mountain bikers. Most people complete the ride in two to four days, depending on fitness and time constraints. And you can ride it in either direction: we've described it from east to west so you can enjoy a sunset at the end and little more descent.

On the Way through Wales

You'll be on quiet lanes as you leave Knighton, but it's only a couple of miles before your tyres taste dirt as you climb into the Welsh hills. There's a pub at Llanbadarn Fynydd for lunch after about 16 miles (26km), and it's roughly the same distance again to the town of Rhayader, which makes a great spot to break the journey on the first day. The reason for this is that there's some excellent singletrack for mountain-biking around Rhayader, especially along the Elan Valley. These are narrow, natural trails with some rocky descents, and if you're a keen mountain-biker, it's certainly worth spending a day doing one of the loops here.

Machynlleth's CAT

A couple of miles north of Machynlleth is the Centre for Alternative Technology, which not only imagines a more sustainable future for the planet, but also offers courses in how to reduce your environmental footprint: learn about low-tech compost toilets, beekeeping and logging with a horse as well as heat pumps, wind turbines and solar power. You can also join walks to enjoy the dawn chorus of birds and spot nocturnal wildlife. At a higher level, the CAT is an innovation hub for researching how Britain can become a zero-carbon country by 2040, and is celebrating its 50th anniversary in 2023 with construction of a smart new visitor experience.

Leaving Rhayader after breakfast, remembering to stock up on Welsh cakes – a sweet flatbread with dried fruit – you'll head south on lanes before circling the Garreg Ddu Reservoir and its elegant 19th-century dams, designed by civil engineer James Mansergh to supply water to Birmingham. Detour up to Craig Goch for the most spectacular of the six dams (left). Keeping Claerwen Reservoir to your left, you'll follow a gravel doubletrack along the edge of a hillside. Expect sheep and drizzle. After about 30 miles (48km) you'll pass the village of Pontrhydygroes, where lead and silver were mined. It's an industry long-since departed from this valley, but the Miners Arms pub remains and offers the opportunity for lunch. Or try Cwtch cafe, which serves homemade food. Stretch your legs with a walk down to the Ystwyth River as it tumbles through the gorge.

The route now doubles back eastward, past more mineworks. Plenty of people stay in Llangurig, at around the 75 mile (120km) point, but there's also a campsite and wild camping in the area. Over its final quarter, the route continues the up-and-down theme, climbing all the way to Glaslyn Nature Reserve at about 1800ft (550m). Nearby there's Cadair Viewpoint, from where you can look out over Snowdonia National Park and the peak of Cadair Idris in the distance. As you approach the coast, the landscape becomes busier. It's largely a descent down to Dovey Junction train station, where the River Dyfi flows into the Irish Sea. There's plenty to do in the area, from birdwatching and walking on the broad, sandy beaches of Ynyslas to the Museum of Modern Art in Machynlleth. But mountain bikers will again want to check out Machynlleth's purpose-built trails in Dyfi Forest, graded blue, red or black according to difficulty.

Trans-Cambrian Way

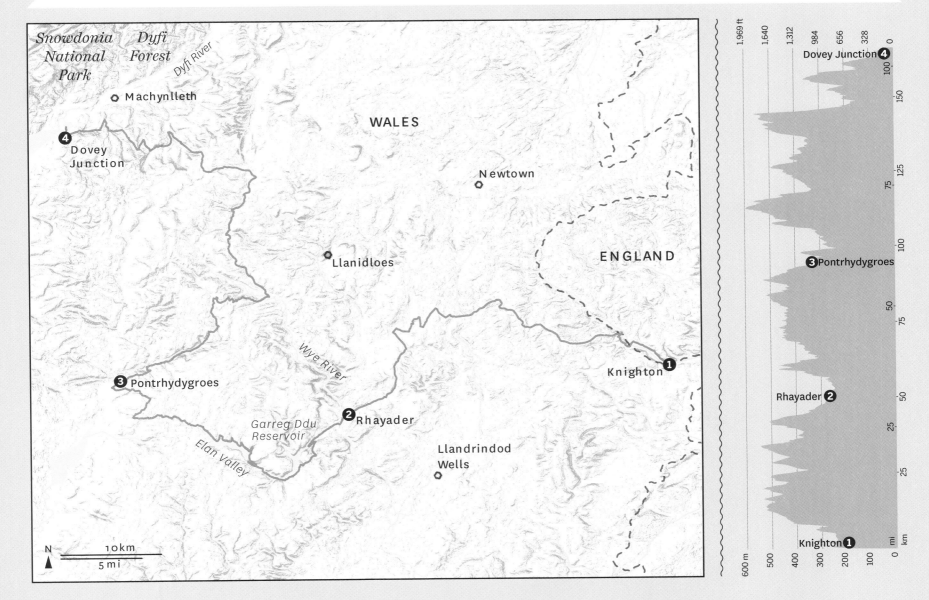

Snowdonia
National
Park

Dyfi
Forest

Dyfi River

Machynlleth

WALES

④ Dovey
Junction

Newtown

ENGLAND

Llanidloes

Wye River

③ Pontrhydygroes

Knighton ①

② Rhayader

Garreg Ddu
Reservoir

Elan Valley

Llandrindod
Wells

N

10km
5mi

Elevation profile (right):

1,969 ft — 1,640 — 1,312 — 984 — 656 — 328 — 0

Dovey Junction ④

③ Pontrhydygroes

Rhayader ②

Knighton ①

600 m — 500 — 400 — 300 — 200 — 100 — 0

150 — 125 — 100 — 75 — 50 — 25 — 0 mi / km

→ Distance: 163 miles (262km)   → Ascent: 31,265ft (9530m)   → Difficulty: 4

Trans-Dolomiti

Italy

Explore the exceptional beauty of the Dolomites on this challenging loop on history-rich trails through mountain meadows, which gives the perfect excuse to fuel up on Italy's delicious food and drink.

Plan and Prepare

Logistics

The loop starts from the town of Brixen, close to Italy's border with Austria. Brixen can be reached by train in around 4hr from Milan, the closest major Italian city, with a change at Bolzano. However, the rules around taking bicycles on Italian trains are complicated. It's a lot easier to travel on a direct Deutsche Bahn train from Innsbruck in Austria in about 1hr 30min; bike spaces can be reserved.

Hazards

The amount of often steep ascent on this route means that fitness will be a factor: make sure that you allow adequate time when route planning. Also, bear in mind that the trails will often be relatively busy with hikers, so take care and always give way. Some of the descents are fast and loose, so be careful with a laden bike.

Gear

Although the tracks aren't too technically testing, a mountain bike is preferable to a gravel bike as the wider tyres will help on the rougher descents. Take some spare brake pads, too. There's no lack of places to buy food and water so you may not wish to carry a full cooking set-up. If you're planning on overnighting in mountain refuges, you'll need a sleeping bag and bivvy for back-up.

Info

With the high-altitude climate, it's best to ride in the peak season, from June to September. October is also possible but check weather forecasts carefully. Wild camping is forbidden in this region. There are several mountain refuges along the route that can provide shelter. You will also be passing close to plenty of villages with accommodation. There's lots of route info at bikepacking.com

The Trans-Dolomiti route was finessed by the nomadic German couple Franzi Wernsing and Jona Riechmann, also known on social media as Tales on Tyres. They're based in southern Germany so the Dolomites of northern Italy is a very accessible playground. One of Europe's highest mountain ranges, the Dolomites themselves are very distinctive. Originally known as the 'Pale Mountains', it wasn't until the end of the 18th century that the newly discovered form of limestone characteristic of the range was given the name 'dolomite', after French geologist Déodat de Dolomieu. Made up of fossilised coral reefs formed some 250 million years ago, these jagged peaks were pushed up skyward by the movement of the African and European tectonic plates.

Franzi and Jona's route makes a clockwise loop around these dramatic mountains, taking in winter-sports resorts such as Cortina d'Ampezzo and Alta Badia – which gives you an inkling that this a physically arduous experience that takes most riders five or more days to finish. But the rewards can be enjoyed with every turn of the trail as fabulous vistas open up, and with every stop at a cafe or restaurant for an espresso or a plate of polenta with cheese from the Aosta Valley.

A jagged profile

Head south out of the town of Brixen, follow the milky Eisack River, with a stash of pastries for the day and the knowledge of the whopping 7388ft (2252m) of climbing to cover over the coming 23 miles (37km). After you turn left away from the river, a gravel track ascends into grassy alpine pastures. At an altitude of 7560ft (2304m) above sea level, the Rifugio Genova Schlüterhütte awaits. As at many of the refuges along the route, a bed at this large lodge can be reserved in advance.

War stories

Horrific accounts of war abound in these mountains, where many of the tracks you ride were made as a result of military manoeuvring. Following WWI skirmishes between Italian and Austro-Hungarian regiments in 1916, the latter took control of the Col di Lana near Cortina. Lacking the firepower to engage, the Italians spent three months chiselling a tunnel into the rock beneath the Austro-Hungarian position. On 17 April 1916, the five tonnes of nitroglycerin packed into the tunnel was detonated. More than 100 men died and the mountain lost 100ft (30m) of its elevation. In all, some 18,000 WWI soldiers died fighting for control of the Col di Lana alone.

Descending on dirt trails, don't be distracted by the sublime views of grassy hillsides punctuated by alpine huts (and the occasional marmot). You can pick up supplies as you pass through the villages of Longiarù and Piccolino, but the day's big goal could be the ski town of Cortina d'Ampezzo, about 43 miles (69km) to the east (though with far less climbing than on the first day). The trail takes in mixed forests and the valley floor as it crosses into the Parco Naturale di Fanes-Sennes-Braies, dominated by three large plateaus where alpine species such as capercaillie birds and mountain hares thrive. Look up and you might spy a golden eagle.

Cortina d'Ampezzo is the easternmost point of the loop. This affluent Italian town isn't especially cheap, but out-of-season accommodation is better value, and there are huts before the town if you prefer to save a few euros. Leaving Cortina d'Ampezzo, there's a very stiff road climb up to views of the Cinque Torri rock formation. These slowly collapsing spires are at the heart of Cortina's rock-climbing scene, which is one of the world's best.

Continue up to the highest point of the route at 7700ft (2347m), then enjoy another long off-road descent to Colle Santa Lucia. There are several villages with places to overnight around here.

Next you'll circle the amazing emerald-green waters of the Lago di Alleghe, below Monte Civetta. The lake was formed by a landslip in 1771, which submerged five villages. You'll probably want to spend another night at a lower elevation before taking a gondola up to the Passo Fedaia, at the foot of the Marmolada mountain resort. Once up into the mountains again, you'll be pedalling between alpine resorts before looping around to shadow the A22 autostrada back to Brixen and the route's end.

Trans-Dolomiti

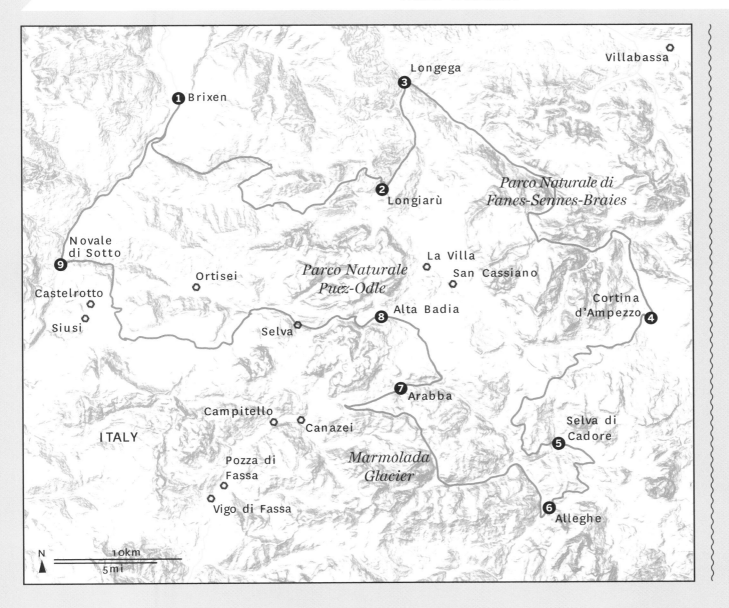

Villabassa

Longega ③

Brixen ①

Longiarù ②

Parco Naturale di Fanes-Sennes-Braies

Novale di Sotto ⑨

Ortisei

La Villa

San Cassiano

Parco Naturale Puez-Odle

Castelrotto

Siusi

Cortina d'Ampezzo ④

Selva

Alta Badia ⑧

Arabba ⑦

ITALY

Campitello

Canazei

Selva di Cadore ⑤

Pozza di Fassa

Marmolada Glacier

Vigo di Fassa

Alleghe ⑥

N

10km
5mi

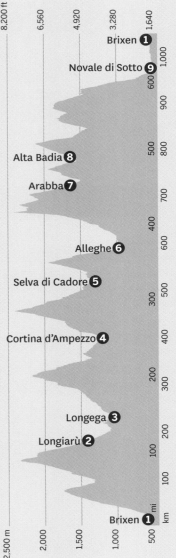

8,200 ft
6,560
4,920
3,280
1,640

Brixen ①
1,000
Novale di Sotto ⑨
600
500
Alta Badia ⑧
800
Arabba ⑦
700
400
Alleghe ⑥
600
Selva di Cadore ⑤
500
400
Cortina d'Ampezzo ④
300
Longega ③
200
Longiarù ②
100
Alleghe ⑥
100
Brixen ①
mi
km
500
Brixen ①
2,500 m
2,000
1,500
1,000

→ Distance: 147 miles (237km)   → Ascent: 9790ft (2984m)   → Difficulty: 2

West Kernow Way

England

Loop around Cornwall's Land's End and the Lizard on this moderate route that takes in Neolithic stone circles, ruins and remnants of mining history, plus gorgeous sea views from coastal paths, pretty fishing villages, sandy beaches and some irresistible fish-and-chip meals.

Plan and Prepare

Logistics

The route follows a figure-of-eight loop around the Cornish transport hub of Penzance, which can reached by train from local stations or direct from Exeter (in about 3hr) or by express train from London (around 5hr). On trains from London, you'll need to reserve a space for your bicycle in advance; this is not usually necessary for off-peak local trains.

Hazards

There's not a lot to worry about in Cornwall. Biting insects may be a problem in some areas, so pack insect repellent; steep hills and getting lost on the moors are other minor concerns. Carry water and wear sunscreen in summer. Cornwall's holiday-season traffic, often squeezing down narrow lanes with poor sightlines, is perhaps the biggest hazard.

Gear

The route can be ridden on gravel bikes with wider, grippy tyres (for the occasional muddy conditions) or on a mountain bike. A standard touring or road bike will struggle with some sections. You will also be grateful for a wide gear range as a few slopes are very steep. An electric bike is also an option and can easily be recharged along the route.

Info

The best time to ride is from May to October. Short sections of the route can be waterlogged after rain or in winter, but much of it is rideable year-round; summer sees the most pleasant conditions, of course. There are lots of accommodation options, from unofficial camping spots to B&Bs in fishing villages. The route was designed by Cycling UK (cyclinguk.org), which offers lots of useful info and maps on its website.

Since the 1970s, walkers have enjoyed a National Trail, the South West Coast Path, that guides them around the edge of the gorgeous county of Cornwall. With warm weather and some of the UK's best beaches, this region at the toe of Britain is one of the nation's most popular holiday destinations. It's also rich in history and is home to a distinctive Celtic culture, including a language, Cornish, formerly almost extinct but now enjoying a revival.

Until recently, cyclists looked on enviously at Cornwall's offerings for hikers but, in 2021, the dedicated West Kernow Way bikepacking route was launched by Cycling UK, formerly the Cyclists' Touring Club, which has been advocating for cyclists since 1878. Kernow is the Cornish name for Cornwall, deriving from the Celtic word for 'headland' or 'horn', and the route forms a figure-of-eight loop in the far west of the county, starting from the busy hub of Penzance. While the West Kernow Way currently covers only a fraction of the South West Coast Path's distance – and only Cornwall's far west corners of Land's End and the Lizard – it's a great introduction to the region and very accessible from the rest of Britain.

In addition to the sandy coves, tiny ferries and secluded smugglers' villages that most riders will be expecting, you'll also encounter a number of fascinating and unexpected features of Cornish history. The route touches on a lot of the region's mining heritage and also includes several so-called 'lost ways'. These are former public paths such as the Tinners Way, a track used by horse-drawn carts for centuries and marked on 17th-century maps, but long since disused and forgotten. The West Kernow Way knits these historic tracks into the route's patchwork of lanes, bridleways and other trails as a way of restoring access and encouraging their use once more.

Penzance to Porthcurno

Penzance's train station is pretty much on the seafront, so getting onto the trail is straightforward: just head to the shoreline and turn right. The early sections of the route are a little misleading, being on surfaced roads, but once you reach the pretty fishing port of Mousehole (pronounced 'mow-zel') things get quieter. Away from the coast road, the lanes dip in and out of valleys. What you'll first notice is how tropical the vegetation is here in comparison to the rest of the UK. Everything is larger and a more vibrant shade of green, with some of the lanes almost becoming tunnels through the foliage. After about 13 miles (21km), a detour leads to Porthcurno and the open-air Minack Theatre, which was cut into the granite cliffs here in 1930 in order to stage a production of Shakespeare's *The Tempest*; you'll want to come back and see a play above the waves.

Land's End to the Tinners Way

A couple of miles further on is Land's End, the most westerly part of mainland Britain. You may spot a few other cyclists arriving or setting off for John O'Groats in Scotland, the mainland's northeast tip. The actual site is as heavily touristed as you'd expect. Back on the main West Kernow Way, you'll get a taste of gravel on the next section, but first there's the pretty Cot Valley to conquer as well as a pass through the town of St Just, the epicentre of the region's tin mining. Back on the coast, you'll find many reminders of that industry in the disused engine houses overlooking the sea (left); one, the Levant Mine and Beam Engine, has been restored, with a working 1840s steam engine.

Turning east, you'll jump on the Tinners Way, an age-old track that's in the process of becoming an official right of way once more.

Mining

For centuries, many Cornish toiled as miners, digging deep to find rich deposits of minerals and ores, including iron ore, copper, gold, china clay and, crucially, tin. The region is littered with prehistoric forts, evidence that as far back as the Bronze Age, Cornish metals were being dug up to make weapons and armour. During the Industrial Revolution, when all these materials were in high demand, mining brought huge wealth to the area, and railways were built to expand the trade. But by the end of the 19th century, prices had collapsed and Cornwall was suddenly one of the poorest places in Britain. Today, it's tourism that brings in the gold, and ruins you pass on this ride are all that's left of Cornwall's mining industry.

A Cornish glossary

The Cornish language has Celtic roots and is descended, like Welsh and Breton, from the ancient Common Brittonic language. This glossary should help you decode some of the words in local placenames.

Als, alt – a cliff

Bal – a mine

Bron – a hill

Carn – a heap of rocks

Dinas – a hill fort

Enys – an island

Goon – moorland

Kelly – a grove or copse

Lan – a monastic enclosure

Maen, mēn – a stone

Mēn-an-Tol – a stone with a hole

Mēn scryfa – a stone with an inscription

Nans – a valley

Pen – a headland

Pol – a pool

Porth – a cove

Praze – a meadow or common

Ruan – a river

Towan – a sandhill

Tol – a hole

Tre – a house or dwelling

Wheal – a mine or shaft

Zawn – a chasm

This section of the route climbs up onto moorland and is the least-populated part of the ride – and somewhat eerie if the fog has come down. It's also the most challenging in terms of navigation, with many conflicting tracks disappearing over the moors – keep your wits about you. If you pass Mên-an-Tol (two upright menhirs flanking a hollow, ring-shaped stone) and the Nine Maidens stone circle, you're going in the right direction. There are some rough trails as you descend down to St Erth via Nancledra. This is where the crossover in the figure-of-eight route comes. By St Erth you will have done around 45 miles (72km), but you could push on another 10 miles (16km) to Porthleven if you'd like to spend the night in a fantastic little harbour town with good food options.

Porthleven to the Lizard

Beyond Porthleven lies what is for many riders the best part of this route: the Lizard, a rounded headland that feels like a world unto itself. To reach it, you'll be cycling along the coast with the sparkling sea a constant distraction over your right shoulder. It also means that you'll be cycling down and up some steep and sometimes sandy slopes as the route dives down to tiny coves and back up the other side. It's hard work on a loaded bicycle, but there's often an ice-cream as a reward. There are two sides to the Lizard: there are some very busy areas with day-tripper-crammed car parks, but once away from the crowds it's a beautiful place. The fishing village of Coverack (lower left) makes a stunning location for lunch, about 35 tough miles (56km) beyond Porthleven. Then turn inland on lanes that lead towards Helford. Rather than taking a dogleg inland, you could hop on a ferry across the Helford River to the Ferry Boat Inn, but note that it's a very small boat with space for at most two bicycles at a time (if there are not many other passengers).

Closing the Loop

However you reach Constantine, this is as far east as you'll go. The route, alternating between lanes and rough (and sometimes muddy) tracks, now heads north to Portreath on Cornwall's north coast through more mining landscapes and also more built-up areas. Rest the legs in the sea (or rent a board) for a surf on Portreath's sandy beach (it's another overnight option if you're not camping), then make your way back southwest to the official end of the West Kernow Way at Marazion, where St Michael's Mount looms over the bay. This last inland leg has a little bit of everything, with mining history and Neolithic landmarks such as the Giant's Quoit. From Marazion, it's just a 20-minute ride back to Penzance.

West Kernow Way

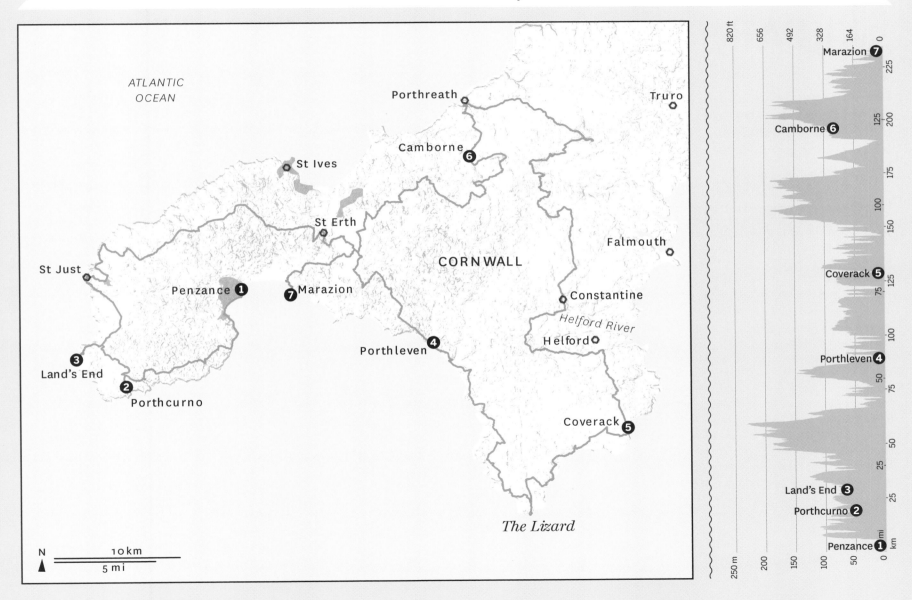

ATLANTIC
OCEAN

Porthreath

Truro

Camborne **6**

St Ives

St Erth

Falmouth

CORNWALL

St Just

Penzance **1**

Marazion **7**

Constantine

Helford River

Helford

Land's End

3

Porthleven **4**

2

Porthcurno

Coverack **5**

The Lizard

N

10 km
5 mi

Marazion **7**

Camborne **6**

Coverack **5**

Porthleven **4**

Land's End **3**

Porthcurno **2**

Penzance **1**

820 ft   656   492   328   164   0

250 m   200   150   100   50

→ Distance: 1550 miles (2500km)   → Ascent: 75,500ft (23,012m)   → Difficulty: 2

Wild Atlantic Way

Ireland

Encounter empty beaches with dolphins dancing in the distant waves, endless green fields and entrancing towns and villages where the pubs buzz with music and chatter. You can ride the whole Wild Atlantic Way or select short and sweet sections.

Plan and Prepare

Logistics

The full Wild Atlantic Way route runs between Malin Head on the Inishowen Peninsula in the north, and Kinsale in County Cork to the south. Derry (Londonderry), across the border in Northern Ireland, is about 35 miles (56km) south of Malin Head and has rail connections with Belfast (bikes are permitted). You may require extra travel documents for the border crossing. In the south, Kinsale is just an 18-mile (29km) ride from Cork.

Hazards

Rain, rain and more rain: the west coast of Ireland is famously one of the wettest places in Europe (those lush fields are green for a reason). High winds are sometimes a problem, too. But with adequate wet-weather kit, or a little luck, it's all survivable. Other than the weather, watch out for tourist drivers in the summer, who may not know how to share the road with people on bicycles.

Gear

Any regular road or gravel bike will suit the task: traditional touring bicycles will have appropriate mounts for panniers, but modern bikepacking bags can be fitted to most bicycles. You'll likely find a mountain bike too slow, given the surfaced lanes, but it's a personal choice. Be sure to carry puncture-repair kit and, given the likely rainfall, some lubricant for the chain.

Info

The optimum time of year to ride is from May in late spring to early autumn in September, but you can enjoy beautiful days in April or October – it's all down to the vagaries of the weather fronts crossing the Atlantic. In terms of the best direction, it's thought that riding south to north may offer a slightly greater chance of a tailwind.

Stretch Ireland's crinkly west coast out into a straight line and it would reach far further than the distance between London and Rome. But, instead, it is compressed into a coastline that curves around the west of this small island, taking in countless small bays and beaches, giant cliffs, tiny villages and the occasional town that feels like it's on the edge of the known world – to the west, the next city is New York. And in between roils the stormy Atlantic Ocean, bringing spray-laden winds, cetaceans and enough rain to turn the gentle hills a bright green.

The Wild Atlantic Way is an Irish tourism initiative that opened in 2014. It takes in famous sights, such as the Cliffs of Moher and the Dingle Peninsula, but also a large number of places that wouldn't otherwise attract many visitors. Given the route's extreme length, it's perfectly reasonable to select some appealing sections to tick off first if you don't have three or four weeks free to ride the whole thing. For example the coast south of Galway that covers the Burren and the Cliffs of Moher in County Clare, looking out to the Aran Islands, is a popular segment; another is the bike-friendly Beara Peninsula in County Cork to the southwest.

South to north

If you were to ride the entire Wild Atlantic Way from south to north, then the quiet country lanes of the Beara Peninsula are among the first you'll find. Fuel up on an Irish breakfast that includes Clonakilty black pudding before heading off into the drizzle. The southwest coastline has no lack of ups and downs and if the weather clears up you may spot minke whales from the seaward cliffs, or at very least the lighthouses that warned sailors of this treacherous coast.

Highlights

At intervals along the Wild Atlantic Way lie what are termed 'signature discovery points' – highlights of the route. There are just 15 in total, and they include natural wonders and human constructions. From the south, some of the most interesting are the Lusitania Museum, dedicated to the world's fastest transatlantic liner, sunk in WWI and, a little further on, the craggy island of Skellig Michael. After the soaring Cliffs of Moher (below), come back down to earth at Derrigimlagh Bog. Then there's pretty Killary Harbour and Keem Bay followed by a series of headlands, from Downpatrick's rock-stacks to Cionn Fhánada's lighthouse, ending at Malin Head at the top of the Way.

The most southwesterly point of Ireland is Mizen Head. Heading north, the Wild Atlantic Way zigzags in and out of the southwest's bays, so tightly spaced that you'll feel like almost reaching across the inlets. After the beautiful Beara Peninsula and pretty fishing villages such as Portmagee Harbour (left), most of which can offer a pint of Beamish at the end of the day and a bed for the night, you'll loop around the larger Castlemaine Harbour. At the tip of the Dingle Peninsula, the contemporary architecture of the Blasket Centre houses a museum that tells the story of the Blasket Islands' community. It's a great place to learn more about the Irish language.

Around Galway

Further up the coast, once you've passed the sheer Cliffs of Moher, you'll arrive at Galway City, one of the heartlands of traditional Irish music. Most pubs, such as Tigh Neachtain, host nightly trad music sessions. Just off the Galway coast are the Aran Islands, the largest of which is Inis Mór, reached by ferry from Doolin. Cycle around the windswept island to find fields hemmed by dry-stone walls and the remarkable prehistoric fort of Dún Aonghasa. Back on the mainland, discover some of the west coast's white-sand beaches on the 60-mile (96km) stretch between Killary Harbour and Keem beach, where you can soothe hot feet in cool, turquoise water.

Another of County Mayo's natural highlights is Downpatrick Head (left), where crumbling rock-stacks are home to puffins and other seabirds. More coastal towns, including County Mayo's largest, Ballina, offer sustenance and somewhere to sleep for passing cyclists. The next county is Donegal, where Killybegs is another perfect village to explore shortly before you reach Slieve League, some of the highest cliffs in Europe. It's still 130 miles (210km) to Malin Head and the northern end of the Way.

Wild Atlantic Way

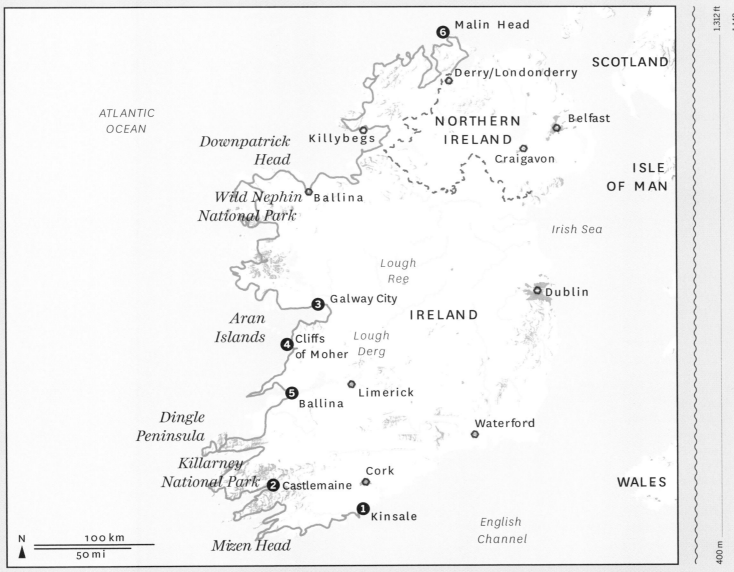

ATLANTIC
OCEAN

6 Malin Head

Derry/Londonderry

SCOTLAND

*Downpatrick
Head*

Killybegs

NORTHERN
IRELAND

Belfast

ISLE
OF MAN

Craigavon

*Wild Nephin
National Park*

Ballina

Irish Sea

*Lough
Ree*

Dublin

3 Galway City

IRELAND

*Aran
Islands*

4 Cliffs
of Moher

*Lough
Derg*

Limerick

Waterford

5 Ballina

*Dingle
Peninsula*

*Killarney
National Park*

2 Castlemaine

Cork

WALES

1 Kinsale

*English
Channel*

Mizen Head

N

100 km

50 mi

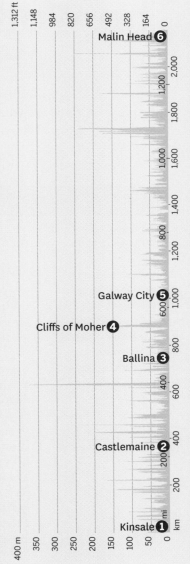

1,312 ft
1,148
984
820
656
492
328
164
0

Malin Head **6**

2,000

1,200

1,800

1,000

1,600

1,400

Galway City **5**

Cliffs of Moher **4**

Ballina **3**

Castlemaine **2**

Kinsale **1**

400 m
350
300
250
200
150
100
50
0
km

→ Distance: 241 miles (388km) → Ascent: 28,195ft (8594m) → Difficulty: 3

The Wolf's Lair

Italy

The Apennines are the spine of Italy, running down the centre of the country. This wild route, just east of Rome, plays around on some of these mountainous vertebrae, circling three national parks in the little-visited region of Abruzzo.

Plan and Prepare

Logistics

The route starts just outside the city of L'Aquila at the archaeological site of Amiternum, and is designed to loop back around clockwise. Rome is the closest transport hub, with buses to L'Aquila.

Hazards

The local shepherds' dogs – large, white guardians of the flock – can cause problems and may require a detour. The dogs are there because of the wolves and although there have been no recorded attacks on humans in recent times, there were deaths attributed to wolves during the 19th century. Brown bears also live in these mountains but are typically shy and elusive. It's advisable to make some noise while riding.

Gear

The route is designed for a gravel bike with chunky tyres (40mm or more), but a hardtail mountain bike may be more comfortable on some of the rougher sections. There are a few short, steep climbs where low gearing is helpful but generally gradients are less than 10%. A reliable bike is key, as there are few bike shops on the way.

Info

May to the end of September is the prime time to ride, though August tends to be too hot for the available (limited) water supplies; riding earlier in spring could mean more mud from the snowmelt. September is probably the perfect month. Remember that at the higher altitudes it will get much colder quite quickly at night.

The Wolf's Lair ride through Abruzzo was designed by bikepacking buddies Francesco D'Alessio and Giorgio Frattale, also known as photography and filmmaking duo Montanus. They were living in the city of L'Aquila when the earthquake of 2009 hit; several years later they started exploring their backyard wilderness on bikes, eventually composing the route they christened the Wolf's Lair.

The name comes from the local lupine inhabitants, who are thriving in the three national parks that the trails traverse – Gran Sasso, Maiella and Abruzzo – plus the regional park of Sirente Velino. The wolves don't seem that interested in bikepackers but they do prey on the abundant deer and wild boar around these mountains, some of the highest in central Italy. Punctuating the beautiful landscapes are fortified villages and medieval castles, long abandoned or at least only used by shepherds during the summer. The trail that connects many of these mementoes from earlier ages is mainly off-road, covering singletrack, doubletrack and gravel roads. There are places to camp and refill water bottles, but fewer opportunities to pick up food supplies – plan ahead.

Parco Nazionale del Gran Sasso

Leave the ruins of Amiternum, founded by the pre-Roman Sabine people, and head east into Gran Sasso for some of the highest reaches of the route. You'll be passing through pastures as you climb into an ancient landscape, reaching an elevation of around 5400ft (1645m). After about 30 miles (48km), the pretty walled town of Santo Stefano di Sessanio appears. As is common in rural Italian towns, there's an ageing and dwindling population here (currently around 100); new residents aged under 40 are encouraged by subsidies, especially if they intend to start a business.

There's accommodation in Santo Stefano di Sessanio or you can just pick up some snacks and continue onward. The trail swoops down to Rocca Calascio, a 13th-century castle sitting on a hilltop at 4790ft (1460m) and overlooking the Valle del Tirino and the Navelli plains below. It was designed for defence and surveillance rather than luxury living, with four stout towers at each corner, and has been derelict since an earthquake in 1703, although you can walk or ride right up to it. In the eerie village beneath the fort (population about 100), cafes offer refreshments. It's strange to think that 500 years ago this place had 1500 inhabitants, supporting the 30,000 shepherds who roamed the Abruzzo hills with some three million sheep.

Deeper into Abruzzo

Plenty of bikepackers camp near Calascio. The limestone path then climbs up to a high plateau in the Gran Sasso, a frontier-like landscape that was often used as a location in Spaghetti Western movies. Descending through forest, the doubletrack leads down to the Aterno-Pescara River, which flows from the mountains and into the Adriatic. Crossing the river and a motorway, you'll find yourself in a built-up area but you'll soon be climbing steadily into the Parco Nazionale della Majella; after 20 miles (32km) you'll reach the Passo San Leonardo, where there's food and camping.

Heading south along a broad basin at 3500ft (1067m), you're now on the Altopiano delle Cinque Miglia (Five-Mile Plateau), an open karst landscape that gets very cold in winter and has thwarted many armies in the past. More recently, it has been crisscrossed by shepherds and their flocks, which are often guarded against wolves by several mountain dogs. These dogs can be very protective and sometimes you'll need to figure out a way to give them a wide berth. They're just doing their job.

Abruzzo's cuisine

Spared the spotlight that Tuscany, Piedmont and Puglia enjoy, the cuisine of Abruzzo has changed little over the centuries. Whether you're sitting beachside or in a mountain hamlet, the food on your plate will be humble and hearty, honouring local ingredients. Lamb is big here. *Arrosticini* (below) is a classic dish: skewers of local lamb, seasoned with salt, pepper, rosemary and olive oil and cooked over a barbecue until tender. They're served with pickles and a glass of the local Montepulciano d'Abruzzo red wine. Otherwise, lamb is cooked with the ubiquitous local *diavolino* (little devil) chillies, or in a ragù with *chitarra* (egg pasta). More portable are the *pizza scima*: thick, crunchy flatbreads similar to focaccia.

Heading north

Eventually, you'll cross over into the Parco Nazionale d'Abruzzo, Lazio e Molise at the Passo Godi ski station, where you can pick up supplies. The surface switches from steep and unpaved to paved, making the ascent a little easier. After about 10 miles (16km) of easy riding you'll reach Lago di Barrea, a large artificial lake surrounded by towns and villages, the most interesting of which is historic Civitella Alfedena. Constructed from the region's pale limestone, it has buildings and alleys that date back more than 1000 years, although the landmark Saettèra tower was built in the 16th century to defend against raiders. Now a relatively busy tourist centre in the summer season, there are places to stay, eat and wash before the return leg of your ride.

It's about 90 miles (145km) back to the start in L'Aquila but as you leave Civitella Alfedena you'll be back in the wilder reaches of the national park, albeit riding on a surfaced road through forests. In the surrounding mountains live goat-like chamois, considered a separate species to the chamois of the Alps, being more slender with longer horns. The chamois here have recovered in numbers thanks to the park's conservation efforts – as has the Marsican brown bear, the emblem of the national park itself, which was created in 1923 to protect this ursine subspecies. There are only around 50 Marsican bears in the wild today; back in the Roman period they were captured in order to fight gladiators in Rome, and later persecuted by farmers and hunters. Try to find time for a bear-spotting tour.

As you head north, alternating between roads and unpaved tracks, the scenery is arguably less spectacular than on the east side of the loop, and there are a few more towns along the way. But it's a beautiful ride and the gradual descent back into L'Aquila is a worthy reward at the end of Wolf's Lair.

The Wolf's Lair

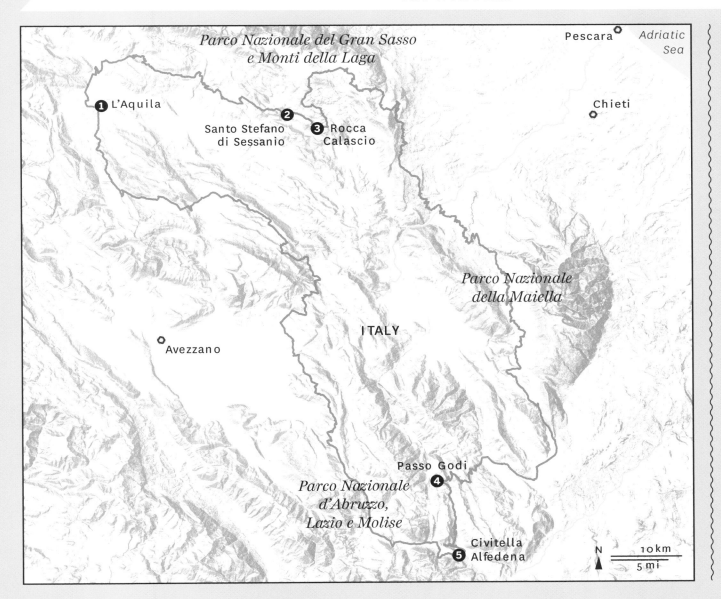

Parco Nazionale del Gran Sasso
e Monti della Laga

Pescara

Adriatic
Sea

1 L'Aquila

Chieti

2

3 Rocca
Calascio

Santo Stefano
di Sessanio

Parco Nazionale
della Maiella

ITALY

Avezzano

Passo Godi

4

Parco Nazionale
d'Abruzzo,
Lazio e Molise

Civitella
Alfedena

5

N

10 km

5 mi

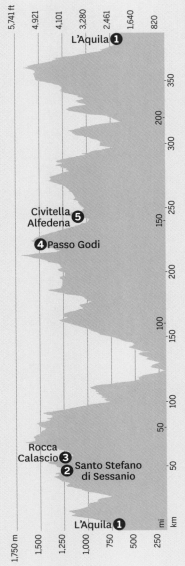

5,741 ft

4,921

4,101

3,280

2,461

1,640

820

L'Aquila **1**

350

200

300

Civitella
Alfedena **5**

250

4 Passo Godi

200

150

100

100

Rocca
Calascio **3**

50

2 Santo Stefano
di Sessanio

L'Aquila **1**

mi

1,750 m

1,500

1,250

1,000

750

500

250

km

→ Distance: 218 miles (350km)   → Ascent: 11,191ft (3411m)   → Difficulty: 2

King Alfred's Way

England

Pedal through 10,000 years of history on this loop through southern England around King Alfred's ancient kingdom of Wessex. An ideal, easygoing introduction to bikepacking, the route takes in both the South Downs Way and the Ridgeway national trails.

Plan and Prepare

Logistics

Most people start the loop from one of the towns or cities with a mainline rail connection; these include Reading, Farnham, Petersfield and Winchester. The choice will depend on which line is most convenient, although all connect with London, which is about 1hr by train from the stations mentioned. Winchester is the official start point and the route is designed to be ridden in a clockwise direction.

Hazards

King Alfred's Way passes through Ministry of Defence land around Salisbury Plain; obey any signs, observe access closures during firing practice and don't pick up any objects. Some of the route is on flint tracks and the sharp stones can cut tyres: carry spare tubes, a puncture-repair kit (for tubeless set-ups too) including a tyre patch or boot, and a pump. Other sections are on chalk, which is perilously slippery when wet.

Gear

The terrain varies from mud to hardpacked dirt and rocks with a lot of surfaced lanes, so a gravel or touring bike with a minimum of 38mm tyres would be the quickest option. But a mountain bike might bring more comfort and control on a few of the off-road sections. However, people have completed the route on a huge variety of bikes. You can camp, or travel light and stay in accommodation.

Info

Visit cyclinguk.org for route info, maps and accommodation advice. Most people take around four days to complete the route, which is deceptively hilly. Outside of the warmer months (April to October) there's a likelihood that sections will be unpleasantly muddy. For accommodation, there are lots of campsites and B&Bs catering to cyclists. It's possible to wild-camp but check with the landowner first. You're never more than a few minutes away from shops.

King Alfred's Way is a route designed and pieced together by the Cycling UK organisation. That means that although it's not signposted (yet), there are detailed directions available, an established infrastructure of food and accommodation providers along the route, and a very lively and informative Facebook group. That makes it a good choice for novice bikepackers, who can gain support and encouragement to make a multi-day trip. There are also lots of options depending on how you want to ride the loop: you can carry all your kit and camp and cook out, or sleep between clean sheets, enjoy hot showers and eat at pubs and cafes. Your call. The other great advantage is the route's accessibility: cyclists can jump on or off at numerous points.

So, what type of cycling is offered on the King Alfred's Way? Well, a little bit of everything. The route connects a couple of England's long-distance off-road trails – the South Downs Way to the south and the Ridgeway to the north – using a mix of lanes and bridleways (off-road tracks that riders of horses and bicycles are permitted to use). There are a few steep hills (up and down) and some (short) tricky sections, but the vast majority of the route isn't intimidating. The official start point is Winchester, once the capital of the Anglo-Saxon kingdom of Wessex, and that highlights the other unique attraction of this ride: the history through which you pass.

The heart of Wessex

From the Westgate next to Winchester Castle, you'll head west towards Salisbury, slipping through slumbering suburbs before segueing onto lanes and tracks towards Sparsholt village (the name means 'wood where spear shafts were made'). Look out for the first of many Bronze Age burial barrows (or mounds).

© Pannier.cc

After crossing the Test River, one of the world's top fly-fishing spots thanks to its beautiful chalk riverbed, the route climbs up a chalk down (the misleading name actually comes from the Old English for hill: 'dūn'). Once on higher ground, you'll be pedalling past fields of crops. After about 25 miles (40km), you'll come to Old Sarum, a circular Iron Age fort that then became a Roman settlement – complete with long-gone temples – and later saw the addition of a Norman castle and cathedral before being abandoned by the year 1500: layer upon layer of history.

At this point, Salisbury is a short diversion south but most riders will press on towards Stonehenge, probably one of the most famous prehistoric sites in the world. The henge – a circular earthen enclosure around the iconic bluestone monoliths – is 10 miles (16km) from Salisbury but requires a tricky road crossing to reach (take care and follow Cycling UK's advice). There's no shortage of serious research to read about Stonehenge, but suffice to say that the earliest construction dates back to 3000 BCE. But, amazingly, it's arguably not the most amazing prehistoric site on this route: that might be Avebury in the Vale of Pewsey.

Avebury comes at about the 65-mile (105km) mark and is home to the world's largest stone circle. Not only that but there are Bronze Age barrows at Silbury Hill and West Kennet, all of which forms part of a remarkable prehistoric panorama when viewed from the Ridgeway.

Alfred's Wessex

Wessex was the Anglo-Saxon kingdom, defined by its resistance to Viking raiders from around the year 870 CE onwards. It encompassed much of southwest England, including what are now the counties of Hampshire and Wiltshire. Wessex was ruled from his capital, Winchester, by the young King Alfred from 871 to 899. He was only 22 when he assumed the throne but proved to be an exceptional leader: militarily, diplomatically and politically, but also in his championing of literacy. By 886, he had captured London and united the Anglo-Saxons for the first time. But it wasn't plain sailing. The first few years of his reign were spent fighting marauding Danes, and he had to retreat to a fort on the Somerset marches to the west. Gradually the tide turned thanks to Alfred's foresight: he created fortified 'burhs' (strongholds) so that no part of Wessex was more than 20 miles (32km) from refuge, and also built a navy of fast warships. Just as important was his initiative to translate Latin texts into Anglo-Saxon to educate the population. He died in 899 and was buried in Winchester, the only English ruler to be known as 'the Great'.

reaching Reading. This is another change of pace and you'll be riding through an extremely affluent and genteel part of the country. Depending on the schedule you've set, you may be anticipating another overnight stop around here. The largest city on the route, Reading, is approaching and you'll need to be on top of the navigation; the route tries to follow low-traffic lanes. This is also probably the least enjoyable section, but thankfully you're soon out of urban England and back in the greenery. There's a change of terrain, from chalk to sandy ground, but the history lessons continue. After exiting Reading on the way to Farnham, a trip of 33 miles (53km), you can divert to Silchester, the ruin of a Roman town. More recent history is apparent in the WWII defences in the area and in the town of Farnham, where the 12th-century castle hosted wartime research into camouflage.

The Ridgeway

The wonders of Neolithic Avebury are visible from the Ridgeway, an ancient road running east to west across southern England, and used for more than 5000 years by Saxon armies, Stone Age drovers, medieval merchants and modern-day hikers and bikepackers. In total, the Ridgeway extends for 87 miles (140km), all the way to Ivinghoe Beacon in Buckinghamshire, but you'll only be using it as far as Goring. As the name suggests, the Ridgeway hugs the high ground, which means that the views are fabulous but there are also significant climbs. Along the way you'll pass such sights as the Uffington White Horse, a graceful 360ft (110m) chalk figure of a horse, seemingly snapshotted in motion (left). The horse is thought to date from the pre-Christian Bronze or early Iron Age.

From Goring, after about 110 miles (177km), you'll drop down to the River Thames before

The South Downs

After Farnham, the landscape turns to sandy heathland, punctuated by pine trees. You'll circle Frensham Ponds and then climb up to the Devil's Punchbowl, a great viewpoint. On the way, take a rest amid the ruins of Waverley Abbey, a 13th-century Cistercian monastery that was demolished by King Henry VIII when he formed the Church of England. From Waverley, it's a short ride towards the South Downs in the distance, via the Shipwrights Way. The final section of King Alfred's Way follows the South Downs Way from South Harting to Winchester for 30 miles (48km). It's a beautiful and challenging finale, with some big hills, usually with an Iron Age fort perched on top. Although the surface is quite fast-rolling, be sure to savour the orchids and butterflies of this ancient Downland landscape before finishing in King Alfred's former home town.

King Alfred's Way

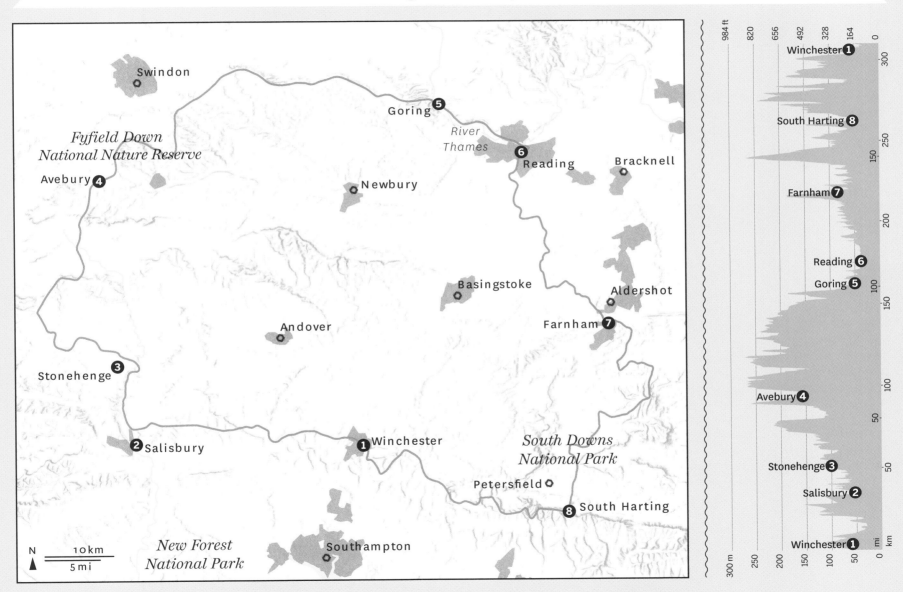

➔ Distance: 423 miles (680km)   ➔ Ascent: 41,550ft (12,665m)   ➔ Difficulty: 5

Montañas Vacias

Spain

For experienced cyclists, the Montañas Vacias loop is an escapist's dream. It ranges over an inland region east of Madrid known as Spain's Lapland – not for the climate (though it can be cold) but for its depopulated desolation.

Plan and Prepare

Logistics

This loop starts from the town of Teruel, around 2hr from València by direct Media Distancia (mid-distance) train; these have limited spaces for bicycles and there's a small fee to pay, and you'll probably have to book and pay in advance. But you don't need to dismantle the bike. You can also reach Teruel directly by train from Zaragoza (2hr 30min).

Hazards

This is a very isolated route at a higher elevation, bringing with it all the weather-related hazards you'd expect. It can get very cold, very windy or even snowy, at any time of year. Dress accordingly. There are very few settlements along the way so plan ahead for food and water, and what to do in an emergency. Also, do not light campfires.

Gear

There's a lot of ascent so keep weight as low as possible. The route is manageable on a robust gravel bike with 40mm+ tyres, but a 29er mountain bike with front suspension might be the better option for most. Ensure that you have the means to carry and purify water. A bivvy bag and sleeping bag are essential.

Info

Ideal months to ride are May and June in spring, or September and October in autumn; it's otherwise too hot or too cold. There are about a dozen refuges along the route in which you can overnight. Wild camping is prohibited in many parts of Spain, including some of the parks and protected areas on this route. There a handful of legal campsites, however. See montanasvacias.com for some very detailed route info.

The Montañas Vacias route was devised by Spanish bikepacker Ernesto Pastor, who wrote about it in Lonely Planet's *Epic Bike Rides of Europe*. His intention in creating the ride was to introduce a region of Spain that has missed out on the tourism benefits enjoyed by the coasts and cities. He hoped to encourage bike riders to visit this vast, high-country plateau, known as the Serranía Celtibérica, where villages have been emptied of the younger generations. Although this arid area could pass for the set of a Spaghetti Western, its local nickname is the Spanish Lapland, due to there being so few people hereabouts. The ride's terrain covers lots of ridges of red earth, and sparse forests threaded with doubletrack and rough gravel roads. And as it covers 423 miles (680km), plan for eight to 10 nights away.

Up into 'Lapland'

Pastor's hometown is Teruel, one of the very intermittent settlements on the route. It's the start point for Montañas Vacias, which heads west and anticlockwise into the wilderness. Teruel lies at an elevation of 3000ft (914ft) and it's one of the lowest points on the loop, with high spots topping out at 6500ft (1981m). It's not a ride that you should start without some fitness training. From Teruel, the route climbs steadily on an off-road track towards Albarracín (right), which is regularly voted one of Spain's most beautiful towns, the peach-coloured tiles of its rooves clustered along a ridge and shielded by medieval fortifications. The first walls were built in the 10th century by its Berber rulers and the town has since changed hands countless times, suffering especially during the Spanish Civil War in the 1930s. It's an interesting place to stay overnight and one of the few places along the route in which you can find a comfortable bed.

Stargazing

With so few people in the region and few flight paths, the night sky is extra dark here and, as a result, the stars are beautifully bright. This makes the Serranía Celtibérica ideal for stargazing sessions as you sit in the silence of the night, tired after a day on the bike. One of the best spots from which to stare at the night sky is the Javalambre plateau, where a simple stone shelter provides the perfect setting. Head to the top of the Collado del Buey, at 5640ft (1719m) in Parque Natural Puebla de San Miguel, where there's a basic refuge. To take good starscape photos, keep the f-stop of your camera low and allow the shutter to open for about 20 seconds.

Beyond Albarracín, the next point of interest is the Parque Natural del Alto Tajo (left), where the Iberian Peninsula's longest river, the Tagus, has its source, flowing west all the way across Spain to Lisbon and the Atlantic Ocean. You'll follow it for the next 60 miles (100km), more or less, into the province of Guadalajara. At this point there's the option of shortcut back to Teruel that takes in several castles, but if you continue you'll be entering the real Spanish Lapland of this ride: pine forests that extend into the distance, deep in the Serranía Celtibérica mountain range.

At Puente de San Pedro you say farewell to the Tagus as you turn back to loop eastward again; take the opportunity for a dip in its chilly turquoise waters. There are a few stone refuges in the vicinity, including La Falaguera and Vado Salmeron, so you can shelter overnight. After about 160 miles (257km) you'll be leaving the Alto Tajo Nature Reserve (and its camping restrictions) and passing through small hamlets in which to restock provisions. Soon you'll be in the Parque Natural de la Serranía de Cuenca (lower left). Rivers have cut through the limestone plateau here to create deep gorges, while other distinctive mushroom-shaped rock formations are due to this high landscape once being at the bottom of a sea. It all adds to the otherworldly feel of the Montañas Vacias.

The highest point of the ride is coming up: the Pico de Peñarroya at 6653ft (2028m), with views across the Sierra de Javalambre being the reward. Here the route turns west again back to Teruel. Throughout, it helps to remember the purpose of Ernesto Pastor's ride: to bring life back to the empty mountains again – so try to bring a little Spanish of your own and chat to the locals when you stop for *almuerzo* (brunch).

Montañas Vacias

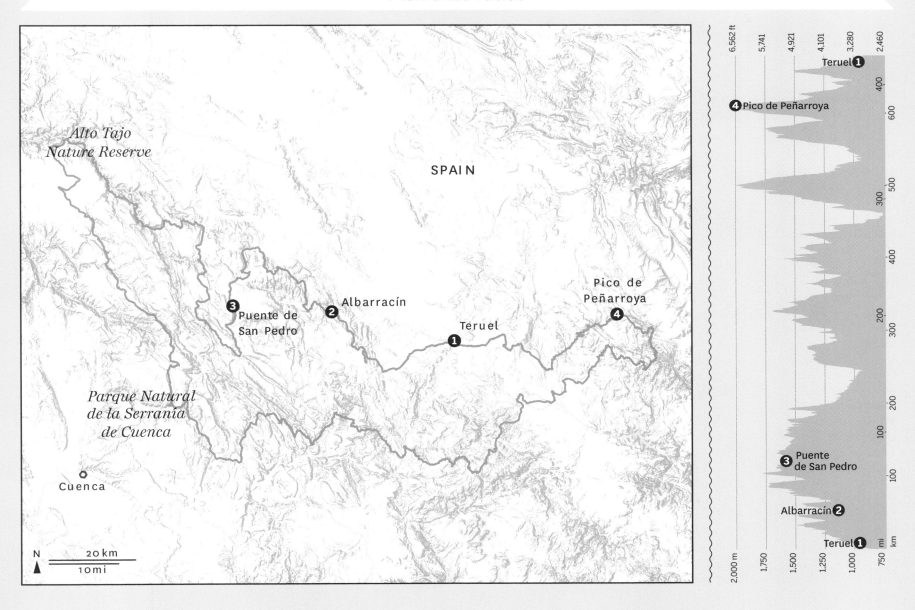

➡ Distance: 373 miles (600km)   ➡ Ascent: 33,000ft (10,058m)   ➡ Difficulty: 3

Tuscany Trail

Italy

This annual bikepacking race probably has the most beautiful pitstops in the world: Florence, San Gimignano and Siena. But if you're not racing the trail, you can adapt the route in your own time for a tour of Tuscany off the beaten path.

Plan and Prepare

Logistics

The route starts from Massa in the north of Tuscany, and ends at Capalbio Scalo in the south. Both towns are connected to Pisa by direct trains (Massa is 30min north, Capalbio 2hr south); Pisa is also connected by fast services to Rome via Florence. On regional Trenitalia trains in Tuscany, tickets are usually required for bicycles and there may be restrictions on timing.

Hazards

As this isn't an overly remote region, there are few real hazards to consider. However, the distance and terrain (there are a lot of steep hills) are certainly challenging for anybody other than a super-fit cyclist – be prepared for the physical exertion, especially during the summer. Some of the surfaces are loose so watch out on descents; and be aware that you'll be sharing roads with vehicles.

Gear

For the race event, most riders will be using hardtail mountain bikes or gravel bikes with the chunkiest tyres that will fit. A lot of the route is off-road and on quite steep or rocky slopes, so a mountain bike has the necessary grip and gearing. You'll probably need to carry some shelter, although the route does pass through places with overnight accommodation.

Info

The Tuscany Trail race typically takes place in late May, which is an ideal time to ride before the heat of summer. Autumn is another sublime time, with grape harvests and warm days. But there's a risk of rain during either season. Winter will bring a lot more mud and some snow. You can find detailed information on the event at tuscanytrail.it

The majestic Tuscan cities of Florence, San Gimignano and Siena are dream destinations for many people: medieval wonders packed with masterpieces by Botticelli and Michelangelo and defined by their Gothic architecture. However, this bikepacking ride across Tuscany is certainly no picnic. As the route replaces main roads with rough tracks across the wilder corners of this very hilly region, the Tuscany Trail is a considerable challenge: don't be misled by images of gently undulating gravel lanes with a distant hilltop town glowing golden in the afternoon light.

The route was originally pioneered by Andrea Borchi (the brain behind bikepacking.it) as a way to explore the most natural parts of his home region and it soon became, if not a serious race, then a semi-competitive rally. At its inaugural event, 80 bikepackers participated (half completed the route), and there are 10 times as many taking part today. Borchi's vision was that people would be able to follow the itinerary, at their own pace, throughout the year. But don't underestimate how adventurous the off-road cycling really is; as Borchi explained in an interview with bikepacking kit specialists Apidura: 'I like narrow, unpaved paths that cross woodland. I like being far from busy roads and seeing landscapes from high above. I like climbs, especially the most difficult ones.' You have been warned. Tuscany Trail racers take four or five days but casual riders could double that and have time to explore the Tuscan towns along the way. The other important thing to note is that the race route changes each year, sometimes skipping cities like Lucca or Florence, although most of the route options are of a similar distance.

There are, however, a number of constants: classic Tuscan scenery such as the Val d'Orcia; enthralling cities; and numerous villages in which you can rest, eat and drink if you're not trying to beat the clock.

Towards Florence

Depending on the route you're taking, the first destination is likely to be Lucca after about 33 miles (53km). Every bit the architectural equal of Florence and Siena, Lucca's monumental *mura* (city wall) dates from the 16th and 17th centuries, when the wealth of the Renaissance created a number of feuding city-states, leading to the defensive hilltop positions and huge fortifications that many retain today. From the footpath along the top of Lucca's ramparts you can see the Apuan Alps to the north. If you're taking it easy, stop in Lucca for the night; otherwise continue towards Vinci, birthplace of Leonardo da Vinci. Be aware that the surface on the approach to Vinci can become very muddy after rain, and there are some difficult climbs.

There's another ridge to conquer before the city of Florence appears below. After a tricky off-road descent, the Tuscany Trail takes you into the heart of Florence. If you're choosing to camp, there are options just outside the city, but if you don't plan on passing this way again soon, you may prefer to book a roof over your head and enjoy some time sightseeing in the heart of the Italian Renaissance. Florence straddles the Arno River, which is a useful navigation tool. On the north side are the Duomo, the Galleria degli Uffizi and the Galleria dell'Accademia, home to Michelangelo's iconic *David*. It's the scale of the world's most famous statue that is staggering: carved from a single block of marble, he stands 17ft (5m) tall and weighs 19 tonnes.

Siena's Strade Bianche

'I always look forward to Strade Bianche as it's one of the most beautiful races of the season' – so says Olympic cycling champion Greg Van Avermaet. Yes, the cypress-lined 'white roads' of Tuscany around the city of Siena are the playing field for one of the road-racing season's classic bike races. The Strade Bianche takes place in March every year, just as the region is waking from its winter slumber. Competitors set off from Siena on a 115-mile (185km) loop around the city on some of the white-gravel tracks that you'll ride on the Tuscany Trail. The racers might not have time to appreciate their surroundings, but the spectators can explore this beautiful city, devised, as Unesco writes in its description of the World Heritage Site, as 'a work of art that blends into the landscape.' Siena's fortifications date from its long-running feud with neighbour Florence: in fact, Siena's Fortezza Medicea was built by Florentines to keep the Sienese from taking back their city in the 16th century. Aside from the ice-cream shops, not a lot has changed since then, with Siena's street plan retaining its Gothic townhouses and palaces, vegetable gardens growing inside the city walls and fountains still fed with water from underground tunnels.

To Siena and beyond

From Florence, the route becomes much more hilly with some hard climbs, some of the hike-a-bike type. But the classic Chianti scenery of vineyards and villas perched on ridges makes up for the sweat and tears. Being in Italy means starting the day with an espresso, and further refills are not usually far away. It's about 30 miles (48km) to the town of Sambuca and usually about the same again, depending on the exact route, before you spy the spires of San Gimignano on the horizon. These famous towers date from the 11th century and were built as a way for neighbouring families to outdo each other. More than 72 were constructed, but only 14 still stand. The Tuscany Trail takes you inside the historic heart but, again, you can camp on the outskirts of town or take a room in the centre.

Part of the trail in this region follows the Via Francigena, a pilgrims' path that travels from Canterbury in England to Rome. Much of this signposted route from the Swiss border to Rome is rideable on a bicycle (see viefrancigene.org). The Tuscany Trail now heads for Siena, which is usually about halfway along the route. The city's charms include the Piazza del Campo, almost entirely ringed with medieval buildings and with Siena's striped Gothic cathedral dominating one side. The square is the venue for the notorious 90-second Il Palio horse race, and the finish line for the Strade Bianche. The entire city is of a manageable size and it's very rewarding to see where various alleys lead.

South of Siena, riders enter the Val d'Orcia, another world's-most-photographed place that somehow lives up to the hype. White limestone roads snake into the distance, framed by Montepulciano grape vines, olive groves and wildflowers. It's fast riding, passing through pretty hilltop towns like Pienza and Pitigliano before looping westward, back to the coast and the finish.

Tuscany Trail

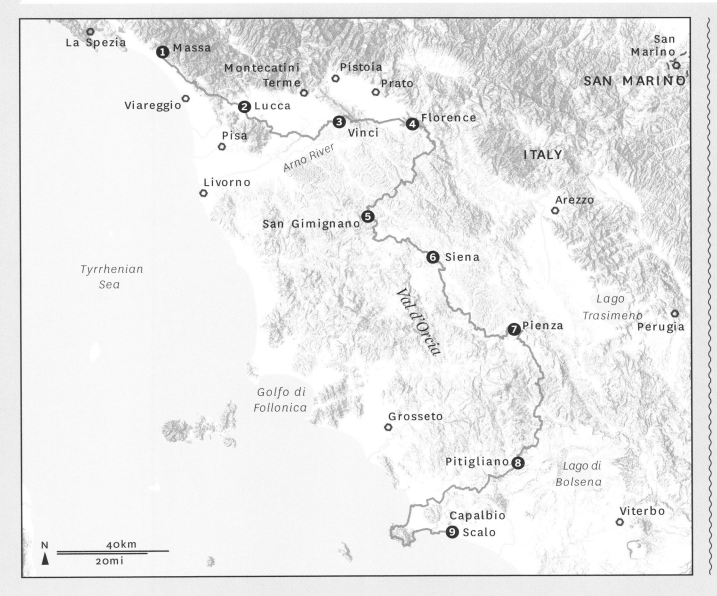

La Spezia

1 Massa

Montecatini
Terme

Pistoia

Prato

Viareggio

2 Lucca

Pisa

3

Vinci

4 Florence

Arno River

Livorno

ITALY

San
Marino

SAN MARINO

Arezzo

5

San Gimignano

6 Siena

*Tyrrhenian
Sea*

Val d'Orcia

*Lago
Trasimeno*

Perugia

7 Pienza

*Golfo di
Follonica*

Grosseto

Pitigliano **8**

*Lago di
Bolsena*

Capalbio
9 Scalo

Viterbo

N

40km

20mi

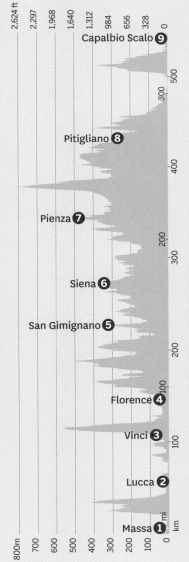

2,624 ft
2,297
1,968
1,640
1,312
984
656
328
0

Capalbio Scalo **9**

Pitigliano **8**

Pienza **7**

Siena **6**

San Gimignano **5**

Florence **4**

Vinci **3**

Lucca **2**

Massa **1**

800m
700
600
500
400
300
200
100
0

500
400
300
200
100
0
mi
km

→ Distance: 776 miles (1250km) → Ascent: 23,000ft (7010m) → Difficulty: 1

La Vélodyssée

France

Skip from seaside town to surfy beach and back on this sedate ride along France's west coast between Brittany and the Basque Country. Delicious regional specialities, ever-changing as you go, keep you pedalling, and the sea is always near for a refreshing dip.

Plan and Prepare

Logistics

The route runs from Roscoff on the Brittany coast to Hendaye on the Spanish border. You can reach Roscoff by train from Paris via Morlaix (through which the route passes anyway); it's quite complicated to get to Roscoff by ferry from the UK. Hendaye is connected to Bordeaux by a fast and direct train (2hr 30min), and from Bordeaux it's easy to transfer to other major cities by train.

Hazards

There are few hazards to worry about here. Some of the route crosses or uses busy roads, so take care around traffic and ensure you're visible and have lights as required. The weather is variable, with rain likely along the coast: be prepared with waterproofs. The route is also quite hilly in the north but considerably flatter in the southern half.

Gear

Any standard bicycle will be suitable if it can carry the luggage you require. Most of the route is on surfaced bike paths or roads, so fast-rolling tyres are recommended. A touring bicycle would be best but electric bikes are also an option since there are places to charge them overnight (if you're not camping). You can also decide whether to carry cooking kit or eat out along the way.

Info

Spring can be quite wet but is otherwise a pleasant time to ride; early autumn is also an enjoyable period. The peak of summer will bring lots of tourist traffic to beaches and some high temperatures. The official website (cycling-lavelodyssee.com) has detailed practical info, including GPX files and profiles of 38 short segments making up the whole.

The Vélodyssée is truly an odyssey, hugging the west coast of France from the tip of Brittany to the Basque border with Spain. It's a long way, but we've rated the ride as easy for several reasons: it uses predominantly surfaced and traffic-free bike paths and roads; it's generally well signposted, so navigation is not too challenging; and it never ventures far from a town with a railway station, or a village with a soft bed for the night and warm croissant waiting in the morning. These factors make it a very approachable bikepacking trip for novices, or for those who don't want to overly exert themselves.

But that's not to say that it is without challenges. In the north, the Vélodyssée fights its way over the frequent hills of Brittany and the Loire, often into a salty headwind straight off the Atlantic ocean. Then in the lower third there are some quite tedious sections of long, straight roads through Les Landes region, though these are redeemed by the proximity of some great surfing beaches.

We also discounted the distance as a factor in our rating for the simple reason that most people will tackle the Vélodyssée in stages rather than in one go. And its structure of connecting small towns along the coast mean that it is easy to cycle one-way and then hop on a regional train (on which bikes are typically accepted).

This also enables riders to prioritise some of the many highlights of France's Atlantic coast. From north to south these include the Breton culture and Celtic mythology of the first 100 miles (160km); the area around La Rochelle and Île de Ré, with cycling paths along the pretty seaside; and the beaches, surf breaks and sophisticated towns of Biarritz and Saint-Jean-de-Luz in the very southwest.

© Cass Gilbert

Southbound

The Vélodyssée can be ridden in either direction and it's a gamble as to whether the wind will be a help or a hindrance. But starting from Roscoff, way out on the coast of Finistère (the end of the land), you're guaranteed a strong breeze. The route starts by heading inland towards Morlaix and Carhaix through stone-walled Breton lanes. Brittany's distinct personality shines through in its language and placenames, its landscape of granite and river valleys, and the Celtic myths and Neolithic monuments that abound. Cycling through Brittany is a brilliant way of exploring this densely packed region, not least because of its pride in its bike-racing history. Eventually you'll reach the first of several canals you'll follow, leading south past manor houses, Cistercian abbeys and the Lac de Guerlédan. Throughout there are small villages and towns, such as gorgeously medieval Malestroit, in which you can stay at a B&B or pitch a tent. More waterways guide you south towards Nantes in the Pays-de-la-Loire, the first city to cross.

From Nantes, the Vélodyssée follows the Loire to the coast proper and you'll get a taste of the region's maritime history – and its oysters. By the time you reach Saint-Jean-de-Monts you'll be pedalling through sand dunes and pine forests, and although the sea temperature will still be bracing, the beaches will become more appealing for a dip. Fishing boats are swapped for yachts at Les Sables d'Olonne, start- and finish-point for the Vendée Globe solo round-the-world race. The landscape changes again, becoming flat marshland with huge skies above as you approach La Rochelle, the next large city on the route and a former trading post with an interesting Protestant history – hence the towers that defend its port. It's also the jumping-off point for a trip to the Île de Ré.

The Île de Ré

Just offshore from La Rochelle, the Île de Ré has long been a haven for French holidaymakers and British visitors, attracted by its colourful harbours, chic resorts and the very family-friendly cycling. Although measuring just 19 miles by 3 miles (30km by 5km), the island has more than 60 miles (100km) of cycle paths, mostly separated from what little traffic exists. The Île de Ré is also very flat, making it almost an alternate cycling universe – a little Amsterdam in the sun. The capital (and also an Unesco World Heritage Site) is Saint-Martin-de-Ré, where an artisanal ice-cream parlour offers a world of dreamy flavours. Unwind watching sunset over the marshes with a glass of white wine and the island's other speciality: oysters.

La Vélodyssée extensions

The southern end of the Vélodyssée is in Hendaye, but the ride's end can also be the start of further explorations. From here it's about 30 minutes by train across the border to Spain and the city of San Sebastián (below), known for its gastronomic food scene. If you've cycled this far there's no reason not to continue onward for a taste of *pintxos* (Basque tapas) with a glass of the region's Rioja wine. The train line continues along the coast so in theory you could catch a ferry north. Or, from Hendaye, backtrack to Bayonne, from where you can catch direct trains to the gateway of the Pyrenees, Pau, or the hiking hotspot of Saint-Jean-Pied-de-Port; both are about an hours' journey away by rail.

Beyond Bordeaux

South of La Rochelle, the atmosphere of the coastal towns becomes more about summer holidays, with broad sandy beaches that gradually become surfier the further south you go. You'll be cycling through some very gentle terrain, typically of beaches backed by pine forests, until you reach the handsome town of Royan, where a ferry crosses the Gironde estuary. Now you're in the Médoc – wine country. Just down the Garonne River, which forms the Gironde estuary, lies the city of Bordeaux, surrounded by some of the world's most renowned names in wine. It's not actually the climate that gives Bordeaux's wines their quality but the gravel in the soil, washed down from the Pyrenees over the ages. The Vélodyssée doesn't venture into Bordeaux, but there is cycle path there from Lacanau.

Continuing south, the section from Lacanau-Océan takes in giant sand dunes around Arcachon Bay, then follows a rail trail south into Aquitaine's Landes region. The cycling becomes even easier, with a bike path scything through the pine trees but rarely heading uphill. The ocean is ever-present on your right, with sideroads down to beaches and such small towns as Mimizan-Plage. Unless you're an aspiring surfer, this final quarter can be a slightly repetitive stretch, but can be ridden very quickly thanks to the Vélodyssée's regular green signposts.

Interest returns at Capbreton and the surf beach of Hossegor. A further 20 miles (32km) south lies the city of Bayonne, capital of the Basque Country, a transport hub and a base for exploring Basque culture. This is another region that attaches great importance to its own language (Euskera), its folklore, food, sport and history. The next few stops come in quick succession: the faded glamour of Biarritz (left), with its grand hotels and spas; the stylish resort town of Saint-Jean-de-Luz, a former fishing port; and the Vélodyssée's end at Hendaye.

La Vélodyssée

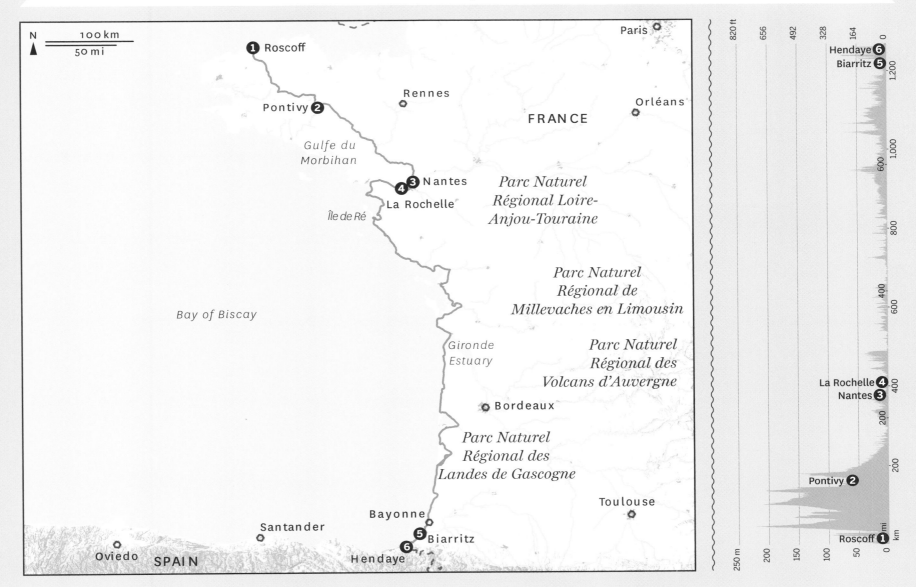

N
100 km
50 mi

1 Roscoff

Paris

Rennes

Pontivy 2

Orléans

FRANCE

Gulfe du
Morbihan

Parc Naturel
Régional Loire-
Anjou-Touraine

3 Nantes
4
La Rochelle

Île de Ré

Parc Naturel
Régional de
Millevaches en Limousin

Bay of Biscay

Gironde
Estuary

Parc Naturel
Régional des
Volcans d'Auvergne

Bordeaux

Parc Naturel
Régional des
Landes de Gascogne

Toulouse

Santander

Bayonne

5 Biarritz

Oviedo   SPAIN

6

Hendaye

820 ft   656   492   328   164   0

Hendaye 6
Biarritz 5

1,200

1,000

800

600

400

La Rochelle 4
Nantes 3

200

Pontivy 2

Roscoff 1

250 m   200   150   100   50   0
km

➡ Distance: 134 miles (215km)   ➡ Ascent: 6000ft (1830m)   ➡ Difficulty: 1

John Muir Way

Scotland

Ride Scotland's John Muir Way coast to coast, from Glasgow to Edinburgh, taking in history, industrial heritage and some natural beauty on an accessible bikepacking trip that's ideal for novices.

Plan and Prepare

Logistics

Trains to the start of the John Muir Way in Helensburgh take about 1hr from Glasgow's Queen Street station; from the end of the route in Dunbar, it's a 30min train trip into Edinburgh Waverley station. ScotRail permits bicycles on its trains, but try to avoid rush-hour travel. There's a frequent fast service between Edinburgh and Glasgow, and both cities are well connected to the rest of the country.

Hazards

Scottish dangers tend to be seasonal. Wet and windy weather may strike at any time between September and May; during the warmer months (May to September), beware the midge. This minuscule biting insect is especially voracious at dawn and dusk, so cover up and wear repellent. You'll also be sharing the road with drivers, who are probably a greater danger.

Gear

You can ride the route on almost any bicycle, so long as it can carry some luggage in panniers or frame-bags. A modern touring bike will probably be the quicker option, but gravel or mountain bikes are perfectly acceptable; due to the modest amount of ascent, you could even ride it on a folding bike. As the route passes through Scotland's central belt, there are plenty of places to stay and eat, so you don't have to carry a tent or cooking kit.

Info

Timing depends on whether you're keen to avoid bad weather. Summer has the greatest chance of dry days (and the longest hours of daylight), but early autumn is also a fine time to ride. Much of the route is waymarked, but you can find additional map downloads at johnmuirway.org

Scotland's right-to-roam laws mean that the routes across the northern nation available to bikepackers are limited only by riders' tolerance for mountains, midges and the occasional bog. The terrain is typically rocky and the hills unrelenting. But the John Muir Way is different. This route, if you're taking advantage of the likely tailwind, traces a coast-to-coast path west to east across the central belt of Scotland from Helensburgh, northwest of Glasgow, to Dunbar, east of Edinburgh. When compared to other routes in Scotland, it travels through some relatively populated parts (on quiet lanes and gravel paths) and also remains fairly flat, with only around 6000ft (1830m) of ascent over the whole distance. That makes it an easygoing introduction to cycle touring that could take anything from two to four days, depending on your definition of leisurely.

The route passes by remnants of the Roman Empire's northern frontier as well as monuments to Scotland's 19th-century industrial heritage. But it takes its name from the Scottish conservationist and writer John Muir, who was born in 1838 in Dunbar but is best known for his achievements in the US, where he was instrumental in the formation of America's national parks.

Leaving the Clyde

From Helensburgh, the John Muir Way follows lanes to the southern tip of Loch Lomond (right) and then past Balloch Castle (actually a 19th-century construction by a banker) before one of the biggest climbs of the ride, up towards Strathblane. This is also the most remote stretch of the route, with the Campsie Fells to your left. After the descent, you'll pick up the Forth & Clyde Canal towpath, which offers easy pedalling and some moments of natural beauty as you watch wild birds go about their day on and around the water.

John Muir

Is John Muir the only Scot to have two eponymous long-distance trails on different continents? The Scottish writer, naturalist and activist was born in 1838 in Dunbar, now the end of Scotland's John Muir Way. In 1849, his family emigrated to the US and settled in Wisconsin; in 1868, aged 30, he landed in San Francisco and made California his home. He co-founded the Sierra Club and campaigned for Yosemite to be protected as a national park. Later, when showing then-president Theodore Roosevelt around, he lobbied for more protection of wilderness areas. Today, California's long-distance John Muir Trail passes through the Yosemite, Sequioa and Kings Canyon national parks.

Running between the Firth of Clyde and the Firth of Forth in Edinburgh (a firth is an inlet), the canal opened in 1790 and was vital for trade, allowing quicker cross-Scotland passage than the route around the coast. After about 40 miles (64km), the towpath takes you past Bar Hill, a Roman fort which was the high point of the Antonine Wall. This barrier of turf extends eastward for about 37 miles (60km) from Old Kilpatrick on the River Clyde near Glasgow to Carriden near Bo'ness, and was the northwestern frontier of the Roman Empire. As far as the Romans were concerned, anywhere north of the wall was fraught with danger. Along the length of the Antonine Wall, as it hugged the high ground, Bar Hill was one of 16 forts constructed by the Romans.

To the Forth

Scotland's engineering prowess is on unforgettable display at Falkirk. This is where the Forth & Clyde Canal meets the Union Canal, and an idea was needed to replace the series of 11 locks required to link the two. The elegant solution was the gigantic Falkirk Wheel (left) rotating boat lift, which opened in 2002. Learn a bit more about Falkirk's history at the 14th-century, chateau-style Callendar House, a few minutes' further along the route; and from the Wheel, take a 20-minute detour to see the beautiful *Kelpies* sculptures, inspired by the horses that powered Scotland's canals. Back on track, you'll pass the lofty Avon Aqueduct before meeting the Forth River, which will lead you to brutal Blackness Castle, a 15th-century fortress and prison, and then the Forth Rail Bridge, an Unesco World Heritage Site, as you approach Edinburgh. The sights come thick and fast now. You'll pedal through Holyrood Park in central Edinburgh and return to the invigorating sea air at Musselburgh. The John Muir Way now hugs the coast all the way to the ruins of Dunbar Castle, overlooking the harbour and town of Muir's birth.

John Muir Way

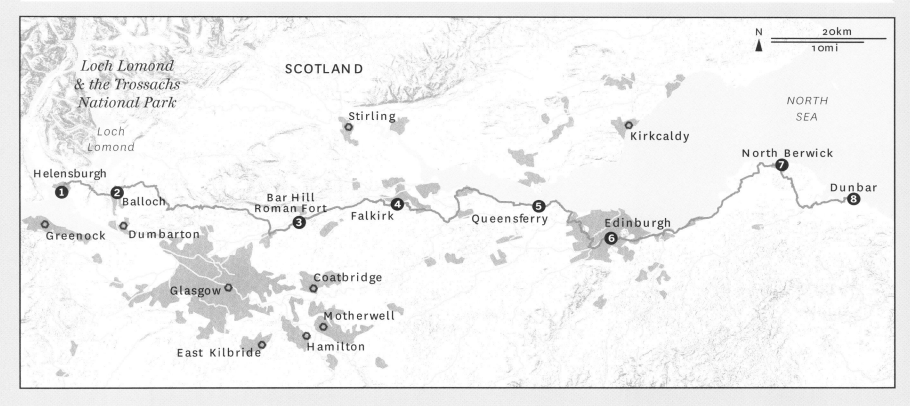

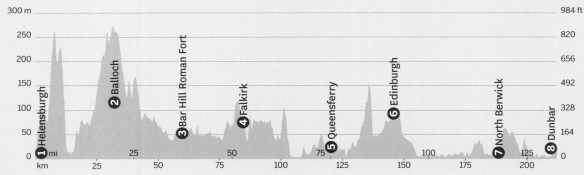

➡ Distance: 267 miles (430km)   ➡ Ascent: 33,690ft (10,269m)   ➡ Difficulty: 4

Vuelta de Vasco

Spain

Dive into the Basque Country on this demanding multi-day loop around a diverse corner of Spain. Discover world-class food and drink in San Sebastián, a famed art gallery in Bilbao, peaceful wildernesses and a unique local language and culture.

Plan and Prepare

Logistics

This loop starts from Bilbao, the largest city in the Basque Country, which has a fast train connection (just over 5hr) from Madrid. However, your bike will need to be packed (in a bag or box) within specific dimensions, and you'll need to book a space for it when buying your ticket. Since this route is a loop, you could also start from San Sebastián or any other spot on the circuit.

Hazards

The numbers tell the story: there are a lot of steep ascents on this route, so fitness and experience are factors to consider. The Basque Country also receives a lot of inclement weather, especially up high in the mountains, so watch out for storms of thunder, hail, rain, snow or all of the above. Some of the sections are far from help so take care on the rougher trails.

Gear

Most people will be happiest on a mountain bike with (at least) front suspension. The route isn't generally rough but lower gearing will help on the climbs. While you can stay under a roof on most of the route, there are sections through national parks where you may need to camp, so carrying a tent or shelter is the best course of action; water purification kit is also useful.

Info

August and September tend to see the lowest rainfall; autumn is also a beautiful time to ride in the Basque Country. Wild camping is typically not permitted in Spain's natural parks, so plan around that restriction. There are a few mountain lodges and, where the Vuelta de Vasco connects with the Camino del Norte, some *albergues* (pilgrim hostels). There's detailed info at bikepacking.com or from route designer Lars Henning at tourintune.com

Northwest Spain seems like a world apart from the rest of the Iberian peninsula: green rather than arid, with a unique local culture and language that is reflected in everything from local customs and history to food and drink. El País Vasco – the Basque Country – is an enthralling place to explore by bicycle, but it's certainly not an easy place. Note the stats of this circuit, through two of the region's key cities and three of its natural parks: divide the distance by the ascent and you'll see that this is an unforgivably hilly ride, with some of the climbs steep enough to require you to push your laden bike. But despite that, the Vuelta de Vasco offers a rewarding insight into a place that is rich in natural beauty and fascinating culture. The route was created by Lars Henning, who recommends riding the loop in a clockwise direction. From Bilbao, it follows the coast to the culinary hotspot of San Sebastián, turns inland to the Parque Natural Aralar, passes through the regional capital of Vitoria-Gasteiz, and heads back to Bilbao via the vast Parque Natural de Gorbeia.

Goodbye Bilbao

Leaving Bilbao, the riding is relatively level as you head towards the Atlantic coast along quiet lanes and greenways, including sections of the Camino del Norte pilgrimage route that heads north toward Santiago de Compostela. You'll reach the fishing village of Lekeitio after about 33 miles (53km), where you can paddle in the surf on the sandy Karraspio beach. Along the whole route there will usually be a range of accommodation options: you can opt for credit-card touring and stay in hotels, hostels or B&Bs. Or carry a tent and camp, bearing in mind that in Spain, wild camping is generally illegal without prior permission from landowners.

© Cass Gilbert

San Sebastián

The first Spanish restaurants to receive three Michelin stars were in the Basque Country. But Basque cooking was originally family food, and it took a long time to become fashionable. Today, Basque food retains its strong community links, and experimental cooking clubs, known as *txokos*, are a widespread (albeit male-only) tradition. San Sebastián is where chefs from the around the world come to enjoy creative cooking: 'You could make the argument that there's no better place to eat in Europe', said Anthony Bourdain. The historic quarter's grid of lanes are packed with crowded bars, each serving *pintxos* (local tapas) with a glass of sparkling wine or a beer.

Following the coast for another 45 miles (72km) leads you into the city of San Sebastián (left), but by avoiding the busy highways the route does get a bit steep and rugged in places. San Sebastián itself is a joy to explore, so spend some time here before hopping back on the bike. Turning deeper inland and into the Navarra region, the route jumps on the Vía Verde del Plazaola, a greenway that follows the old railway from San Sebastián to Pamplona, using tunnels blasted through mountains (bring bike lights). The trail meanders through vivid green countryside, its steep slopes dotted with sheep and occasional whitewashed houses. All that rainwater has to go somewhere, and there are abundant springs at which you can refill water bottles.

Into the wilds

After a steady climb up to the town of Lekunberri, stock up on Basque snacks (energy-rich local cheeses, chorizo, pastries and figs) before the first of three natural park crossings. The Sierra de Aralar takes you to the second-highest point of the trip and the highland landscape opens up: broad vistas, sweeping gravel trails and some roaming ponies. It's about 30 miles (48km) between towns here so you might not need to camp out.

From Lizarraga-Ergoiena, you'll segue straight into the next natural park in the Sierra de Urbasa, with more up-and-downs on rough gravel tracks. Picking up the Vía Verde de Vasco-Navarro (a repurposed train line) takes you into the Basque capital, Vitoria-Gasteiz – another interesting city to explore, both architecturally and culturally. Its medieval heart dates from the 12th century, with Gothic flourishes everywhere, but it's surrounded by artfully designed 19th-century suburbs. Stay a day or two. The final stage covers the toughest climb of the route, up into the Parque Natural de Gorbeia, before dropping down to the endpoint in Bilbao.

© Mark Read / Lonely Planet; Cass Gilbert

Vuelta de Vasco

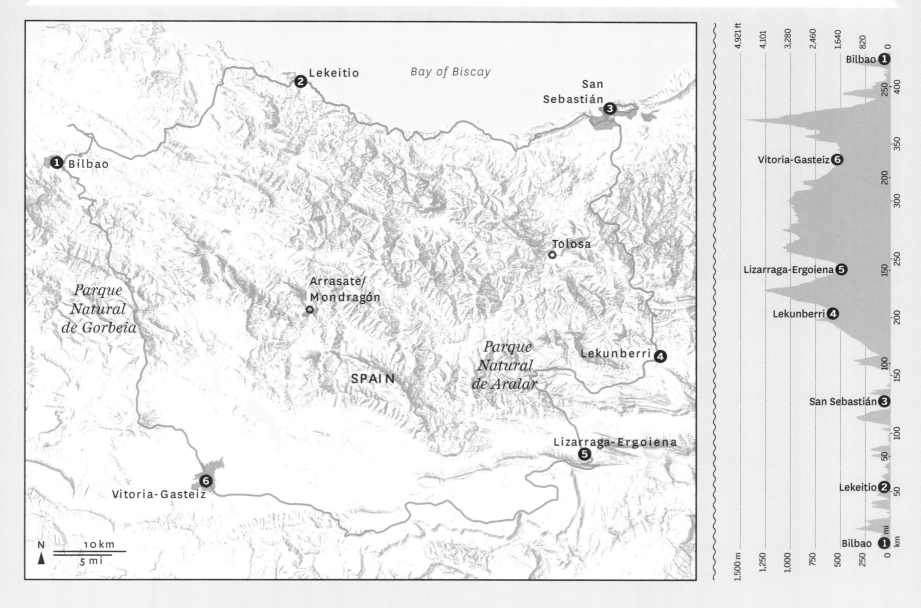

Bay of Biscay

Lekeitio ②

San Sebastián ③

① Bilbao

Tolosa

Arrasate/
Mondragón

*Parque
Natural
de Gorbeia*

*Parque
Natural
de Aralar*

SPAIN

Lekunberri ④

Lizarraga-Ergoiena ⑤

Vitoria-Gasteiz ⑥

N
10 km
5 mi

4,921 ft
4,101
3,280
2,460
1,640
820
0

Bilbao ①
Vitoria-Gasteiz ⑥
Lizarraga-Ergoiena ⑤
Lekunberri ④
San Sebastián ③
Lekeitio ②
Bilbao ①

400
350
300
250
200
150
100
50
0 mi

1,500 m
1,250
1,000
750
500
250
0

250
200
150
100
50
0 km

More to ride

Six more superb routes in Europe

Iron Curtain Trail
Germany

Distance: various
Difficulty: 2

EuroVelo's EV13 route, the Iron Curtain Trail, follows that great geopolitical fissure from the Barents Sea to the Black Sea, through Norway, the Baltic nations, Poland, Germany, the Czech Republic, the Balkans, Romania, Bulgaria and beyond to Turkey. It's not yet complete but will cover more than 6214 miles (10,000km) when finished. However, the German section is mostly signposted and ready to ride. The history of the Iron Curtain means that there are some fascinating sites to visit along these quiet roads and bike paths. But if you want to get further off the beaten track, consider the Iron Curtain Gravel Trail, a 426-mile-long (685km) trail crafted by Markus Stitz that runs from the Harz mountains to the Czech border (maps available via komoot.com).

Trans Dinarica Trail
Slovenia, Croatia, Bosnia & Hercegovina

Distance: 758 miles (1220km)
Difficulty: 3

The multi-use Trans Dinarica Trail (above) was designed by local enterprises to encourage visitors to explore the Western Balkans by bicycle, and currently covers Slovenia, Croatia and Bosnia & Hercegovina. It's a sister trail to the Via Dinarica hiking route, which extends into Albania, Kosovo and North Macedonia. The Trans Dinarica starts in Slovenia's Soča Valley, famous for its watersports, then rolls through the foothills of the Julian Alps beside the Italian border before dipping into Croatia for a foray into the forests of Risnjak National Park. Next it shadows the Adriatic before a transfer takes riders across the border and into Bosnia & Hercegovina, where it visits Mostar and Sarajevo.

Ronde van Nederland
Netherlands

Distance 860 miles (1384km)
Difficulty: 1

Holland's long-distance cycling routes, known as LF routes, are an easy way of exploring this cycle-friendly nation. Most use traffic-free bike paths that are wide and well made. Some of the classic trips include the LF Kustroute along the North Sea and Wadden Sea coastlines; the popular LF Zuiderzeeroute around an inland sea and through national parks and historic towns; and the LF Vechtdalroute linking quiet Dutch villages. But put some of the LF routes together and you get this fantastic 860-mile (1384km) circuit of the Netherlands. Dunes, dykes, canals, sculptures, megaliths, polders, towns and villages feature. Completing the Ronde van Nederland earns riders a special certificate.

Tour du Mont Blanc
France, Switzerland & Italy

Distance 105 miles (169km)
Difficulty: 3

File this trip under 'do now, while you can'. Climate change is causing the glaciers of the High Alps to melt, which means that the stability of these mountains is changing and, increasingly, that trails such as this loop around western Europe's highest peak are diverted or closed due to rockfalls and other dangers. But while it's possible, the Tour du Mont Blanc is a fantastic challenge for mountain bikers, who need only carry enough kit for three or four nights spent in refuges. Most start at Chamonix and will enter three separate countries on their ride. They'll also cross rivers, climb several passes above 6500ft (1981m) and eat their own weight in pastries.

Torino–Nice Rally
Italy & France

Distance: 435 miles (700km)
Difficulty: 3

Beginning life as an annual bikepacking rally – a non-competitive group ride – designed by James Olsen, this gorgeous route explores some of the lesser-known alpine regions between Turin in Italy and Nice in France, and can be ridden at any time between late June and early September when the higher parts are free from snow. Riders take a mixture of rough gravel tracks and trails, with some road diversions available if needed. Bikes are usually hardtail mountain bikes, but gravel bikes with chunky tyres will also be fine. And accommodation can be in some of the mountain *refugios* (below) on the route or under canvas, depending on preference. There's a lot of ascent, obviously, so most need eight or more days if stopping to savour the views and the local food.

Great North Trail
UK

Distance: 825 miles (1328km)
Difficulty: 3

Snaking north from England's Peak District National Park to the tip of Scotland, the Great North Trail touches on some of the UK's greatest cities and its wildest open spaces. This is a mountain-bike route for experienced cyclists if attempted as a single trip, but it's easy to break it up into sections. The first leg borrows the Pennine Bridleway, which hugs the ridge of hills between Manchester and Leeds before entering the patchwork of stone walls and green fields in Yorkshire Dales National Park. The route then crosses the open moors of Northumberland National Park, and heads into the Scottish Borders at the mountain-biking hub of Peebles before visiting Edinburgh and Glasgow and taking on the real mountains of Scotland on its way to John O'Groats.

Contents

Americas

Ruta Maya de los Cuchumatanes (Guatemala)	228
The Baja Divide (Mexico)	232
The BC Trail (Canada)	236
Camino dél Puma (Peru & Bolivia)	240
Colorado Trail (USA)	244
Green Mountain Gravel Growler (USA)	248
Oregon Timber Trail (USA)	252
Ruta Chingaza (Colombia)	256
The Tahoe Twirl (USA)	260
Tree to Sea Loop (Canada)	264
The Great Allegheny Passage (USA)	270
Katy Trail (USA)	274
Kenai 250 (USA)	278
Cowichan Valley 8 (Canada)	282
Finger Lakes Overnighter (USA)	286
Trans Ecuador Mountain Bike Route (Ecuador)	290
More to ride	294

→ Distance: 329 miles (529km)   → Ascent: 53,684ft (16,363m)   → Difficulty: 4

Ruta Maya de los Cuchumatanes

Guatemala

The Sierra de los Cuchumatanes are the highest non-volcanic mountain range in Central America so you'll feel like you're on the roof of Guatemala, cycling quiet backroads among pines, cloud forest and karst outcrops. There's a rich indigenous culture to get to know too.

Plan and Prepare

Logistics

The route begins in Quetzaltenango and finishes in the market town of Chichicastenango, but can be ridden in either direction. If you're flying into Guatemala City, a tourist shuttle van is recommended for transport to/from the start or end points. Cheaper regular 'chicken buses' (converted ex-USA school buses) service most of the towns on this route. Carry sufficient cash for the tour, as ATMs are unreliable outside cities.

Hazards

Guatemala is a tropical country, but as this route lies in the cooler highlands, and the highest sections reach 10,000ft (3048m), you'll experience both high humidity and chillier (occasionally close to freezing) nights on the plateau. Thunderstorms can be expected in any season. Dogs will often chase cyclists, but seldom become genuinely aggressive; they will usually calm down if you stop moving.

Gear

A rigid or hardtail mountain bike, equipped with bikepacking luggage and generous climbing gears, is the most suitable. You'll encounter steep and sometimes rough dirt roads, but also long stretches of smooth pavement, so a fast-rolling knobbly tyre in the range of 2.2in to 2.4in is ideal. There are no high-end bike shops on the route, so bring spare brake pads, tubes/sealant and basic tools for repairs.

Info

Little English is spoken, so you will need a basic grasp of Spanish to get by. There are numerous guest houses (*hospedajes/ posadas*) on the route, and these are preferable to camping due to hassles with pitching on private property as well as privacy and security. If you do camp you should try to seek permission, but expect to have curious locals checking out your tent. GPX and more info: bikepacking.com/routes/ruta-maya-de-los-cuchumatanes

Guatemala is an enchanting and challenging country for bikepackers: the hills can be steep and the roads are sometimes full of potholes, but with the rigours of riding comes the chance to encounter a vibrant indigenous culture, along with a Central American landscape that is as diverse as it is mountainous. There's often a volcano on the horizon, or a shimmering lake nearby – and when there's not, you'll either be deep in pine forest enjoying quiet dirt roads, or distracted by yet another market full of colourful textiles, thronged with local people resplendent in traditional dress.

To Todos Santos Cuchumatan

The route kicks off in Guatemala's pleasant 'second capital' Quetzaltenango (Xela), soon reaching the village of San Andrés Xecul, which features a remarkable, intricately painted yellow church. A relatively gentle paved road then climbs deeper into the highlands to the small town of Momostenango, a good place to stop for the night. Beyond here the surface turns to smooth dirt and follows beautiful conifer forest on a rolling ride most of the way through to the lively, blue-collar mestizo city of Huehuetenango. From here you head up on to the unique Cuchumatanes plateau via the legendary 4000ft (1219m) Manzanas climb on a steep dirt road. The plateau is dotted with karst outcrops and distinctive spiny maguey (agave) plants. The route then drops to the colourful municipality of Todos Santos Cuchumatán, which is an essential stop and an opportunity to witness some of the best of Guatemalan high-country culture. The traditions of the Mam people are very visible here, with the menfolk in their striped outfits and women often working hard at looms creating richly coloured textiles.

Maya heritage

The Maya people, for whom the highlands are home, have their roots in the Maya civilisation which flourished in Central America between 2000 BCE and the arrival of the Spanish in the late 1400s, and stretched from southeastern Mexico, through modern-day Guatemala and Belize and into western Honduras and El Salvador – most of the cultural region of Mesoamerica, where pre-Columbian societies flourished. The temples of the former Maya city-states of Mexico's Chichén Itzá and Palenque (below) and Guatemala's Tikal are among the most recognisable symbols of this ancient culture, along with the *traje* (traditional outfits) worn by indigenous Maya peoples today.

Beyond Todos Santos, the route tackles a tough section of more remote mountain riding through to San Miguel Acatan and the Pett Junction. While vehicles will be few, there are occasional towns, villages and *tiendas* for meals, supplies and bottled water. Climbing out of the Rio San Miguel presents the biggest challenge of the ride, but commitment is well rewarded with a glimpse of this spectacular steeply-walled valley and its isolated inhabitants.

San Mateo Ixtatán to Nebaj

The out-and-back pavement ride to the mountain town of San Mateo Ixtatán is well worthwhile for an opportunity to stay in a traditional Chuj Maya township, where you'll see many women in traditional *huipil* (colourful tunics). The return to Pett Junction can easily be made by minivan or chicken bus. From Pett, the legs get a gentler – but still hilly – ride, through small towns and eventually back up to the heights of the Cuchumatanes plateau before dropping down a huge dirt-road descent to Aguacatán.

Sacapulas is the next stop, nestled deeply in an arid valley, and from here the road climbs again on pavement over the forested sierra to Nebaj, one of three Ixil Triangle Maya towns which long held out against the Spanish conquest. Traditions and traditional dress are strong here. The valley is a great place to spend a day or two exploring a couple of further-flung Maya villages, Chajul and Acul, taking in local culture and trying speciality foods. The return climb can be made by chicken bus.

Chichicastenango

From Sacapulas the ride finishes with an easier day of mixed pavement and dirt through to Chichicastenango; arrive on a Thursday or Sunday to see the famously colourful and lively market, when Maya groups pour into town for the day.

Ruta Maya de los Cuchumatanes

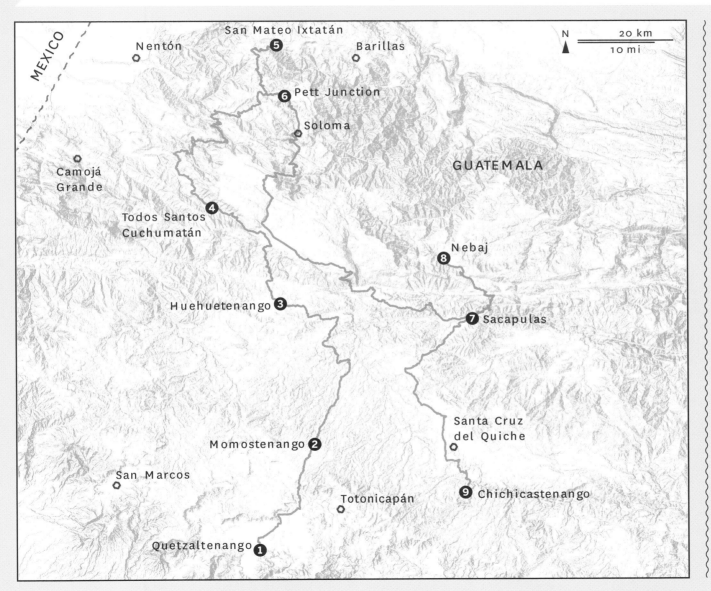

MEXICO

Nentón

San Mateo Ixtatán **5**

Barillas

6 Pett Junction

Soloma

GUATEMALA

Camojá Grande

Todos Santos **4**
Cuchumatán

Nebaj
8

Huehuetenango **3**

7 Sacapulas

Momostenango **2**

Santa Cruz
del Quiche

San Marcos

Totonicapán

9 Chichicastenango

Quetzaltenango **1**

N ▲   20 km
       10 mi

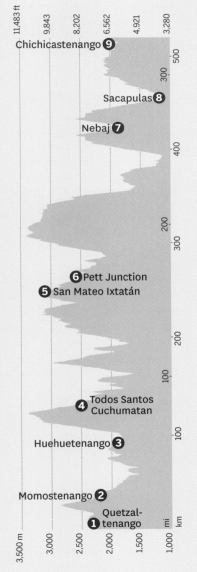

11,483 ft   9,843   8,202   6,562   4,921   3,280

Chichicastenango **9**

Sacapulas **8**

Nebaj **7**

6 Pett Junction
5 San Mateo Ixtatán

4 Todos Santos
Cuchumatan

Huehuetenango **3**

Momostenango **2**

Quetzal-
tenango **1**

3,500 m   3,000   2,500   2,000   1,500   1,000   km   mi

500
300
400
200
300
200
100
100

→ Distance: 1671 miles (2690km)　　→ Ascent: 91,636ft (27,930m)　　→ Difficulty: 5

The Baja Divide

Mexico

Sun-scorched sand, cactus-pricked hills and fishing and surfing settlements are all part of this challenging adventure down the Baja California peninsula. The ride culminates at Los Cabos, where the unique marine environment offers the possibility of some whale-watching.

Plan and Prepare

Logistics

Most people ride north to south, catching a flight home from La Paz, San José del Cabo or Loreto, all of which have international flights to the US and Canada, often with a connection at Los Angeles' LAX. Alternatively, there's also a northbound bus. At the start, you can either ride straight from San Diego (such as from the airport) or start from Tecate on the Mexico–California border, about an hour's drive from San Diego.

Hazards

There are certainly potential hazards to be aware of on Baja California. The hot climate and lack of water is something to consider – you will need to carry many litres of water on some sections of the route. You're also a long way from help or a hospital at certain points. Be aware, too, of your personal safety after dark, much as you would elsewhere in North America. Some animals, such as rattlesnakes, are low-level risks.

Gear

It's possible to complete the ride on almost any bike, but those that have the easiest experience are typically on mountain bikes, with large-volume tubeless tyres (3in) to cope better with the sand and the thorns. You'll need to carry a lot of water so plan to wear a hydration pack and have plenty of bottles to fill. For navigation, a GPS unit is essential. Wear sun protection at all times.

Info

Winter is the best time to ride the Baja Divide; the nights might be chilly, but the days will also have a welcome coolness too – aim for November to March. You'll likely need to wild camp (although there are occasional motels), but this is usually without problem. Most riders average 30-50 miles (48-80km) per day, although the fastest-known time is just over 10 days. Check bikepacking. com for the latest info.

Baja California, the slim peninsula of Mexico south of San Diego and sandwiched between the Sea of Cortez and the Pacific Ocean, has long been the sort of place where hedonism meets adventure. Its coast has drawn surfers since the 1940s; by the 1960s and 1970s Hollywood celebrities were partying at the southern tip of Baja in Los Cabos – Keith Richards married Patti Hansen here in 1983. And for the adventure, Baja's untamed terrain is the venue for perhaps the world's most dangerous motor race: the Baja 1000.

But there's another side to the peninsula, one that takes in deserted dirt roads, remote ranches and dewy sunrises over Pacific coves. This is the Baja Divide, an undeniably challenging route running the length of the peninsula. It was created by record-breaking endurance cyclist Lael Wilcox and Nicholas Carman (aka Gypsy by Trade). Due to the rough backcountry conditions, it's one for experienced bikepackers, who know how to plug the fifth cactus-caused hole in a tubeless tyre that day. But despite demoralising stretches of energy-sapping sand and loose, rocky climbs, it's a ride that teaches you a bit about yourself and also offers moments of beauty.

Biking Baja

The 60 miles (100km) from San Diego to the border at Tecate is a preview of what's to come: rough, rocky climbs and scrubby desert. Tecate is usually a safer and less stressful border crossing than Tijuana to the west, but do check up-to-date advice as situations can change quickly in Mexico. Generally, it's worth acknowledging that there is violent crime in Baja (such as carjackings and muggings), as there is throughout North America, but the Baja Divide route takes you into more out-of-the-way locales and, with a bit of common sense, the vast majority of riders don't report any problems.

Sea of Cortez species

The narrow and calm stretch of sea between mainland Mexico and the Baja peninsula is a Unesco World Heritage Site thanks to its amazing marine ecosystem. At the top of the food chain are blue whales, which feed on krill at the opposite end of the chain. The whales arrive in Loreto Bay in February and March to give birth to their calves. Also near the top of the food chain is the Humboldt squid, a voracious 6ft (2m) deep-sea predator; you're unlikley to catch sight of a giant squid, but on a sea-kayak tour around Espíritu Santo, one of 244 Sea of Cortez islands, you'll be able to view a sea lion colony and an abundance of bird life. La Paz is the best base for exploring the marine park.

Crossing into Mexico, your first taste of Baja will be a big off-road climb up to 4700ft (1432m) but, thankfully, it's not representative of the route as a whole. Dirt roads pass through tiny communities of a handful of inhabitants, where you can pick up snacks. To avoid buying plastic bottles of water, top up for a few pesos at the water filtration taps that you'll find in many grocery stores.

After about 200 miles (322km), you'll reach the Pacific coast for the first time and have the opportunity to dip your toes in the cold ocean. Fishing villages and surfing communities punctuate the coastline. The days take on a kind of rhythm now: early starts, with a siesta under shelter during the heat of the middle of the day. The landscape is extremely arid so the only vegetation that thrives here are cacti, and their thorns are a frequent annoyance for bikepackers in Baja. Carry a lot of spare sealant and rubber plugs for tubeless tyres.

The route crosses the peninsula to the Sea of Cortez side at beautiful Bahía de los Ángeles and then meanders back to the Pacific at Laguna San Ignacio. This is one of Baja's prime whale-watching spots, where grey whales reside from January to April each year. If you take a whale-watching boat tour, make sure to select a responsible operator, who will wait for whales to approach the boat of their own free will.

Laguna San Ignacio is about halfway along the route, and you now enter southern Baja, which is more developed. The section from San Ignacio to La Paz, taking about two weeks, is regarded as a highlight of the Baja Divide, passing through several former Spanish missions. And from La Paz there's a convenient 200-mile (322km) loop around Parque Nacional Cabo Pulmo and the artsy town of Todos Santos to finish.

The Baja Divide

N 200 km
   100 mi

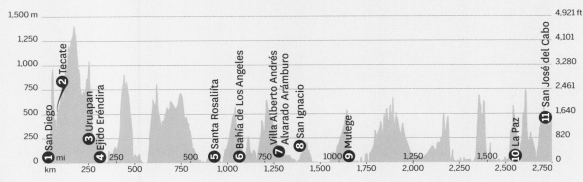

➡ Distance: 743 miles (1195km)   ➡ Ascent: 46,663ft (14,223m)   ➡ Difficulty: 3

The BC Trail

Canada

Traverse the interior of British Columbia, winding your way to the Rockies on this epic succession of interlinked rail trails across trestle bridges and wild rivers. Beguiling towns along the way offer beers and mountain-bike trails.

Plan and Prepare

Logistics

Getting to and from either end of the BC Trail is not easy. The full trail runs between Cultus Lake Provincial Park, about 75 miles (120km) east of downtown Vancouver, and Fernie, which is about 115 miles (185km) south of Calgary and without much public transport. Getting a lift to Cultus Lake is helpful. From Fernie, one option for those without their own vehicle is to cycle the Great Divide Trail to Banff, from where you can catch a bus to Calgary.

Hazards

There's quite a long list of hazards for any long-distance ride through backcountry Canada. Large animals, whether elk, bear or cougar, can be dangerous; inform yourself of best-practice responses to all three. Smaller creatures – mosquitoes and biting flies – may also be an annoyance. Extremes of climate are also a hazard. Check forecasts for heatwaves, rain or snow. Riders will also be far from assistance on some stretches of trail.

Gear

Although some of the route is along rail trails, don't underestimate how rough the surface will be for much of the way. A mountain bike with the largest-volume tyres you can fit will add some comfort. A gravel bike is not advised by many riders who have completed the BC Trail, but might suffice for short sections. You'll also need to carry water, and camping and cooking kit; bear spray is recommended, too.

Info

The prime time to ride is from late June to September; outside of those months there's a risk of snow and rain. During the summer, be sure to carry water as the heat can be intense. Numerous campgrounds offer basic facilities and there are also regular towns and motels. Check bikepacking.com for reams of useful BC Trail info; for details of the province's mountain-biking destinations, check mountainbikingbc.ca

You can trace the economic development of Canada through its railways. The country's first railroad, between La Prairie on the St Lawrence River and Saint-Jean-sur-Richelieu just east of Montréal, was opened in 1836. Bit by bit, sleeper by sleeper, railroads headed west, wherever there was trade to be done. By November 1885, the final rail of the Canadian Pacific Railway was laid at Craigellachie in British Columbia (still a long way from the west coast), and rail extensions in the early 20th century saw southwest British Columbia served by trains for the first time. Given Canada's uncompromising landscape, constructing these railroads was an enormous engineering feat: on the Kettle Valley Railway, for example, the Trout Creek Trestle Bridge was built to span 619ft (188m) across and 238ft (72.5m) above Trout Creek canyon floor. It's still a spectacular, if not slightly scary, construction.

The point of this history lesson is that the BC Trail pieces together several of these former railroads, and their vertiginous trestle bridges, with sections of gravel forestry roads, a bit of highway and some other connecting trails in its journey across southern British Columbia. That's not to say that this route is routine in any way: the distance and terrain are daunting and the actual conditions of the rail trails are often rough and corrugated, making for sometimes slow and uncomfortable progress. Even though 90 percent of Canadians live with 150 miles (240km) of the route, the BC Trail takes riders into wilderness where cell phone coverage is minimal, so preparation is important for this ride. But it also passes by some classic BC mountain-biking destinations including Nelson in the Kootenays and Penticton in the Okanagan Valley. And where there are mountain-bikers, there are usually great breweries, fun trails and friendly faces in the community to show visitors around.

Mountain-biking BC

British Columbia is one of the world's most renowned mountain-biking destinations. The scene was pioneered in the province's west during the 1990s and early 2000s: places like Vancouver's North Shore Mountains, Squamish and the Whistler ski resort attracted the world's best riders and set a high bar. Today, few self-respecting BC towns are without their own trail networks. Along the BC Trail, the best biking towns include Fernie, Cranbrook, Nelson and Penticton, where volunteers craft flowing trails through the forest and often-arid interior landscape. Local bike shops are usually good sources of advice; Canadian trails are graded from green for beginners to double-black-diamond for local riders with god-like skill levels.

West to east

The BC Trail is rideable in either direction. If you start from the Cultus Lake Provincial Park, out west, the first challenge is the rough-and-ready trail from Chilliwack Lake to Hope, which is often overgrown. Some riders start from the town of Hope as a result. Once you're past the Coquihalla Summit (4081ft/1244m), you'll join rail trails for much of the 125 miles (200km) to Penticton. This is the former Kettle Valley Railway, and although the surface varies in its state of repair, it is at least straightforward to navigate. There are towns along the way in which to rest and restock: Princeton is a good bet, at the junction of Similkameen and Tulameen rivers.

Penticton, at the foot of Okanagan Lake, is another good spot to pause, not only thanks to its great mountain-biking trails but also because you're entering the Okanagan Valley's wine-growing region, with many wineries offering tastings. Prefer hops to grapes? This small city has eight craft breweries (the most per capita in BC). Off the bike, there's also paddling and climbing to try here.

Continuing north towards Kelowna city (which has a bus link with Vancouver), the Kettle Valley Rail Trail veers into Myra Canyon, where timber trestle bridges span airy drops (previous page). It's a popular spot for sightseers so expect extra traffic. With more than half the route still to travel, continue onto the Columbia and Western Rail Trail from Midway to Castlegar, up towards the Arrow Lakes and Selkirk Mountains. This area is much wilder and helicopters are widely used as transport by skiers and bikers. It's about 75 miles (120km) from Castlegar to Nelson (lower left), which is the adventure hub of the Kootenays and tempts riders to linger. As you approach the endpoint at Fernie, you'll need to decide whether to ride north to Banff for better onward transport.

The BC Trail

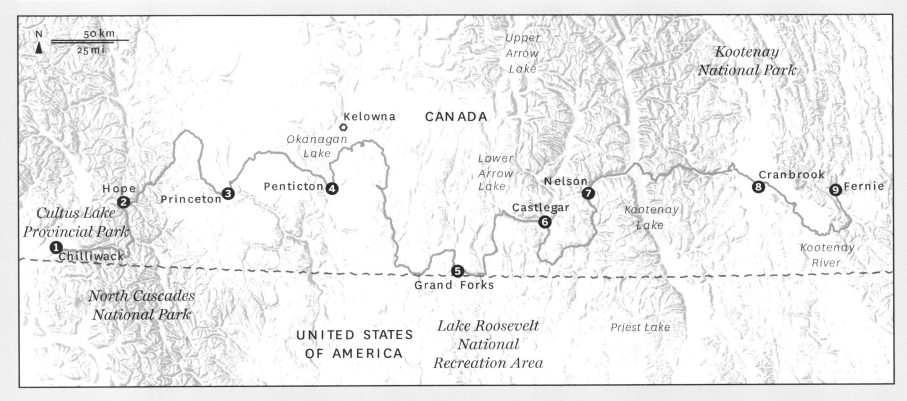

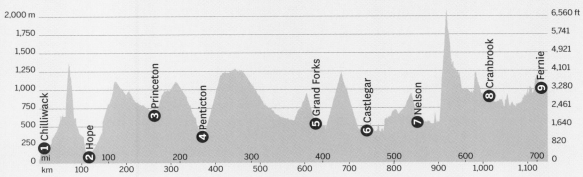

→ Distance: 780 miles (1255km)   → Ascent: 57,569ft (17,547m)   → Difficulty: 4

Camino dél Puma

Peru & Bolivia

This remarkable tour explores the altiplano (or puna), taking in Andean volcanoes, ancient ruins and South America's biggest lake, as well as one of the continent's deepest canyons and its most beautiful cities – all the while immersed in Quechua and Aymara indigenous culture.

Plan and Prepare

Logistics

Arequipa (Peru) is the traditional start point for the clockwise loop, although La Paz (Bolivia) is also a logical place to set off from. Both have international airports. It's also easy to join up with the route from Puno (Peru). Many sections of the Camino dél Puma are serviced by the occasional *collectivo* (communal taxi), convenient if you require transport on the route. A basic grasp of Spanish is essential, as little English is spoken.

Hazards

The Camino dél Puma's high point is just under 16,400ft (5000m) and the average elevation is over 13,000ft (4000m), with many points higher, so acclimatisation is essential before you start the ride. Afternoon thunderstorms can bring lightning, hail or snow during the shoulder seasons. While daytime temperatures can be mild to hot, it can regularly plunge below freezing at night. Dogs will sometimes chase cyclists, but are seldom genuinely aggressive.

Gear

A rigid or hardtail mountain bike with tyres of 2.35in is the minimum to fully enjoy the riding, and a bike with 2.6in to 2.8in tyres is ideal for the sometimes sandy and rocky roads. Pack bikepacking bags with kit for water filtration/ treatment; a tent, mat and warm sleeping bag are recommended, as towns are sparse but camping opportunities abundant. Carry a set of waterproofs, as well as a warm hat and gloves.

Info

This route is best ridden during the southwest altiplano dry season (April to November). Groundwater is relatively common, but you will need to plan for water on some sections, such as around Ubinas and Ticsani volcanoes, so allow for extra capacity. Water in some communities is treated, but check first. GPX and further info: bikepacking.com/routes/ el-camino-de-la-puma

Arequipa is a Unesco World Heritage site, and a memorable city from which to start your ride. There's a lot to see here among stunning Spanish colonial architecture, set against a backdrop of the nearby Misti and Chachani volcanoes, popular goals for summit-baggers.

Onto the Altiplano

The riding begins with a long climb up the vast Pacific Slope of the altiplano to the salt lake of Laguna Salinas, where you'll likely see alpacas, llamas and their wild ancestor, the vicuña. You might also spot viscachas, large rabbit-like rodents which live among rock outcrops. There's opportunity for basic resupply here before you cross a dramatic high-altitude desert landscape past active Ubinas volcano. A sandy stretch of road cuts around the edge of this pleasingly symmetrical cone before climbing over a pass and then dropping into the stunning Río Ichuña. Once in the canyon the route passes several small indigenous pueblos before reaching the larger town of Ichuña, where there is basic accommodation and restaurants. The indigenous people of this region – as along much of the route – are of Quechua descent, and it's common to see people in traditional dress, proud of their culture and traditions.

Chucuito and Lake Titicaca

Beyond Ichuña the steady climbing resumes over the route's high point, a pass on the Continental Divide at just under 16,400ft (4999m), but from here it's (almost) downhill all the way to the shimmering expanse of Lake Titicaca. The hilltop funerary towers (*chullpas*) at Cutimbo are a fascinating example of precision Inca stonework. Chucuito is a pleasant small town, its deeply historic feel contrasting with that of Bolivia's Copacabana, a couple of days' ride away.

Volcanic legacy

Dropping into the Río Tambo canyon, you'll ride through a landscape covered in tephra, volcanic ash and pumice – sometimes in drifts several metres deep, and a relic of the Huaynaputina volcano on the northern side of the canyon. The pyroclastic flow of its catasptophic eruption in 1600 buried entire villages in its wake. It was the largest eruption ever recorded in South America, and continued for several days, devastating all in its wake. Ten villages were destroyed or buried, and the death toll exceeded 1500 people. Quinistaquillas, on the Camino dél Puma route, was one such buried settlement; a completely new village has now been rebuilt on the site of the original, but the surrounding landscape is a constant reminder of the region's volatile volcanic past.

Copacabana has full tourist services and the best food on the route outside of Arequipa. A little further into Bolivia are the most notable pre-Columbian ruins of this tour: Tiwanaku. Wander between monoliths, archways, arcades and a subterranean temple, and take a peek into the site's two decent museums.

The Puna and Ticsani

Back into Peru, with border formalities out of the way at Desaguadero and your bags filled with food, you're set for the apogee of this ride, which tackles a long and remote high-altitude section as it crosses the northernmost margin of the Puna de Atacama back towards Arequipa. You'll pass small villages most days, which allow for limited resupply and sometimes a meal or a bed. After Capasa you'll roll by highlights daily, and may well spot flamingoes in the Vilacota conservation area. If not, you definitely won't miss the volcanoes that fill the horizon: the biggest is 17,743ft (5408m) Ticsani which – with the exception of the rarefied air – is a relatively straightforward hike from the nearby pass. The region's multihued landscape, a spectacular palette of reds, oranges and greys, was formed by the power of long-ago eruptions.

Down to the Río Tambo

Beyond Tiscani lies the Río Tambo canyon, which is roughly twice the depth of the United States' Grand Canyon – riding into it, you'll descend more than 12,000ft (3760m) over 60 miles (96km); it's like cycling into the inside of the Earth. This is a place that's as spectacular as it is harsh, and the heat in the bottom of the canyon can be challenging. While it's a long climb back out towards the finish, the pleasant oasis town of Omate is a good place to rest your climbing legs for the final stretch of the route to Arequipa.

Camino dél Puma

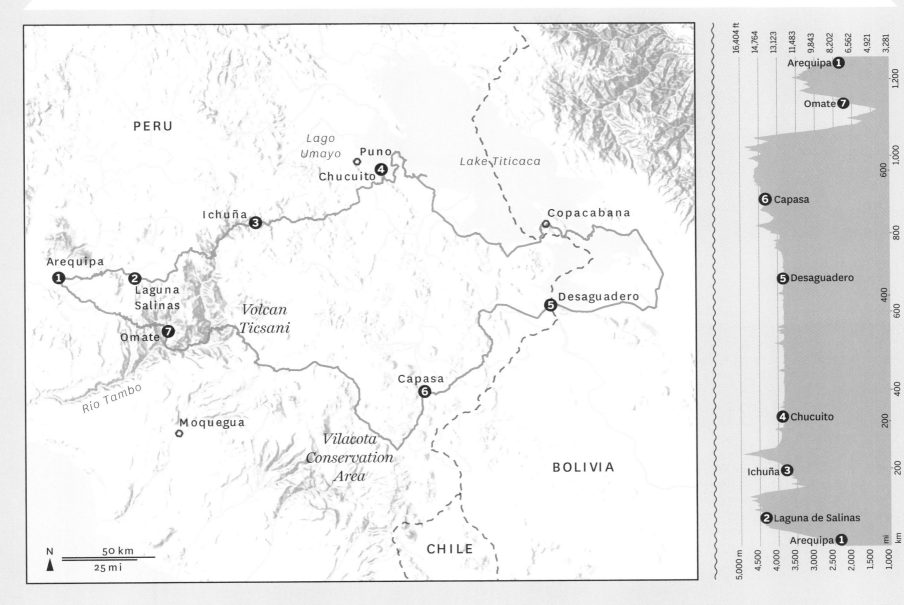

→ **Distance:** 539 miles (867km)   → **Ascent:** 72,500ft (22,100m)   → **Difficulty:** 5

The Colorado Trail

USA

This North American long-distance classic is a mountain-bike adventure high into Colorado's ranges, where dirt trails swoop joyously and climb painfully from one charming town to the next. The Colorado Trail will be up near the top of experienced bikepackers' bucket lists.

Plan and Prepare

Logistics

The trail runs between Denver and Durango, and many bikers ride in that direction: north to south. The trailhead is just outside Denver at Waterton Canyon, but with limited public transport it may be easiest to book a lift from downtown Denver. If there's a group of riders, someone can leave a vehicle in Durango. Otherwise you'll need to arrange transportation to your onward destination (Durango is a 7hr drive from Denver).

Hazards

This route earns its 5-star rating. Much of it is at an extremely high altitude for cycling, which means that riders need to be both physically fit and prepared for life-threatening weather events that include lightning storms with rain, hail or snow. Carry appropriate clothing and know what to do in an emergency. In addition to the elevation, the distance is also daunting. And, there are a black bears after your food.

Gear

The Colorado Trail is undoubtedly mountain-bike country. A lightweight full-suspension bike is ideal, offering extra comfort and control, but many riders manage on hardtails, with or without plus-sized tyres. You'll need to carry a lot of kit: a tent or shelter; sleeping bag; cooking gear and a bear-proof method of food storage; warm and waterproof clothing; and tools and spares such as brake pads and spokes.

Info

There's a lot of very useful information from the Colorado Trail Foundation (coloradotrail.org), including details on transport and how to get back from either end of the trail, plus information on water sources and other essentials. The Foundation's *CT Databook* is also a must-have. The trail's high passes are generally free from snow from July to September. The trail is waymarked but you'll need navigational know-how, too.

Heart pounding at Kokomo Pass, 12,000ft (3657m) above sea level, you notice clouds building over the distant mountains. It's time to decide: press on toward the mountain town of Leadville, 25 miles (40km) ahead, or lose as much elevation as possible and hunker down for another of the frequent summer storms in this part of the Rockies? Riding the Colorado Trail is full of such decisions. This ribbon of dirt is laid pretty much diagonally across the state, where even the lowest point in Denver is at a breathless 5500ft (1676m). Despite being one of the most famous long-distance hiking and biking trails in the US, it still inspires trepidation in the most experienced of outdoorsy folk. As a physical challenge, it earns its difficulty rating with ease. The riding features mammoth climbs and descents in mountain wilderness, with the prospect of extreme heat or cold, rain or dry. But it's a mental challenge too: do you have the confidence to continue into the unknown?

If the answer is yes, then you'll enjoy some of the finest singletrack mountain biking in the world. Long, sinuous trails snake along slopes, speeding through forests and meadows with an ever-present backdrop of the Rocky Mountains. Every now and then you'll have the pleasure of dropping into a mountain town, such as Leadville, Silverton or Breckenridge, for rest and resupply. Many riders take two to three weeks to ride the whole trail, but it's a feat that will stay with you forever.

One factor that does keep the Colorado Trail within the realm of achievable goals is that camping is relatively straightforward. Numerous campgrounds are stationed along the way and wild camping, bearing in mind the obvious ursine precautions, is usually a convenient option. Water is widely available too, from mountain streams, although you should fill up wherever possible.

Colorado 101

Colorado is steeped in mountain-biking history, much as the state's brews are steeped in hops. Some pioneers of the pastime came from Colorado and shared their amazing trails – like the 401 Trail near Crested Butte or Salida's Monarch Crest – with the world. Crested Butte continues to host the world's oldest mountain-bike festival every June. And Durango was the venue for the first official Mountain Bike World Championship in 1990, won by Durango-dwelling legend Ned Overend. Colorado's average altitude of 6800ft (2073m) makes it the US' highest state, perhaps lending local athletes an aerobic advantage. For those whose ethos is more pleasure than performance, the state has some great breweries, and legalised pot in 2012.

Leaving Denver

Once you've made it to the Waterton Canyon trailhead, about 40 miles (64km) from downtown Denver, the trail starts climbing gradually. But it isn't until you're about 100 miles (160km) deep that the altitude hits five figures – and pretty much stays there until Durango. The scenery starts to open up around Kenosha Pass at the 115-mile (185km) mark, as you freewheel across alpine meadows.

The first major break can be made with a detour from Gold Hill down to Breckenridge, where a chilled Kölsch awaits in the Broken Compass taproom (in the opposite direction, Frisco also has some good food options). Back on the trail, the next big section from Breckenridge to Leadville takes in a couple of very high passes, including Kokomo, that may require pushing the bike. Leadville is another legendary mountain town and the stretch from here to Buena Vista contains some of the most varied riding, through the austere beauty of aspen forests and then up again above the trees, pedalling along rocky mountainsides.

Buena Vista to Durango

The southern half of the Colorado Trail is generally acknowledged to be both the most scenic (it's a high standard) and the most mountainous. You can expect to push the bike more frequently, with Sargents Mesa being a particularly tough section. You'll also need to follow the detours for cyclists around the dedsignated wilderness areas. But the trail redeems itself with the rollercoaster ride from Lake City to Silverton (top left), into the San Juan Mountains. Remember that this all occurs at 12,000ft (3658m), although hopefully your body will have acclimated to the rationed oxygen by now. Silverton is another fun town to stop in, before more dirt nirvana and the stunning descent into Durango over the last 100 miles (160km).

The Colorado Trail

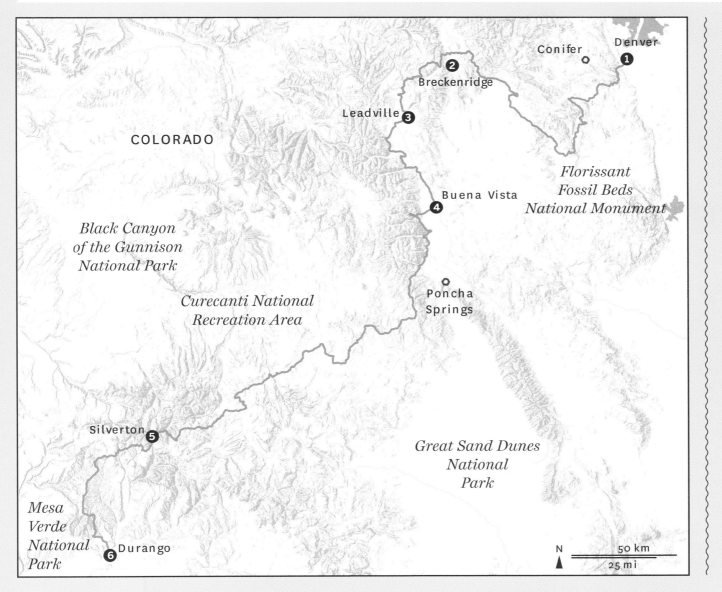

COLORADO

Denver ❶
Conifer
Breckenridge ❷
Leadville ❸
Buena Vista ❹
Poncha Springs

Florissant Fossil Beds National Monument

Black Canyon of the Gunnison National Park

Curecanti National Recreation Area

Great Sand Dunes National Park

Silverton ❺

Mesa Verde National Park

Durango ❻

N
50 km
25 mi

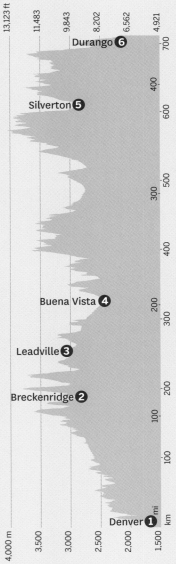

Durango ❻
Silverton ❺
Buena Vista ❹
Leadville ❸
Breckenridge ❷
Denver ❶

→ **Distance: 255 miles (410km)**   → **Ascent: 21,200ft (6462m)**   → **Difficulty: 3**

Green Mountain Gravel Growler

USA

Bikepacking and beer go together like peanut butter and jelly – and this loop connects some of Vermont's finest breweries via farm tracks, rural roads and some fun singletrack. It's a great opportunity to taste some beers that rarely leave the state.

Plan and Prepare

Logistics

The beauty of a bikepacking loop is that you can start and end wherever is most convenient. For most people, that will be Burlington, Vermont's largest city. Amtrak's Vermonter train service from Washington, DC stops here and at many cities in between, including New York and Philadelphia; boxed bicycles are permitted. The Green Mountain Gravel Growler loop also passes through Vermont's state capital, Montpelier.

Hazards

Statistically, Vermont is one of the safest states for cyclists, but you will be sharing road with vehicles at times. Also, it's dangerous (and potentially against the law) to be intoxicated while riding a bicycle, so it's best to leave the beer-tasting until the end of the day's riding. There are black bears in Vermont but more of a problem are ticks, many carrying Lyme disease – research how to remove them.

Gear

The route was designed with gravel bikes in mind, but a hardtail mountain bike might offer more comfort on the few rough sections. A bike with tyres narrower than 40mm might feel a bit out of its depth in places. The amount of baggage to carry is dependent on whether camping is preferred over accommodation at B&Bs. The same applies to food – there's little need to carry cooking kit if you're eating at cafes and pubs.

Info

The ideal time to ride is late summer or early autumn, when you can catch the leaves changing colour. Rainfall peaks in June, with high humidity in July. Note that there's a lot of private property along the route, so always ask before pitching a tent. Dispersed camping is permitted in Green Mountain National Forest. There's lots of useful info at bikepacking.com/routes/green-mountain-gravel-growler

Scouting a new bikepacking route in Vermont was an enjoyable job for bikepacking.com editors Logan Watts and Joe Cruz. Their mission was to connect some of Vermont's acclaimed breweries by quiet, bicycle-friendly paths and, by all measures, they succeeded. Their five-day loop around the heart of the state features more than a dozen great breweries, plus assorted taprooms and pubs. Most riders start from Burlington on the shore of Lake Champlain and follow the route clockwise, arriving at state capital Montpelier at around the halfway point.

For most of the route you won't be further than 25 miles (40km) from a bed for the night, whether in a rural B&B or in one of the towns along the way, such as Stowe (right), Greensboro, Bristol, Waterbury, Middlebury and so on. But it's also possible to camp, asking permission where required; there's a section of the Green Mountain National Forest around Lincoln Gap, between Warren and Middlebury, in which it's possible to camp freely.

Also note that beer, especially brews that are high in alcohol, never improves bike-riding skill or stamina. It's best to save your sampling for the end of the day's ride.

Burlington to Montpelier

Burlington is the base for a couple of excellent breweries: Zero Gravity and Foam Brewers. You could christen the start of the trip with one and sample the other at the end. Burlington itself is a leafy, red-brick city (population 44,743) with a lively waterfront overlooking the islands and peninsulas of Lake Champlain. It's a lovely place to spend some time either at the start or end of the ride. The route shadows the highway out to Waterbury, at about 32 miles (51km), and then it starts climbing, mostly off-road.

Here for the beer

Vermont and Maine vie for the title of the American state with the most craft breweries per capita. Although this is partly because they have low population densities, it also means that each state's residents really do have a lot of breweries to choose between. Something else that Maine and Vermont have in common is that they're in the northeast of the US, a region that has proudly paddled its own canoe in the beer world. When California was making ever-more bitter and hop-heavy India Pale Ales (IPA), the New England states (including Maine and Vermont) were trying out hazy IPAs that swapped bitterness for rich, malty flavour and were redolent with tangy tropical fruit like pineapple.

Something else that sets Vermont and its neighbours apart is the range of beer types produced. There's a lot more to try than the standard IPAs: English-style beer, German lagers and dunkels, Belgian tripels and more. Many brews are creatively named, such as the Bernie Weisse, a 'slightly sour and forward-thinking' wheat ale at Zero Gravity (below). But there's a kicker: many of these beers never leave the state, so the only way to taste them is to tour Vermont – ideally on a bicycle.

You'll pass the historic 19th-century Gold Brook Covered Bridge before reaching Stowe at 60 miles (96km). The reward for your effort is a glass of Heady Topper, a Double IPA from Stowe's The Alchemist brewery, regularly hailed as the best beer in America. It's certainly the archetypal unfiltered and fruity New England ale. The Alchemist's popularity means that you'll need to arrive early to bag a seat. Continuing past a couple more breweries in Morristown and passing through the Green River Reservoir State Park, where campsites are only accessible by boat, the next standout brewery is the family-owned Hill Farmstead, which produces an amazing array of beers: the Edward was one of the best American pale ales Cruz and Watts had ever tasted. This is a pretty but isolated corner of Vermont and some of the tracks between here and Montpelier are very steep and rough, including some singletrack just before Montpelier.

Montpelier to Burlington

Vermont's bijoux state capital, the US' smallest, is historic and handsome. Its Three Penny Taproom offers good food and a menu of 20-plus local beers. The southern half of this loop leaves Montpelier and zigzags through a classically Vermont landscape of wooded hills before meeting the Mad River. There are a few more villages and stores here until you reach Warren, where there's a big off-road climb through Green Mountain National Forest. Beyond Lincoln Gap, it's largely downhill back to Burlington via Middlebury, Bristol and Hinesburg.

Green Mountain Gravel Growler

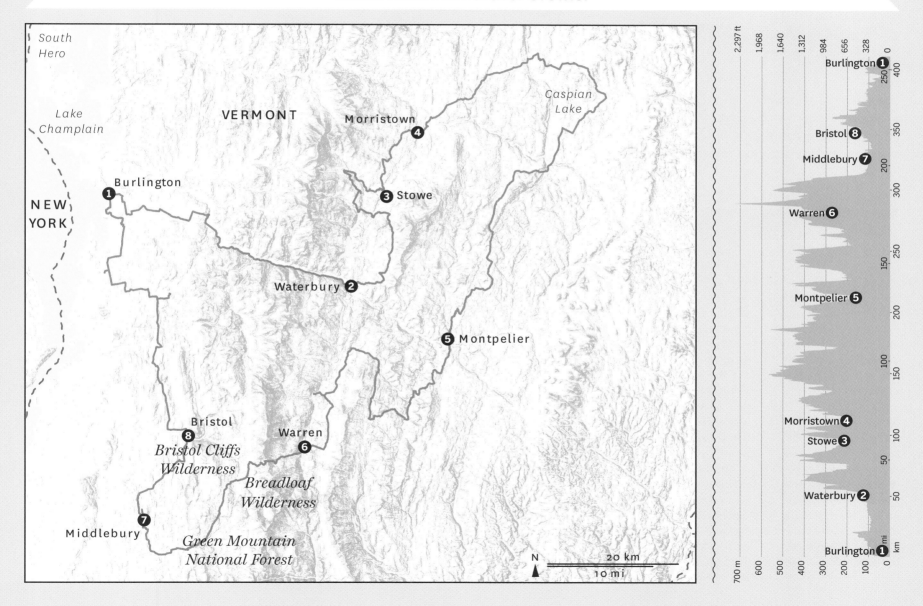

South
Hero

Lake
Champlain

VERMONT

Morristown

④

Caspian
Lake

Burlington

①

NEW
YORK

Stowe

③

Waterbury

②

Montpelier

⑤

Bristol

⑧

Bristol Cliffs
Wilderness

Warren

⑥

Breadloaf
Wilderness

Middlebury

⑦

Green Mountain
National Forest

N

20 km

10 mi

2,297 ft   1,968   1,640   1,312   984   656   328   0

Burlington ①

Bristol ⑧

Middlebury ⑦

Warren ⑥

Montpelier ⑤

Morristown ④

Stowe ③

Waterbury ②

Burlington ①

700 m   600   500   400   300   200   100   0

→ Distance: 688 miles (1107km)   → Ascent: 69,239ft (21,104m)   → Difficulty: 4

Oregon Timber Trail

USA

Traverse the wilds of Oregon on this brilliantly designed long-distance mountain-bike trail between the California and Washington borders. Hopping from community to community via spectacular and varied scenery, it's a great way to experience the Pacific Northwest.

Plan and Prepare

Logistics

You can ride the Timber Trail in either direction, but those doing the full route tend to ride south to north. To reach the start near Lakeview on the Oregon–California border, you can take the Amtrak train from Portland to Klamath Falls and then a shuttle with operators such as Cog Wild. You could also start from Klamath Falls itself. Between the endpoint at Hood River and Portland in the north, Greyhound buses should carry boxed bikes.

Hazards

Weather and wildlife are the chief concerns. At the higher elevations, snow can linger into June and fall again from October. Be prepared, with clothing for all conditions. In the summer, expect extreme heat in places; and water will be in short supply on some sections – plan ahead. Black bears are common in Oregon and food will need to be stored securely away from camps. The mosquitoes are savage: bring repellent and a head-net.

Gear

This route is designed for mountain bikes, whether hardtails (front suspension only) or full-suspension bikes. You'll need to be a proficient and fit rider even if not taking on the full route. Most people carry lightweight camping and cooking kit and a water purification system, since camping sites and streams are plentiful. And because some backcountry sections are far from the nearest town, a first-aid kit is advisable.

Info

The excellent website from the route's creators (oregontimbertrail.org) gives all the details you'll need; bikepacking.com also has tips and advice. Most people ride the OTT from June to October but many do sections at a time, and some legs will be accessible outside those months. Novices might want to book a guide. You can also take advantage of accommodation in local communities on some stretches.

Tall trees, desert, volcanoes and very good coffee all figure in this vertical crossing of Oregon. Extending south to north (or the other way if that works better) across Oregon's interior, the Timber Trail didn't come about by chance. Back in 2015, Oregon's state tourism commission realised the need for a compelling reason for bike riders to visit and stay in the state. What they developed – with the help of the nonprofit Oregon Timber Trail Alliance and a team of trail builders – is truly an epic, world-class mountain-biking experience. The Timber Trail travels through several of Oregon's beautifully wild landscapes on mostly singletrack trails, connecting a number of rural communities, such as Silver Lake, that might not otherwise benefit from many visitors. Cleverly, the trail is divided into four tiers – Fremont, Willamette, Deschutes and Hood – so that riders can tackle just one or two sections at time. Only 50-100 people take on the whole trail in one go each year. You can also break the trail down into smaller day-rides around specific towns in order to gain confidence for bigger trips. 'I believe that experiences in wild places can have a profound impact on our personal growth', says Gabriel Amadeus, founder of the Oregon Timber Trail Alliance.

Fremont and Willamette

Starting in the south on the Fremont tier means jumping into the deep end: this is the highest part of the whole trail and it's a long way from anywhere. The ferns and moss-draped trees of the Oregon you imagine are also absent. Over east, the climate is tinder-dry and you'll pass plenty of fire lookouts in the ponderosa forests. Recent wildfires in Oregon have affected the trail and it's a good idea to check that the sections you want to ride are repaired and open before setting out.

You'll be using the Fremont National Recreation Trail for much of this tier, passing through high-desert towns like Silver Lake at mile 148 (238km), home of the famed Cowboy Dinner Tree diner. After about 200 miles (322km), the trail switches to the Willamette tier and changes character as you cross over the Cascade Range at Timpanogas Lake, into the rain-shadow of the west. From here, the forest of fir, pine, spruce and cedar quickly grows dark, damp and green. The forest floor is loamy and the trees are tall and closely packed, making for brilliant mountain-biking. You'll follow the Willamette River's Middle Fork some of the way, so water is plentiful too. Just over halfway through the 152 miles (245km) of the Willamette tier you'll come to the town of Oakridge, which is a thriving hub of

Oregon's outdoor adventure scene, with hundreds of miles of biking trails. There's also hiking, rafting and, in fall, fungi foraging.

Deschutes and Hood

The Timber Trail meanders back over to the drier east side of the Cascade Range for the Deschutes tier from Waldo Lake onwards. Deschutes is one of the less daunting sections, passing close to another Oregon adventure hub, Bend, but you'll need to carry supplies of food. You'll be riding through some fascinating volcanic landscapes on this leg, with views of Mt Washington from Big Lake. The final tier, Hood, takes you towards the Columbia River via views of Mt Hood from Olallie Lakes, but there are still few places for resupply, so plan ahead.

Oregon's Mt Hood

'These cones or rocks are full of cracks or fissures, as if they had been rent by some convulsion of nature at a remote period... through the crevices in the rock, there is constantly escaping hot smoke or gas of a strong sulphuric odor.' So goes the account of the 1854 summit attempt of Mt Hood by then-editor of the *Oregonian* newspaper, one Thomas J Dryer. His climbing party was aware that they were scaling a stratovolcano (although maybe not that Hood is the highest point in Oregon, at 11,249ft/3429m). But they couldn't have known that 11 years later, Mt Hood would erupt, sending fire, rock and steam into the sky. The stratovolcano, part of the Cascade Volcanic Arc, is currently dormant but it's not impossible that it will spark into life again. In the meantime, Mt Hood is one of the world's most climbed peaks, with more than 10,000 people attempting to summit each year. One reason for its popularity is its accessibility: it's a couple of hours from Portland and can be climbed in a day, most usually via the South Side/Hogsback route. Given the snow and steep slopes, even novices will need to know how to use crampons and an ice axe, and how to stop a fall.

Oregon Timber Trail

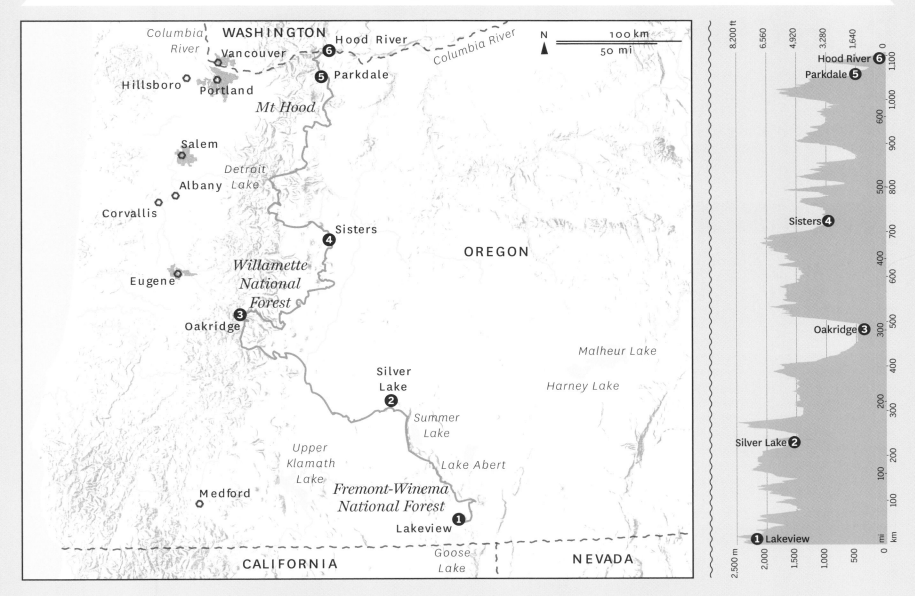

WASHINGTON

Columbia River

Hood River **6**

Vancouver

Columbia River

Hillsboro

Portland

Parkdale **5**

Mt Hood

Salem

Detroit Lake

Albany

Corvallis

Sisters **4**

OREGON

Willamette National Forest

Eugene

Oakridge **3**

Malheur Lake

Silver Lake **2**

Harney Lake

Summer Lake

Upper Klamath Lake

Lake Abert

Medford

Fremont-Winema National Forest

Lakeview **1**

CALIFORNIA

Goose Lake

NEVADA

N

100 km

50 mi

8,200 ft

6,560

4,920

3,280

1,640

0

Hood River **6** 1,100

Parkdale **5**

Sisters **4**

Oakridge **3**

Silver Lake **2**

Lakeview **1**

2,500 m

2,000

1,500

1,000

500

0 mi

0 km

→ Distance: 261 miles (420km)   → Ascent: 31,462ft (9590m)   → Difficulty: 4

Ruta Chingaza

Colombia

Ride up into the highlands east of the Colombian capital, Bogotá, to discover a nature-filled national park and some tranquil dirt-road trails through cloud forests and other vulnerable ecosystems, encountering local communities as you go.

Plan and Prepare

Logistics

Since this loop starts and ends in Bogotá, the logistics are relatively straightforward: just get to Colombia's capital with your bike. The ride starts from Parque Nacional Enrique Olaya Herrera, which is south of Bogotá's lively Chapinero district. Generally, the further north you stay in this neighbourhood the better (avoid Carrera 7 and Carrera 14), although Marly is a safe, student-filled area. Usaquén, north of Chapinero, is even more upscale.

Hazards

Take the usual common-sense precautions you would in any city in the Americas with regard to your personal safety and possessions. Check up-to-date reports on the better areas in which to stay. On the trail, the greatest hazards will be the altitude (watch for signs of sickness, such headaches) and the weather, which will be very changeable. Also, be aware that you'll be sharing dirt roads with vehicles.

Gear

The route's designers recommend using a mountain bike, ideally a hardtail (with front suspension). You could probably manage on a gravel bike, but it wouldn't be as comfortable or as enjoyable. Fit the very lowest gears possible (again a mountain bike will typically have the widest range). Ensure you have adequate clothing for cold and wet weather, but also pack light to save weight.

Info

The route passes through several climatic zones but, generally, the dry seasons are between January and March and during July and August. The temperature is constant year-round but cooler as you get higher, and can be near-freezing at times. Bogotá-based tour operator Tingua Hidden Journeys (hiddenjourneys.co) can assist with airport transfers and bike rental. The most comprehensive source of information on the Ruta Chingaza is bikepacking.com

n early 2020, the bikepacking.com team, including co-founder Logan Watts, began scouting a new route in Colombia in collaboration with environmental organisation Conservation International, which works to highlight the ways in which nature benefits humanity. The route they developed, the Ruta Chingaza, circles out of the capital, Bogotá, and up into the Eastern Andes for a week-long ride through little-seen landscapes – including the páramo, an exceptionally fragile, water-laden ecosystem above the treeline which provides 70% of Bogotá's water supply. 'I always saw bikepacking as a way to tell stories about land-use and conservation', says Logan Watts. 'Bikepacking offers connection to nature like no other form of travel.' By drawing attention to the dependence of humans on the natural world, it's hoped that Ruta Chingaza riders will become more invested in protecting vulnerable places like the páramo.

The route uses dirt roads and a bit of off-piste adventuring to reach the Parque Nacional Natural Chingaza, just east of Bogotá. The whole region lies at exceptionally high altitude: Bogotá is at 8660ft (2640m) above sea level, and riders will gain at least another 3500ft (1067m) of vertical elevation during the loop. This means that acclimatising to the altitude is essential before embarking on the ride. And it also explains why so many successful pro cyclists hail from Colombia: big-names riders like Nairo Quintana and Egan Bernal have grown up accustomed to the thinner air here.

Beginning in Bogotá

The Colombian capital will surprise many first-time visitors, having turned itself around over the last 20 years. It's also a cycle-friendly destination. Every Sunday, city roads are closed to vehicles for the Ciclovía (right), when 1.5 million people enjoy the city safely on foot, bikes and skateboards.

Birding & biking

Home to about 1900 avian species, Colombia is thought to have the greatest diversity of birdlife in the world, and it's well worth using a pocket guidebook or an app to help put names to some of the birds you'll see. The prevalent species will change according to where you are on the route, but in Chingaza, for example, look out for the silvery-throated spinetail, plumbeous sierra finch and black-billed mountain toucan; the dozens of hummingbird species – such as the coppery-bellied puffleg, mountain velvetbreast, tyrian metaltail and blue-throated starfrontlet – are especially entrancing. And yes, the say-what-you-see naming conventions do help identification.

Once you've spent a few days in Bogotá, getting used to inhaling less oxygen than usual, you're ready to set out on the Ruta Chingaza. The first 100 miles (160km) or so uses some surfaced roads and doesn't gain as much elevation as the second half of the route, making it a good warm-up. An initial climb leads to a dirt descent to La Calera, where you can refuel on Colombian coffee and *arepas*, the filled cornmeal patties that are the perfect food for cyclists. The route next passes through Zipaquirá, where a subterranean salt cathedral, carved out 600ft (183m) underground by and for miners, is one of Colombia's wonders. Zipaquirá is also a good place to stop, at about 56 miles (90km) in.

The next landmark is Laguna Guatavita, sacred to Colombia's Muisca people, whose legend tells that a ruler known as El Dorado would cover his body in gold dust for festivals and then jump into the lake to rinse it off. From here, the climbing begins in earnest. The last settlement before Parque Nacional Natural Chingaza is Guasca, but Conservation International is hoping to establish rural projects along the way that can support bikepackers.

Into Chingaza

Much of Chingaza (permit required) lies at over 10,000ft (3048m), which is ideal for the process by which plants of the páramo such as espeletia (or frailejón) capture moisture from the fog and draw it down into the wetland; the water then forms rivers that feed reservoirs. Riders, too, will flow through cloud forest and valleys of mosses, ferns and waterfalls up here, especially between San Juanito (another good place for a break) and Fómeque in the last third of the route. The homeward stretch to Bogotá is extremely challenging, but charming towns such as El Calvario and San Francisco lighten the load.

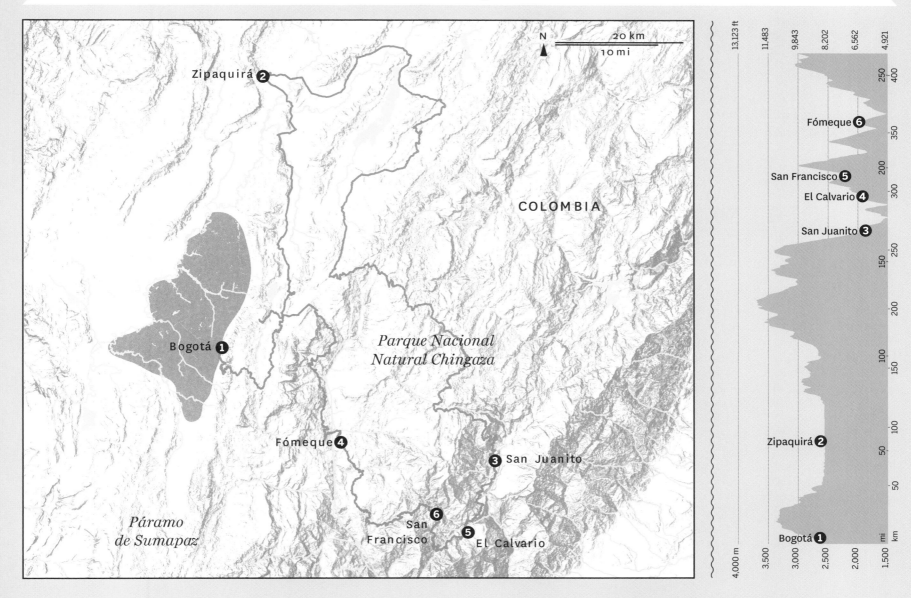

Ruta Chingaza

→ Distance: 190 miles (305km)   → Ascent: 19,520ft (5950m)   → Difficulty: 3

The Tahoe Twirl

USA

Skip the crowds and circle Lake Tahoe by mountain bike through some of the most beautiful scenery in the Sierra Nevada. Rocky trails lead through pine forest and alpine meadows, with lots of camping options.

The Tahoe Rim Trail (TRT) is one of the world's great hiking experiences, looping around this large, beautiful (and very busy) alpine lake through pine forests dotted with giant boulders. But on certain sections through designated wilderness areas, bicycles are banned – enter the Tahoe Twirl, an extended version of the TRT for mountain-bikers that skips the inaccessible parts and adds some sublime singletrack riding north of the lake. Although the Twirl doesn't stray far from settlements (and, indeed, cities) for sustenance, assistance and rest, it does rank as a route suitable only for fit and experienced bikepackers, on account of its huge elevation gain and the added hindrance of high altitude. Riding the whole route in four or five days, at 40-50 miles (64-80km) per day, is a tough physical feat; aim instead for seven or eight.

Plan and Prepare

Logistics

As a loop trail, the Tahoe Twirl can be started from any point. On the California side of the lake, South Lake Tahoe and Truckee are both served by major roads. Truckee is on Amtrak's California Zephyr train line; boxed bicycles can be checked in. On the Nevada side of Lake Tahoe, Reno, the largest transport hub here, is also on the Amtrak line and has an international airport.

Hazards

The altitude will have an effect on people who are not acclimatised to cycling at 9000ft (2743m) or more. And with all the ascent, fitness will be a factor (note that electric bikes are not permitted on the Tahoe Rim Trail). The elevation also means that snow may be present until late in the year, and that weather conditions can change. Black bears are also present, so follow food-storage instructions when camping.

Gear

The Tahoe Twirl was designed as a mountain-bike trail. Much of it is on steep, rocky and sandy singletrack, connected by gravel roads –a mountain bike's wider handlebars, tougher and grippier tyres and more comfortable riding position will help. You'll need to carry camping and cooking kit plus a water purification system. Insect repellent is advised, as is windproof and waterproof clothing appropriate for the mountain climate.

Info

June to September is an ideal time to ride; snow may affect the highest parts of the route into June. After September, there's a greater risk of inclement weather, but you can still get lucky with the forecast. Afternoons also bring frequent rain storms in the mountains. In the sections through the Tahoe National Forest, dispersed camping is free (follow the rules at fs.usda.gov). Check bikepacking.com for more route info.

Reno to South Lake

If you're starting from Reno, the largest city near Lake Tahoe, and heading clockwise, there's a relentless climb for the first 20 miles (32km) or so, generally on gravel roads through forest. It's hot work in the summer but there are streams in which to fill water bottles (do purify the water, there's giardia here). The first payoff comes early enough, however, around Incline Village, where you'll pick up the Flume Trail (right). This famous trail is a bikers' bucket-list favourite, giving great views over the sapphire lake but also requiring utmost concentration: the narrow, gritty path hugs the contour lines and granite buttresses threaten to tip you down the slope. This takes you down to Marlette Lake and then Spooner Lake, where camping is restricted to a campground within the (small) boundaries of Lake Tahoe Nevada State Park. From here you follow the Tahoe Rim Trail south to Kingsbury through fragrant forests of Jeffrey and western white pines at a breathless 8500ft (2591m).

Tahoe Trails

Lake Tahoe is surrounded by excellent mountain-bike trails, graded like ski runs from green then blue to black, and for those with the time to explore further, Tahoe definitely delivers. From the north, Truckee has a network of fun trails on its outskirts, built by the Truckee Trails Foundation. Upper Big Chief has rock features that bring its difficulty-grade to black, but Lower Big Chief and the Sawtooth Trail are both blue, with fast, twisty sections. East of Lake Tahoe, the Flume Trail (below) is part of the Tahoe Twirl. And south of the lake, beyond the suburb of Meyers, there are a couple of classic descents branching off the TRT: Mr Toad's Wild Ride and Christmas Valley.

South Lake to Truckee

It was around Kingsbury that the early Pony Express riders, delivering mail across the west by relay, first crossed the route of the future Tahoe Rim Trail in 1860. But it wasn't until 1984 that construction began on the lake-looping TRT, and the complete trail was opened in 2001. It has become a hugely popular route, and certain sections near trailheads are often busy with hikers during the peak season – so ride with care (the trails, however, aren't nearly as congested as the roads hereabouts).

The highest portion of the Tahoe Twirl is around the south of the loop (the closest trailhead being Big Meadow). The biking is extremely engaging here, on trails that aren't too technically challenging but still adventurous and entertaining as they twist around pine and fir trees and giant boulders. You'll be pushing a laden bike up some of the inclines. In the early summer, a rainbow of wildflowers bloom in the alpine meadows. There's a sustained descent down to Meyers, where you can give your wrists a rest and enjoy some good food. There are places to stay here, too, if you don't want to camp higher up.

After crossing Hwy 50, the next section of the Twirl is on the tarmac of Hwy 89 around the west shore of the lake, passing the photo-op of Emerald Bay. Needless to say, it's not a great experience since the road is narrow and busy with impatient drivers. But after just over 30 miles (50km), it's back onto the dirt at Tahoe City. The route here isn't as rugged as the east or south of the lake but it's great to be among the trees again. Truckee is a couple of hours north and feels like a frontier railroad town – until you look a bit more closely at the independent bookshops and lively bars and restaurants. The final link in the loop back to Reno is on easygoing gravel trails and bike paths.

The Tahoe Twirl

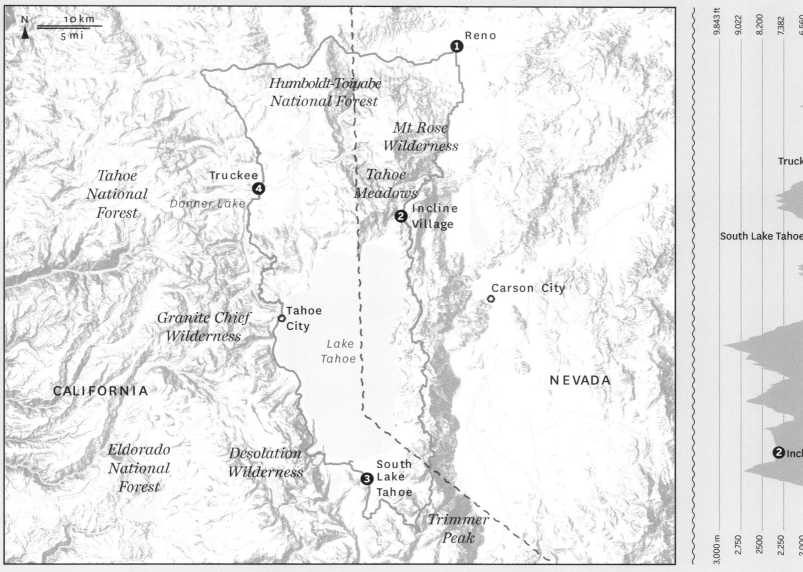

N
10 km
5 mi

Reno **1**

Humboldt-Toiyabe
National Forest

Mt Rose
Wilderness

Tahoe
Meadows

Truckee **4**

Tahoe
National
Forest

Donner Lake

Incline
Village **2**

Tahoe
City

Granite Chief
Wilderness

Lake
Tahoe

Carson City

CALIFORNIA

NEVADA

Eldorado
National
Forest

Desolation
Wilderness

South
Lake
Tahoe **3**

Trimmer
Peak

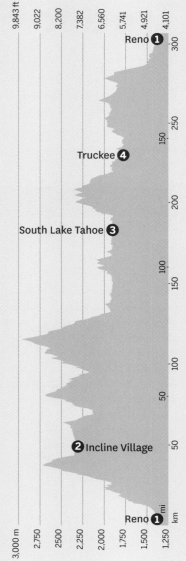

9,843 ft
9,022
8,200
7,382
6,560
5,741
4,921
4,101

Reno **1**

Truckee **4**

South Lake Tahoe **3**

2 Incline Village

1 Reno

3,000 m
2,750
2500
2,250
2,000
1,750
1,500
1,250

300
250
150
200
100
150
100
50
50
mi
km

➡ **Distance:** 647 miles (1041km)   ➡ **Ascent:** 48,631ft (14823m)   ➡ **Difficulty:** 4

Tree to Sea Loop

Canada

Located on the north half of British Columbia's Vancouver Island, the Tree to Sea is an impressive long-distance loop that links together massive valleys, quaint oceanside villages and coastal mountains via a patchwork of gravelled Forest Service roads.

Plan and Prepare

Logistics

The Tree to Sea Loop route starts and ends in Comox on Vancouver Island, which can be accessed by water via the Powell River ferry, operated by BC Ferries, as well as by air via domestic flights to Comox Valley Airport. The closest international airport is in Victoria, at the south end of Vancouver Island, from where there are buses running north to the start of the route.

Hazards

Expect heavy rain and sudden weather changes on the route, especially in the spring and autumn. The area also contains habitat for many wild animals, including bears, cougars and wolves. Always carry bear spray and hang your food at night when camping.

Gear

A gravel bike with tyres of at least 45mm is recommended, but a rigid mountain bike or hardtail would not be overkill. There are many long, steep climbs, so a wide range drivetrain with proper climbing gears is important. There are several major grocery stores and towns along the way, but some fairly remote sections as well: plan ahead and pack accordingly.

Info

Currently a water taxi from Tahsis to Zeballos is required to ride the entire route, and must be booked ahead of time. For charter options and complete route details, head to bikepacking.com/routes/tree-to-sea-loop-vancouver-island

Developed and documented by Miles Arbour of bikepacking.com, the Tree to Sea Loop takes advantage of the gravel roads running north of Campbell River, linking small coastal villages, incredible landscapes and impressive granite mountains into a long-distance, bucket-list bikepacking route. This route travels in both the Nuu-chah-nulth and Kwakwaka'wakw regions, passing through several First Nations communities along the way. These Nations account for almost 20% of the First Nations population in all of British Columbia. Along the way, riders tackling the route will have the chance to whale-watch, explore caves, and unwind at some of the best waterside campsites in the province. The track bundles much of what the North Island offers into a well-rounded route that can be tackled in two weeks, or easily expanded into a 20+ day endeavour with side-trips and rest days.

Though beautiful, this route is no walk in the park. Logistics and coastal weather create a sliding difficulty rating that is both hard to predict and to manage. As presented, the route requires a water taxi from Tahsis to Zeballos, which will be replaced by the Unity Trail that will eventually connect the two communities. It's an expensive ride that's best split between a larger group, but the boat trip is incredibly beautiful and rewarding in its own way. Many of the remote coastal communities have general stores and resupply points that aren't entirely reliable, especially in the off-season, forcing riders to pack several days' worth of food at a time. On top of all that, the unpredictable weather of northern Vancouver Island makes proper rain gear and multiple layers a necessity, especially during the spring and autumn, which are some of the best times to enjoy the Tree to Sea.

Coast to coast: Comox to Zeballos

The route starts and ends at the Comox ferry terminal, just south of Campbell River. While the Old Island Highway (19A) could be used to connect to the ferry up to Campbell River, you can opt to keep things interesting and away from traffic by linking several multi-use paths and sideroads together along the coast, eventually skirting inland just north of Oyster River. From there, a short section of chunky gravel roads sneak behind the Campbell River Airport, joining with the Elk River Mainline, which runs parallel to the paved Gold River Highway (Hwy 28), taking riders all the way to Upper Campbell Lake and the Upper Campbell Reservoir Campground. The next 81 miles (130km) loop up and around Strathcona Provincial Park back down towards Gold River. This section is remote and without services or many established campgrounds so some bikepackers may prefer to ride the highway to Gold River instead.

Some of the most beautiful views of the entire route are between Gold River and Zeballos. After a coffee in Gold River, you'll climb up towards Tlupana Peak, passing by Cala Creek Falls and Upana Caves along the way. It's easy to spend a few hours exploring this massive underground cave system, and Upana also serves as a great place to have lunch. After the massive descent down to Moutcha Bay Resort, the route continues northwest to the beautiful Leiner River Recreation Site and the town of Tahsis. Until the Unity Trail connecting to Zeballos is complete, a water taxi from Tahsis to Zeballos will need to be pre-booked to continue on the route. Otherwise, another option would be to head north from Gold Muchalat Provincial Park, rejoining the route at the south end of Nimpkish Lake.

Esperanza Inlet

The water taxi between the quiet coastal communities of Tahsis and Zeballos is an unforgettable experience. Make sure to book ahead with Zeballos Expeditions and try to link up with another group to keep the cost down. There is a good chance you'll have views of humpbacks and orcas, so keep your cameras ready. There are plans to develop a multi-use trail connecting the two communities, but things are moving slowly. Do your bit to push things along by mentioning your interest in the Unity Trail while you're there!

Ronning's Garden

Tucked away in the forest between San Josef Bay and Holberg, Ronning's Garden is an unmissable, quirky, volunteer-maintained garden. Established around 1910 by Bernt Ronning, the garden is home to exotic trees and plants and is slowly being freed from the invading rainforest. There is no admission fee – but cash donations are accepted.

Caves and the north

The wide gravel climb north from Zeballos leads to the next spelunking opportunity at Little Huson Caves, which are much larger than Upana and equally beautiful; some are above ground. The route continues Port Alice, the next major resupply point; don't forget to stop by Foggy Mountain Coffee Co. while you're there. Next comes one of the more remote sections of the route, to Coal Harbour, looping around Rupert Inlet on Forest Service roads and some rough doubletrack. Mostly rolling, wide gravel roads run north along the long Holberg Inlet before a steep descent to the town of Holberg and the Scarlet Ibis Pub. It's an easy ride out to Cape Scott Provincial Park, where some choose to wild-camp on the magnificent beaches of San Josef Bay.

After a quick stop at the general store in Holberg, follow the Holberg Road east to Port Hardy. Don't forget to stop at the Holberg Shoe Tree at the eastern end of Kains Lake. Port Hardy is a well-established town with campsites, a well-stocked grocery store and a good coffee shop. Skirting the highway, the route continues to Port McNeill, with grocery stores, campgrounds and, most importantly, the world's biggest tree burl. With extra time, consider an optional ferry ride to Malcolm Island and the charming town of Sointula, an old Finnish utopian settlement that is definitely worth a visit. Gravel roads lead to the northern tip of Nimpkish Lake, looping back to the coast and eventually Telegraph Cove. This popular tourist destination has options for lodging, camping and wildlife tours, providing a great layover or lunch spot.

Kissing the Johnstone Strait

Leaving Telegraph Cove, the Tree to Sea heads south along the eastern shores of Ida and Bonanza lakes, two beautiful options for camping and swimming, before arriving in the small town of Woss, just off Hwy 19. The final stretch from Woss to Campbell River has some of the most scenic oceanside camping options on the entire route. Naka Creek rec site, while popular and often busy, has great whale-watching. A long climb and a steep descent lead to the small town of Sayward – head north off-route to Kelsey Bay for more great views. Sayward Junction serves as an important resupply point along the route, with several camping options nearby, as well as a pub (if it's open). East of the Prince of Wales Range, the route passes by McCreight Lake and Stella Lake, both great spots for camping. The last big climb of the route heads south from Elk Bay, towards the highway, and the Iron River Main Forest Service Road towards Elk Falls Provincial Park and Campbell River. The route rejoins with itself just north of Oyster River, following a multi-use rail trail and a short section of the Old Island Highway south from Campbell River.

Tree to Sea Loop

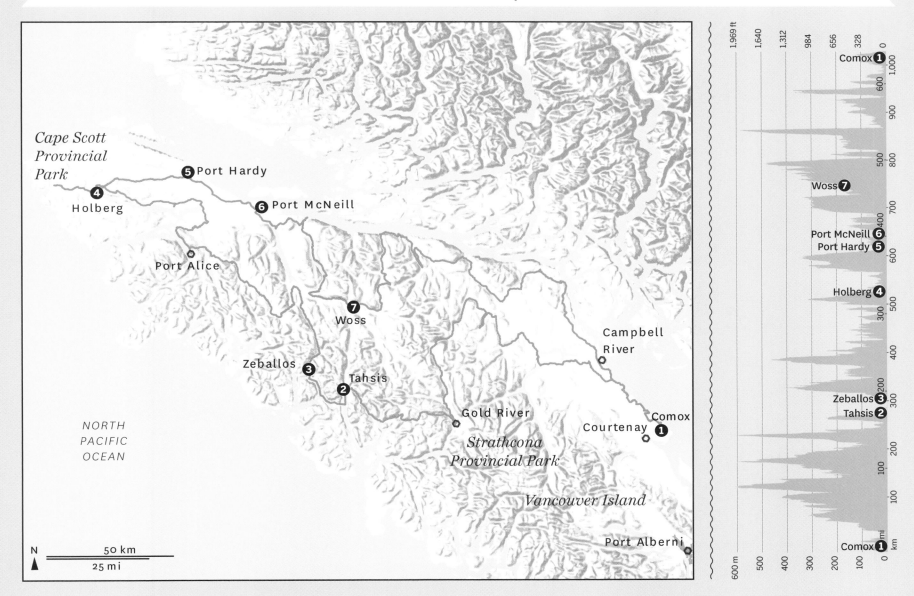

Cape Scott
Provincial
Park

5 Port Hardy

4
Holberg

6 Port McNeill

Port Alice

7
Woss

Zeballos **3**

Tahsis **2**

Campbell
River

Gold River

Comox

Courtenay **1**

*Strathcona
Provincial Park*

NORTH
PACIFIC
OCEAN

Vancouver Island

Port Alberni

N

50 km

25 mi

Comox **1**

Woss **7**

Port McNeill **6**
Port Hardy **5**

Holberg **4**

Zeballos **3**
Tahsis **2**

Comox **1**

1,969 ft
1,640
1,312
984
656
328
0

600 m
500
400
300
200
100
0

1,000
600
900
800
700
400
500
400
300
200
100
0 mi
0 km
100
200
300

→ Distance: 333 miles (535km)　　→ Ascent: 7180ft (2188m)　　→ Difficulty: 1

The Great Allegheny Passage

USA

Ride through Pennsylvania, Maryland and centuries of history on the GAP, tracing gravel trails, repurposed railways and the C&O Towpath between Pittsburgh and Washington, DC. You'll experience amazing architecture, natural beauty and numerous riverside towns along the way.

Plan and Prepare

Logistics

This route, from Pittsburgh to Washington, DC, features both the Great Allegheny Passage (GAP) and the Chesapeake & Ohio (C&O) Towpath. Both cities are easy to reach by train, plane or car – and as there's a direct Amtrak service, Capitol Unlimited, between the two, you can take the train back to the start in about 7hr (bicycles are permitted but advance reservations are required).

Hazards

Take note of the weather forecast: a lot of rain can mean floods, washouts or landslips along sections of the route. Also, some stretches are quite isolated so be sure to carry water and food. Bring lights (there are some long tunnels) and a lock for when you leave your bike unattended. In terms of wildlife, black bears have been sighted along the trail, but you're much more likely to meet mosquitoes.

Gear

Almost any bike can complete the GAP. At worst, the surface is a bit bumpy along the C&O Towpath. A gravel bike would be ideal; a mountain bike might be a little slow. An electric bike is possible. Mudguards (fenders) are recommended. You can decide how much gear you need to carry: it's possible to stay in B&Bs and inns the whole way, or use campgrounds. Carrying some cooking kit is advised.

Info

For the best weather, ride in June, July or August – but note that these are also the busiest months for bookings and other traffic on the trail. There are lots of free hiker-biker campgrounds or better-equipped public campgrounds (for a fee). The official route website (gaptrail.org) has a list of options and a lot of other useful information in a authoritative guidebook.

The Great Allegheny Passage starts from the Point State Park in central Pittsburgh where the Allegheny, Monongahela and Ohio rivers meet. Flowing in different directions, these waterways shaped modern Pittsburgh by spurring the city's rapid industrial development (learn more about them at the Carnegie Science Center, across the water, named after the Scottish-American industrialist who led the region's steel industry and became one of the wealthiest people in history). The GAP follows the Monongahela River out of town and then tracks other waterways to Cumberland, Maryland, where it meets the Chesapeake & Ohio Canal Towpath, which takes you the rest of the way into Washington, DC. Together the two trails are known as the GAP.

Gradients are minimal over the whole distance. Indeed, after 135 miles (217km), the route is largely downhill. With navigation that is mostly straightforward and the fact that you're never more than 20-30 miles (32-48km) from the next town, the GAP is a relatively accessible cycle-touring experience for novices. All you need to do is work out your ideal average distance and pinpoint a few of the interesting sights along the route and you're ready to roll. Plan on three to six days of riding, depending on experience, to complete the route.

From Pittsburgh

Do linger a while in Pittsburgh. The city has played a huge role in events that have defined the US, including the Revolutionary War, the American Civil War and the Underground Railroad. Half the nation's steel was later produced here, and it was also the birthplace of Andy Warhol: following the Monongahela, the GAP passes through Southside Pittsburgh, where you can explore giant street-art murals and cross the iconic Hot Metal Bridge before reaching Homestead, the heart of the steel industry.

Frank Lloyd Wright

The work of the acclaimed American architect is scattered across the US, from Florida to Oregon. But much of his mid-century work is in the Midwest and the Northeast, and it's possible to visit a couple of houses that he designed along the GAP. Foremost is Fallingwater, which was completed in 1939 and is a classic of organic architecture. The house is a 4-mile (6.5km) sidetrip from the route in Ohiopyle, Pennsylvania. Famously, it incorporates a waterfall, with the home's floors cantilevered above the flowing water and bare rock but, amazingly, not in such a way as to detract from the natural beauty. It is quite complicated to visit, however. You'll need to reserve a tour at least two weeks in advance (at fallingwater.org); note too that the lane up to the house is steep. But if Fallingwater is booked solid on the dates you desire, there's another Frank Lloyd Wright in Ohiopyle, even closer to the GAP: Kentuck Knob, another National Historic Landmark. But unlike Fallingwater, which was designed as a weekend retreat for a wealthy family, Kentuck Knob was intended to be affordable for the average American. Book a tour at kentuckknob.com

At McKeesport, the GAP switches onto the smaller Youghiogheny River, tracing a crushed-limestone riverside path into a more rural landscape. West Newton is a good option for a lunch break after about 35 miles (56km), as is Ohiopyle, surrounded by wooded hills, at 77 miles (124km), although there are numerous campgrounds and towns beforehand. The rivers here attract rafters and white-water kayakers, who come to enjoy the rapids.

In the heart of Pennsylvania's maple syrup country, Meyersdale, at 125 miles (201km), is another good stop, with outstanding restaurants and accommodation. On this section, before the terminus of the GAP at Cumberland, riders cross the Eastern Continental Divide, several significant bridges, and the Mason–Dixon Line (which demarcated the free states of the north and the southern states in the Civil War era) before the descent to Cumberland, Maryland.

The home stretch from Cumberland

Epicentre of the Whiskey Rebellion against tax during George Washington's presidency, Cumberland is at the 156-mile (251km) mark, where the GAP connects with the C&O Towpath along the Potomac River. The trail surface, maintained by the NPS, becomes a lot more variable. Passing through the Paw Paw tunnel leads into a green landscape of waterfalls and wildlife. The route follows the border with West Virginia, passing through places of Confederate history such as Harpers Ferry, before entering Washington, DC at Georgetown.

The Great Allegheny Passage

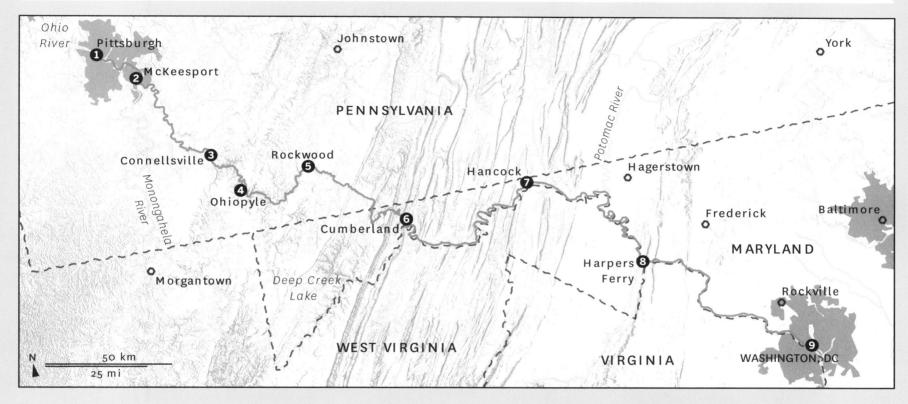

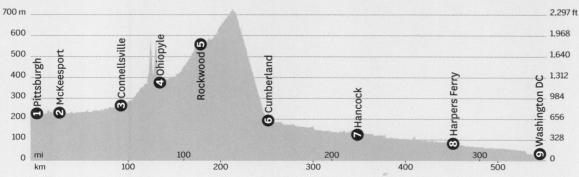

→ Distance: 238 miles (383km)　　→ Ascent: 7900ft (2408m)　　→ Difficulty: 1

Katy Trail

USA

Ride the country's longest rail trail across the Midwest state of Missouri to discover quaint country towns, the thriving city of St Louis, and echoes of the westward movement of settlers that shaped America.

Plan and Prepare

Logistics

The Katy Trail can be ridden in either direction. Machens, just outside St Louis, is the eastern end but many people pick up the trail at St Charles. The western end is at Clinton. Much of the route is on the St Louis to Kansas City Amtrak line, so you can start from St Louis, take the train to Sedalia and ride back. Clinton is about 35 miles (56km) southwest of Sedalia.

Hazards

The summer heat and humidity is a hazard in July and August, so hydrate properly if riding at that time. The surface is good and there are no difficult features on the trail other than a few road crossings. Dangerous wildlife is limited to some venomous snakes, such as copperheads and rattlesnakes.

Gear

A standard road or touring bike is ideal. You won't need especially knobbly tyres and a mountain bike will be much slower. Do carry puncture-repair kit, whether you're going tubeless or not. Insect repellent is essential to keep the bugs at bay. There are private campgrounds if you wish to carry a tent instead of using accommodation; wild camping isn't permitted.

Info

The ideal time of year to ride the route is May, before the weather gets too hot; and September and October, to see some autumn colour. There's food and lodging along the route if you prefer to travel light. Missouri State Parks (mostateparks.com) organises an annual five-day Katy Trail Ride, although it was cancelled in 2021 due to flooding. There's useful info at bikekatytrail.com

When the Missouri–Kansas–Texas (MKT) Railroad gradually closed in the 1980s, one section of the line – from St Charles near St Louis to Sedalia in eastern Missouri – was marked for conversion into a rail trail. This wasn't a novel concept, with the Elroy-Sparta State Trail in Wisconsin dating from 1965, but following the US Congress' deregulation of America's railways in 1980, the rate of abandoned routes quickly surged: it's thought that some 4000-8000 miles of railroad (6437-12,875km) were closed in the 1980s. Only a fraction of the lines earned an afterlife as a rail trail, but the Katy Trail was one of them. Construction started in 1987 and the final sections were completed in the 1990s. The result is arguably the finest rail trail in the US, spanning the north of Missouri along the state's eponymous river.

The appeal of a rail trail to casual cyclists is clear: because the routes follow train lines, and train lines favour flat ground, rail trails tend not to have many steep inclines. And they're often surfaced with gravel, and travel through towns where once there may have been stations. Those factors combine to make them convenient and safe routes for all cyclists.

Starting from St Louis

The Katy Trail is the longest rail trail in the US. It follows the Missouri River, which flows from the Rockies towards St Louis, where it meets the Mississippi. Most riders tackle it from St Charles, on the outskirts of St Louis, to Sedalia, and then have the option of turning south to complete the 39-mile (63km) extension to Clinton. When working out how long to set aside, calculating average speed and multiplying by hours usually gives an accurate estimate – but don't forget to add on time (perhaps days) for sightseeing.

With St Louis' Gateway Arch behind you and the Missouri River on your left, you'll quickly enter a slower-paced landscape of giant limestone bluffs and small-town America. There's regular evidence of the former railroad, such as tunnels punched through solid rock in Rocheport; trestle bridges; and four restored depots. There are no fewer than 26 trailheads along the route that provide restrooms and sometimes water fountains. Towns arrive at frequent intervals, including state capital Jefferson City. Make a small detour for the quaint Missouri town of Hermann, at the 75-mile mark (121km). It's known for its Germanic heritage and as a Midwestern centre of wine production, with several wineries on its outskirts that are open for tastings. After further potential breaks in bijoux Rocheport

or Boonville, arrival at Sedalia offers the choice of completing the whole route by cycling to Clinton (and back), or taking the Amtrak back to the start.

Several spots along the Katy Trail have connections with the Lewis and Clark expedition of 1803 to 1806, as the ride shares part of the same route. Meriwether Lewis and William Clark, with the help of Sacagawea, a young Lemhi Shoshone woman who interpreted local Native American languages for the party, set off westward, stopping at Marthasville and what is now Jefferson City. They weren't the first white people to travel this far west, and the subsequent westward expansion of white settlers didn't benefit the Native American people of the continent, but their journey is significant to the history of the US.

Rail trails in the USA

Somewhat unusually, the Missouri–Kansas–Texas Railroad (known as the MKT or Katy Railroad) on which the Katy Trail is based (or at least the Missouri section of it) ran north to south rather than east to west. It wound up in Texas, connecting such cities as Galveston, Dallas and San Antonio with the northern cities of Kansas City and St Louis, carrying a lot of cattle as well as its regular human passengers. Although only the northern part of the line is now the main Katy Trail, a short section of the old railroad through Houston is now the Heights Hike-and-Bike Trail. Back in the Midwest, there

are several more rails-to-trails conversions to seek out. The Elroy to Sparta route, thought to be the first rail trail in the US, is a bucolic day-ride through southwest Wisconsin. The town of Sparta is the hub for several state cycling trails. In Illinois, the Prairie Path covers some 61 miles (98km) along the abandoned Chicago Aurora and Elgin Railroad, and passes through pretty suburbs such as Glen Ellyn. And up in Michigan, the Pere Marquette Rail Trail, from Midland to Clare, traces a railroad through forests and farmland, and was built to link timber towns.

Katy Trail

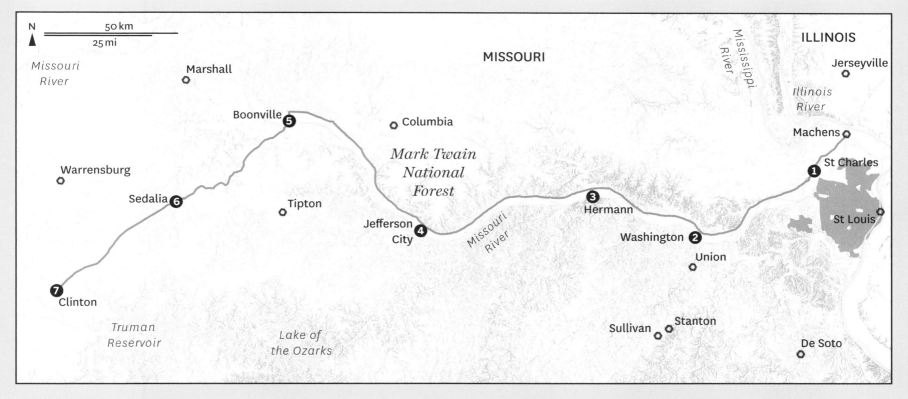

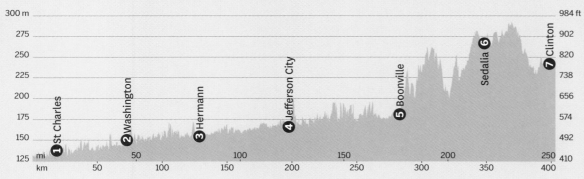

➡️ **Distance:** 255 miles (410km) ➡️ **Ascent:** 21,000ft (6400m) ➡️ **Difficulty:** 4

Kenai 250

USA

Find adventure, clear lakes, great singletrack and possibly some grizzly bears on Alaska's Kenai Peninsula along this well-established multi-day loop. You'll gain a sense of achievement and some once-in-a-lifetime memories on the Kenai 250.

Plan and Prepare

Logistics

The Kenai 250 is a loop, so riders can start from anywhere. However, the most convenient-to-reach settlement is also the largest: Seward. Riders can get to Seward from Anchorage by rental car, bus or Alaska Railroad trains. The latter two typically charge additional fees ($20) for oversized baggage such as boxed bicycles – check current policies. Journey time from Anchorage to Seward is up to 4hr.

Hazards

Backcountry Alaska has no shortage of potential hazards, but all can be managed safely with some education and common sense. Grizzly bears are the most obviously risky residents, but moose can be just as dangerous – research how to interact safely with them. The weather can change quickly, so constant monitoring of the forecast is essential; there are also some water crossings that require care. Note too that there's no cell reception along most of the route.

Gear

This is a mountain-bike route so bring a mountain bike, ideally with full suspension. You won't want to get stuck so carry tools, standard spares such as chain links and spokes, and gear for repairing punctures. Warm, waterproof clothing is a must – as are a tent and sleeping bag, though there are cabins and some small towns with accommodation on the route. You can buy bear spray and bug repellent in Anchorage.

Info

Snow will usually have melted sufficiently by the end of May but will start collecting again come late September. The least rainfall is supposedly in July, but you can still expect to get wet a lot. Much of the route is within the Chugach National Forest and several designated campgrounds have bear-proof lockers and other facilities (details at fs.usda.gov). There's lots of useful info on the route and race at bikepacking.com

There are regular adventures – and then there are adventures in Alaska. This vast state offers supercharged wilderness experiences, but you'll need some outdoors expertise in order to avoid potential problems. Take the Kenai 250 bikepacking route: it's accessible by Alaskan standards, being close to Anchorage on the Kenai Peninsula, but it's also a route that demands backcountry know-how and isn't the right ride for first-timers. That's for several reasons. First, there's the isolation of Alaska, which has the lowest population density of all US states: there are simply fewer towns, shops, emergency services or people around to help. Then there are the living creatures that you'll share the terrain with: brown bears, which can be dangerous if surprised or separated from their cubs; and moose, also a potential hazard if provoked – look for raised hairs and flattened ears. Finally, it can seem as if the land and sky are conspiring against you. It rains a lot, and can become windy or snowy at any instant. And all the rain means undergrowth grows rampantly – by mid- or late summer, many of the trails are overgrown.

The positives? There's certainly an appeal to being on the edge of civilisation, surrounded by a genuinely wild landscape. The scenery is epic and there's always a sense of the elemental power of the natural world. And on this particular route, there's some great singletrack for mountain-biking.

The original iteration of the Kenai 250 route was as a bikepacking race, first held more than a decade ago. The organisers were careful to stress that it was a self-supported race. Most years there were few entrants, perhaps a dozen brave souls. In 2021, 24 people finished from 39 starters, with the winner taking just under 30hr. It's a friendly event with people helping each other out.

Biking Kenai

The route makes a good bikepacking loop that non-racing riders can do in their own time, counting their progress in days not hours. The race starts from Hope, just across Turnagain Arm from Anchorage, but Seward to the south is a larger settlement, has better public transport connections, and may make for a better base, being the gateway to Kenai Fjords National Park. Whether you start from Seward or Hope, you'll be covering the same ground. More than half the route is fun singletrack riding, with rocks and roots providing some extra challenge with a laden bike. The singletrack sections are connected by gravel or surfaced roads, so there's sometimes an easy escape route back to a nearby town.

One of the trickiest sections is the loop around the Russian Lakes region, which is notorious for being bear habitat. You'll notice the bear scat and it's certainly worth carrying bear bells on your bike to warn any ursine locals of your approach. Cooper Landing is the settlement where several trails coincide. It's just south of the highest point of the loop, where the Devil's Pass Trail and Resurrection Pass Trail meet. Another good loop-within-a-loop is the Lost Lake section (above) towards Seward, where the singletrack bike trails meet some of the Iditarod Trail from Seward to Nome, 1000 miles (1610km) away and the endpoint of the epic annual Iditarod dog-sled race. Throughout the Kenai 250 loop, there are campgrounds and rentable cabins offering varying degrees of comfort.

Kenai Fjords National Park

Seward sits on the edge of the Kenai Fjords National Park, and if you've come this far it makes sense to explore the park too. As the name suggests, Kenai Fjords is known for its glacial geology and spectacular coastline. Around 40 glaciers have left their mark on the landscape, although they're all currently retreating, ever-more quickly. They're calved by the Harding Ice Field, which covers 700 sq miles (1813 sq km) of the Kenai mountains. You can take a day-hike to the Harding Icefield from Exit Glacier. Another essential way of exploring Kenai Fjords is by boat or kayak.

This is a marine park, with an amazing roll call of animals that you're likely to spot, including orca, sea otters, porpoises, Steller sea lions and, in spring and early summer, several species of whale, which migrate here to feed. There is weeks-worth of world-class paddling possible in the region, but novices will need to stick to sea-kayaking tours departing Seward, to explore Resurrection Bay and calm Aialik Bay. You'll still be able to see glaciers where they meet the sea. On land you may also spot black and brown bears, mountain goats, moose and marmots.

Kenai 250

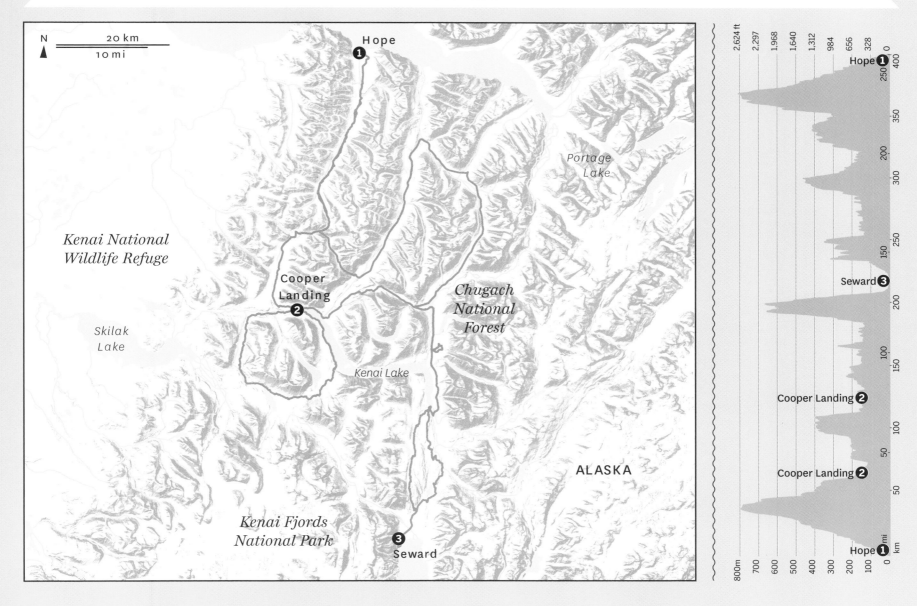

➡ **Distance:** 118 miles (190km) ➡ **Ascent:** 6080ft (1853m) ➡ **Difficulty:** 2

Cowichan Valley 8

Canada

An ideal ride for a long weekend, this figure-of-eight loop winds around parks and lakes in the south of Vancouver Island using bike paths and gravel tracks. It's a soothing and scenic experience in not-too-wild nature.

Plan and Prepare

Logistics

This figure-of-eight loop sets off from Victoria, the island capital of British Columbia. The city sits at the southern tip of Vancouver Island and can be reached from the city of Vancouver, the international gateway to the province, in around 3hr by car or around 6hr if cycling.

Hazards

Be aware that there are some cougars and black bears on Vancouver Island (although there are no brown bears) – but you're much more likely to encounter bugs, so bring insect repellent. The island is regularly battered by storms coming in off the Pacific: check weather forecasts and note that some parts of the trails are prone to washouts after a lot of rain.

Gear

Gravel bikes are ideal for this ride as, indeed, is almost any bike with 35mm tyres or wider. You'll need a modest amount of luggage-carrying capacity (less so if you've booked a cabin rather than a camping spot). A water purification system is useful since there are abundant water sources. You will likely have cellphone coverage for much of the ride.

Info

There's no wilderness camping along this route, but there are several official campgrounds in the provincial parks that you can use (book ahead during the peak summer season). There are also private campsites and cabins available. Although summer (July and August) is a fine time to ride in Vancouver Island's mild climate, don't discount off-peak trips. Check bikepacking.com for more information on the route.

There's a general rule of cycling adventures that rides involving ferries are a good thing. For most people, this relaxed route starts off with a ferry trip to Victoria and it gets you into the right frame of mind: mellow and meditative. And there's another ferry to take across Mill Bay.

The ride, which Miles Arbour and friends stitched together from a number of existing and signposted trails, follows a figure-of-eight north of Victoria up to Lake Cowichan and back through fragrant pine woodlands and some interesting First Nations sites. With regularly spaced campgrounds (most people will spend one or two nights out) and a route that is mostly surfaced with few natural obstacles to tackle, this is a family-friendly trip, doable by capable younger children. That said, there are some sustained climbs with steep sections towards the start and a few stretches of trail that are rougher than the rest.

Leaving Victoria

The starting point of the Cowichan Valley 8 is easy to find: it's British Columbia's Parliament buildings. From there riders pick up the Vancouver Island portion of one of the world's longest cross-country trails, the Trans Canada, stretching across the country from the Pacific to the Arctic. But you're only following a short stretch of it: winding through Victoria's backstreets and into the surrounding farmland as it co-opts the Galloping Goose Regional Trail out to Glen Lake, then heading north onto the gravel Sooke Hills Wilderness Trail, which bears the brunt of the uphill work. The effort is rewarded with views of the Waugh Creek Falls before you cross a suspension bridge across the Goldstream River (named after a short-lived gold rush here in the 1860s). The descent takes you down to Shawnigan Lake, about 31 miles (50km) from the start.

Lake Cowichan and back

The next bridge is more spectacular: the Kinsol Trestle over the salmon-rich Koksilah River is one of the highest free-standing wooden trestles in the world. It's the largest of several trestles along the Cowichan Valley Trail (CVT), which is the route you'll take up to Lake Cowichan. The CVT is an easy gravel path that follows the Cowichan River to the town of Lake Cowichan, which is a popular place to take a dip in the water (there are also several public beaches beside Shawnigan Lake). The official motto here is 'slow down, savour life', which is a reasonable exhortation given the many cafes and pubs. But you can't stay forever and the return ride to Victoria is just as enjoyable. Riders take the CVT south via Cowichan River Provincial Park and

the Stoltz Pool Campground. The ferns and moss on the trees are a reminder of Vancouver Island's temperate coastal rainforest climate.

After 75 miles (121km) you'll reach Duncan (population 5000, and the smallest city by area in Canada), where you can top up your caffeine reserves. There's a large Cowichan Tribes community in Duncan and a number of totem poles, each with a biography of the carver, who should be acknowledged if posting a photo on social media.

After Duncan, riders cross the Kinsol Trestle again and then skirt the north shore of Shawnigan Lake before catching the ferry across Mill Bay, which runs year-round. Then it's back into downtown Victoria on the Lochside Regional Trail.

Vancouver's First Nations

You'll be pedalling through First Nations Territory on this ride and if you wish to learn more about the traditional custodians of the land, the British Columbia Assembly of First Nations offers a great introduction (bcafn.ca). Of the population of Vancouver Island (some 864,800 people), about 5% are First Nations, which is the highest proportion of any region in British Columbia. Around Victoria and Cowichan, there are several First Nations groups including the Cowichan Tribes, a group of some 5000 people concentrated around seven traditional villages: Kw'amutsun, Qwum'yiqun', Hwulqwselu, S'amuna', L'uml'umuluts, Hinupsum and Tl'ulpalus. About half

its members live on the Cowichan Tribes Reserve.

In Victoria itself, the Songhees First Nations comprise five main families and several smaller families, part of the Coast Salish people. This is an ethnically and linguistically related people who live along the North American coast northward from Oregon. Traditionally, the Coast Salish were fishers, harvesting Pacific salmon. Coast Salish villages featured longhouses that could accommodate large families, with beams or posts carved and painted to honour family ancestors. Many of these First Nations groups are still recovering traditions and artwork lost after the arrival of Europeans.

Cowichan Valley 8

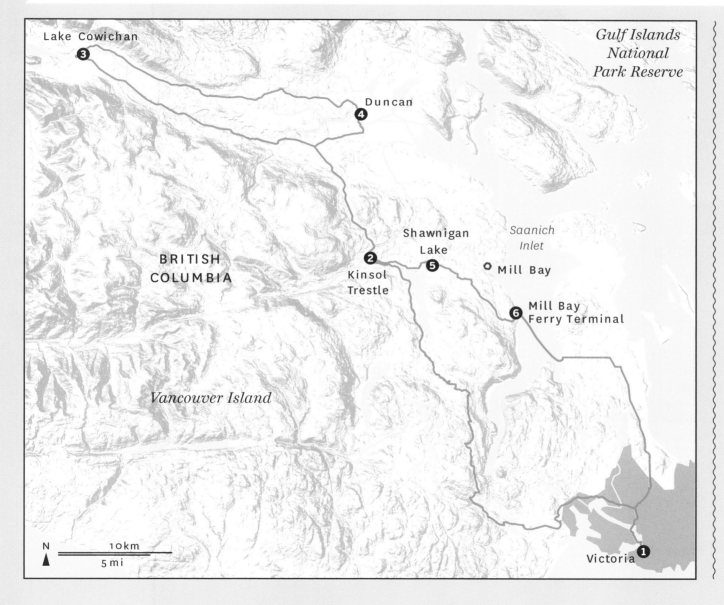

Lake Cowichan ❸

Gulf Islands National Park Reserve

Duncan ❹

BRITISH COLUMBIA

Kinsol Trestle ❷

Shawnigan Lake ❺

Saanich Inlet

⬡ Mill Bay

Mill Bay Ferry Terminal ❻

Vancouver Island

N
10km
5mi

Victoria ❶

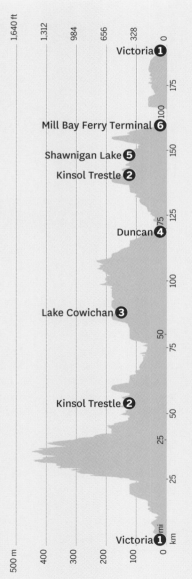

1,640 ft
1,312
984
656
328
0

Victoria ❶
Mill Bay Ferry Terminal ❻
Shawnigan Lake ❺
Kinsol Trestle ❷
Duncan ❹
Lake Cowichan ❸
Kinsol Trestle ❷
Victoria ❶

500 m
400
300
200
100
0 km

175
100
150
125
75
100
50
75
50
25
25
0 mi

→ Distance: 62 miles (100km)   → Ascent: 4050ft (1234m)   → Difficulty: 2

Finger Lakes Overnighter

USA

Enjoy a taste of the open road in New York State's wine country. This summery sojourn takes in backroads, rail trails and some off-road tracks for a fun loop through farmland and forest.

Plan and Prepare

Logistics

The route starts in Watkins Glen, as it's the largest town on the loop – but you could dive in from anywhere that's convenient. There's limited public transport to Watkins Glen. Buses from New York City typically require a change at Ithaca, so driving will likely be the best option. You should be able to leave your car overnight in the town or, if you notify park authorities in advance, at the Watkins Glen State Park overflow lot.

Hazards

Although this route is rated at the easier end of the scale, there are still hills that may prove daunting to novice bikepackers. The main hazard, when walking or camping in the brush, are ticks, which can spread diseases. Do a thorough check of your body and research how to remove ticks safely. Also, you might need to cross a field containing cows: exercise caution, as some can be feisty.

Gear

A gravel bike would be ideal for this route, if fitted with some wide, grippy tyres, but mountain bikes are also fine. There are some loose and rocky climbs but most of the route is on backroads. Carry a lightweight tent, mat and sleeping bag plus whatever stove or coffee-making kit you require in the morning. A filter will save you carrying water all the way. Insect repellent is advised.

Info

The ideal time to ride the route is spring (during April and May) or autumn (September and October) when the foliage is at its finest. Summer is also acceptable but there will be more bugs, more people and more humidity. There's useful information at bikepacking.com; check fs.usda.gov for details on camping in Watkins Glen State Forest.

The rural Finger Lakes region of upstate New York is best known as a place of wine-touring weekend retreats for stressed-out city dwellers. But if you're just as interested in riding bikes as tasting cool-climate Pinot Noir (or perhaps combining the two activities), then a weekend of bikepacking is an equally good opportunity for bonding with buddies. At just 62 miles (100km), with a moderate amount of ascent, this loop around the farms and forests of Finger Lakes could be completed in a day by a regular cyclist. But that's not the point: this is more of a slow-down-and-smell-the-roses type of ride (that will still challenge novice bike riders). It was created by Jim DeWitt and developed by Miles Arbour as part of bikepacking.com's Local Overnighters Project.

The route heads south down the Catharine Valley Trail (a former rail line), loops back north via Odessa, the only other village on the way, then circles around the Finger Lakes National Forest before returning southward to Watkins Glen. Most people carry a tent (share the burden with friends) and pitch it at a campground in the national forest before heating up food and perhaps opening a bottle to share.

Watkins Glen and around

Watkins Glen lies at the southern tip of Seneca Lake, one of the long, slender lakes that lend this region its name. It's a pleasant town with a harbour, handsome Gothic Revival architecture downtown, and a farmers market on Fridays where you can pick up locally grown produce if you want to go gourmet on the ride. North along the lake lies the Seneca Lake Wine Trail; again, you could tie in a visit to a winery or two. East is Watkins Glen State Park, distinguished by some dramatic gorges and waterfalls.

Riding the loop

From Watkins Glen, the route heads out on the gravel Catharine Valley Trail south to Millport via Montour Falls. This is a leafy introduction to the ride, following the former Northern Central Railway. After Millport, turn left onto the first (but not last) sustained climb, which continues for more than 5 miles (8km) but delivers some fine views. The route levels out on quiet country backroads, punctuated by grain silos, before a descent into Catharine, where another abandoned railway leads to Odessa and your last chance to buy provisions.

From Odessa, which is at the 21-mile (34km) mark, it's worth pressing on northward, bypassing Texas Hollow State Forest in order to reach the Finger Lakes National Forest after about 34 miles

(55km). This is the best destination for camping, but it does mean a longer first day in the saddle. Once you've left the main road and conquered a steep gravel grind into the forest, you have several options. Dispersed camping is permitted so long as you camp more than 200ft (60m) from trails or water: there are some good spots along Chicken Coop or Potomac roads. Of the official campgrounds, Blueberry Patch is regarded as the best, offering toilets, tables and nine sites on a first-come-first-served basis.

The next day, the route loops around the forest on a mix of trails (the No-Tan-Takto through pasture can be slow and muddy but readily bypassed) before you exit the forest and follow a gravel road beside Seneca Lake back to Watkins Glen.

Finger Lakes wine

Finger Lakes is best known for its vineyards, which thrive around these glacier-carved lakes thanks to a fortunate series of microclimates. Although winters are harsh here, the deep lakes moderate the temperatures, protecting the grape vines growing there. Most of the wineries are clustered on or near the shores of three lakes: Keuka, Seneca and Cayuga. Riesling is the standout wine hereabouts but great wines are also being made with other varieties that you'd most usually find in northern Europe, such as Gewürztraminer, Chardonnay and Blaufränkisch. Some success is also being had with Pinot Noir and other red varieties.

Touring some of the wineries, with or without your bike, is a great way to learn a bit more about this unusual region. Vines were first planted here in the 1950s by an Ukrainian immigrant, Dr Konstantin Frank. He believed that some European varieties would survive this far north and was confident enough to open his winery, just west of Keuka Lake, in 1962 (below). Most of the wineries in the region offering tastings, usually for a fee of around $20 and some by appointment only. Bottles of wine can be bought for around a minimum of $20. 'You are catching the burst and growth of a wine region finding itself,' says winemaker Kelby Russell of Seneca Lake's Red Newt Wine Cellars.

© Jim DeWitt; Stu Gallagher

Finger Lakes Overnighter

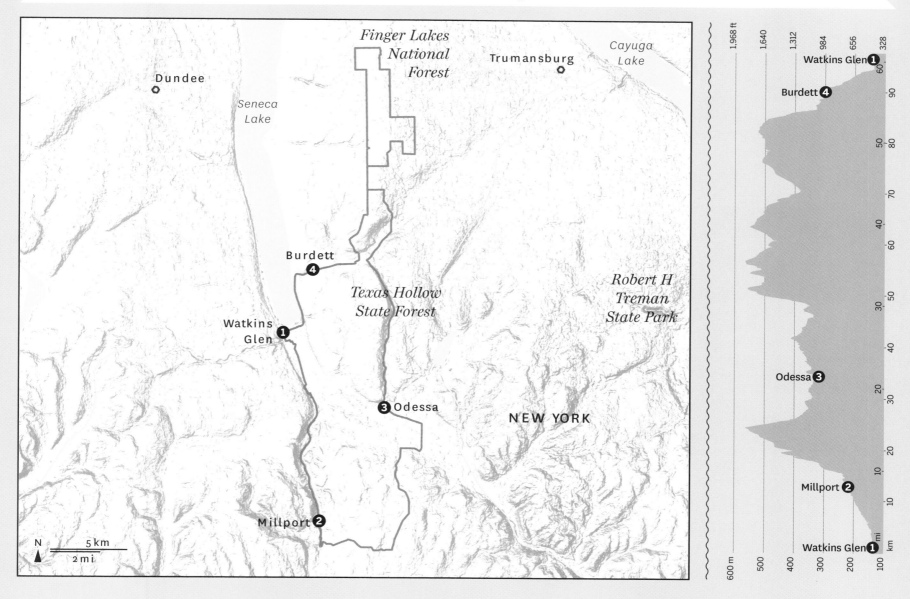

Finger Lakes
National
Forest

Cayuga
Lake

Trumansburg

Dundee

Seneca
Lake

Burdett **4**

Texas Hollow
State Forest

Robert H
Treman
State Park

Watkins
Glen **1**

Odessa **3**

NEW YORK

Millport **2**

N 5 km
   2 mi

1,968 ft
1,640
1,312
984
656
328

Watkins Glen **1**

Burdett **4**

Odessa **3**

Millport **2**

Watkins Glen **1**

600 m
500
400
300
200
100

→ Distance: 858 miles (1368km)   → Ascent: 115,370ft (35,165m)   → Difficulty: 5

Trans Ecuador Mountain Bike Route

Ecuador

Discover Inca legends, colonial-era cities and amazing volcanoes on this high-altitude, off-road route along the length of Ecuador. The nation's natural world will leave you breathless, but regular pitstops at towns and villages make this an achievable goal for experienced bikepackers.

Plan and Prepare

Logistics

The route covers the length of Ecuador from the north at Tulcán to Vilcabamba in the south. Reaching Tulcán from Quito, Ecuador's capital and international gateway, requires a taxi and bus combination via Pifo. But you could also abbreviate the route and pick it up at Tumbaco, just east of Quito. From Vilcabamba, options include buses north or a flight from Ciudad de Catamayo Airport, 43 miles (70km) north, to Quito.

Hazards

Clearly, this is an extremely challenging route even for experienced bikepackers. It's at a very high altitude, reaching over 13,125ft (4000m), so acclimatisation and an understanding of altitude-related ailments is essential. You should also expect changeable mountain weather at any time. Much of the route is very isolated, with limited communications coverage. However, this part of the Andes is generally safe, although some thefts have been reported.

Gear

Mountain bikes are essential, with tyres as wide and robust as will fit. But you'll need to travel as lightly as possibly, given the amount of ascent, so select lightweight camping and cooking kit and carry only what you need. Pack warm and waterproof clothing for the rain and wind, sunblock for the sun and a water purification system for the plentiful water along the route.

Info

The route crosses several climatic zones, but generally Ecuador's dry season is from mid-June to mid-September and is the best time of year to ride. Temperatures will go quite low at night, possibly down to freezing. For navigation, combine a good paper map with a GPS unit (carry a means of charging it). All towns offer accommodation but you'll need to camp in between: choose pitches that are not visible from roads. Check bikepacking. com for more info.

Hummingbirds flit in front of your face while in the distance an active volcano smoulders: Ecuador has both beauty and drama to offer the bikepacking cyclist. Sightseeing highlights and the wonders of the wilderness are revealed on a cross-country route along the Andes through this small South American nation, roughly the same size as the US state of Colorado. Starting from the northern border with Colombia, the Trans Ecuador Mountain Bike Route (TEMBR) undulates up and down in a southerly direction towards Peru. 'Undulates' is an understatement: this is a seriously mountainous land and an average daily ascent of 5000ft (1524m) can be expected. As a result, this is one for experienced and fit riders only.

The route has been pioneered by a party of bikepackers: Cass Gilbert, Nick Gault and, in particular, the Dammer brothers, three Ecuadorians who guide and plot bikepacking routes in between tending their organic farm. It's intended as a slightly less difficult version of the singletrack TEMBR, which consists of many hike-a-bike trails. Instead, you'll be using some cobbled climbs, which hint at the length of time humans have been surviving in these highlands.

As the TEMBR starts in the high páramo, at an elevation of around 10,000ft (3048m), you'll need to have acclimatised before you begin pedalling through clusters of tall frailejon plants. Over the first 150 miles (240km), there are *hostals* and camping spots in which to lay your head at night. And then you reach Otavalo, deep in the green foothills of the Andes. This town is famous as the site of Ecuador's largest market of traditional textiles and handicrafts. It's also a great place to rest and fill up on good food. Beyond, another hard climb leads riders up to Laguna de Cuicocha (right), a water-filled caldera created 3000 years ago after a volcanic eruption (and now a fine camping spot).

Ingapirca

Ecuador's key pre-Columbian archaeological site is about 40 miles (64km) north of the city of Cuenca. This whole region, including Cuenca, has an indigenous history dating back at least 5000 years. The Cañari people settled here around 2000 years ago. Incas invaded and conquered the Cañari in the mid-15th century, then subsequently developed the hilltop site at Ingapirca, building roads that ran all the way to Peru and Colombia as well as buildings, stone calendars and the only Temple of the Sun in the Inca Empire. This ruin is still the focal point for the annual Festival of the Sun, Inti Raymi, celebrated every June. But Ingapirca was short-lived: in 1532 a war between Inca brothers destroyed the settlement, then Spanish conquistadors grabbed its stones for empire-building of their own. Nonetheless, the semi-intact temple and surrounding ruins are fascinating; there's also a small museum displaying Inca and Cañari artefacts.

Riding volcano country

Just over 40 miles (64km) south of Tumbaco, riders enter the enthralling tundra of Parque Nacional Cotopaxi. Its centrepiece, Cotopaxi, is a large, active volcano that began a fresh eruptive period in 2015 after 70 years of slumber. It's the second-highest point in Ecuador, at 19,347ft (5897m), but there a couple of more accessible volcanoes coming up.

Some 60 miles (96km) beyond Cotopaxi, the first is 12,841ft-high (3914m) Volcán Quilotoa. The landscape around Quilotoa is much more agricultural, with fields planted with quinoa and colourful potato varieties, and herds of sheep and llamas tended by shepherds. Quilotoa is a popular destination for backpackers so there are plenty of places to stay and eat. And the Quilotoa Loop is a famous hike (see Lonely Planet's *Epic Hikes of the Americas*) that takes three days or more, passing the volcano's water-filled crater.

Next is the even more imposing stratovolcano, Chimborazo. In fact, although it's not as tall as Mt Everest, at 20,548ft (6,263m), its summit is actually the furthest point on the planet from the centre of the Earth thanks to the bulge around the Equator here. With the help of certified local guides, it's possible to climb above the clouds to the top of Chimborazo in a (long) day, but even if you're not an aspiring mountaineer, the diversion into Chimborazo's wildlife reserve is highly recommended; it's home to hundreds of vicuña (a wild relative of the llama). There are mountain refuges, such as Refugio Jean-Antoine Carrel, in which to overnight.

Continuing south, you're about halfway to the border with Peru but many riders finish the trip at the colonial city of Cuenca, in about 200 miles (320km). Don't miss the Inca ruins of Ingapirca on the way.

Trans Ecuador Mountain Bike Route

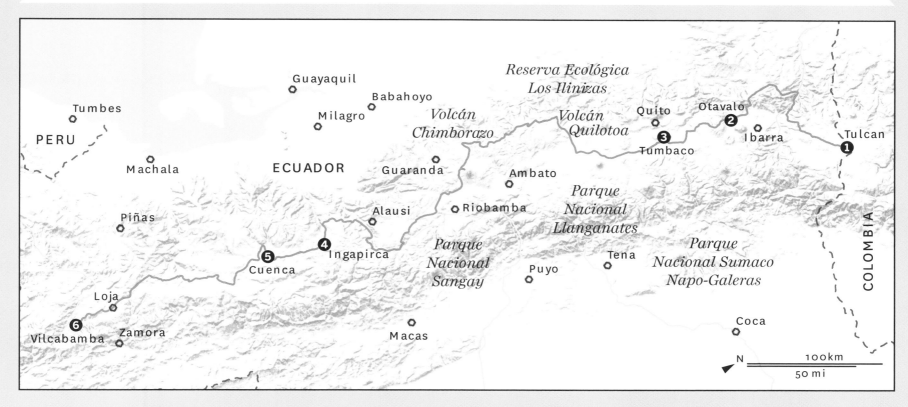

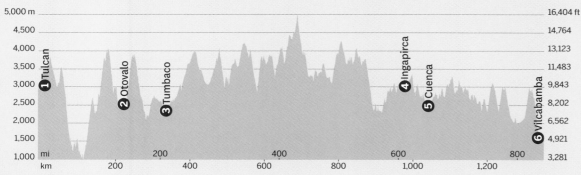

More to ride

Six more superb routes in the Americas

Great Divide Mountain Bike Route
Canada & USA

Distance: 2667 miles (4292km)
Difficulty: 4

The GDMBR traces the Continental Divide of North America from Jasper in Alberta, Canada to Antelope Wells in New Mexico. At times this 'great divide' is as lofty as the snow-tipped Rocky Mountains and at other times it is a desert, but one constant is that water flows off one side to the east from the other side westward. This off-road adventure, perhaps the best-established bikepacking route in the US, is raced annually as the Tour Divide and is an unforgettable test of endurance. Highlights range from Grand Teton National Park to the Gila Wilderness in New Mexico. Taken at your own pace, the amount of ascent remains staggering – but so is the support you receive from people on the route.

Salar de Uyuni
Bolivia

Distance: 110 miles (177km)
Difficulty: 2

Cycling across the salt pans of Uyuni and neighbouring Coipasa is a unique experience and one that is very achievable. The start of this short route is in Sabaya, which can be reached with a couple of bus trips from the Bolivian capital, La Paz. A tailwind should guide you to Uyuni across the arid salt lakes of the altiplano, with another bus ride at the end to get back to La Paz. The first section is across the Salar de Coipasa, salt crystals crunching beneath your tyres (which should be as wide as possible). The lively town of Llica lies between this salt lake and the Salar de Uyuni – and then the silence of the desert returns. It's a journey you can only do in the Bolivian winter (May to October).

East Coast Greenway
USA

Distance: 3000 miles (4828km)
Difficulty: 1

The ECG is a project to build a safe cycling and walking route along the eastern seaboard of the US, through 15 states from Florida to Maine. It's a work-in-progress, with around 1000 miles (1600km) completed, often connecting established bike paths and rail trails through a huge variety of landscapes, from natural scenery along rivers and through forests to urban and industrial communities that are equally enthralling. A favourite and mostly singposted stretch that can be ridden right now is through Maine, from Kittery in the south to Calais in the north for 367 miles (590km). The ECG deliberately doesn't avoid urban centres so you'll cycle into Portland and follow byways and rural roads to places like Brunswick, Camden and Rockland, as well as Maine's largest marsh, Scarborough.

Coast to Coast
Cuba

Distance: 866 miles (1394km)
Difficulty: 4

There's no better way of exploring the Caribbean island of Cuba than by bicycle. For one thing, Cuba's pace of life, outside of its cities, is more attuned to the bike than to the automobile – you'll meet more people and experience more serendipitous moments than if you tour by rental car. Researched by Logan Watts and Joe Cruz of bikepacking.com, this is a largely off-road route across the length of the island, from the eastern city of Santiago de Cuba to Havana in the west; it's a challenging trip and is also known as La Ruta Mala. You might be better off using some of the quiet local roads rather than a dirt tracks. As there's a train service between Santiago de Cuba and Havana that has several stops, including at Camagüey, you could mix train and bicycle if you don't have three full weeks free to ride the whole thing.

The Cabot Trail
Canada

Distance: 186 miles (300km)
Difficulty: 2

Nova Scotia's social history is revealed on this loop around Cape Breton that could easily be tackled in a long weekend. Most people cycling around this wind-scoured outpost of Canada's Atlantic coast start from Baddeck in the southeast and head clockwise. At times you'll be greeted with the tricolore of Acadia, what was once New France and extending over Nova Scotia, Prince Edward Island and New Brunswick. French settlers arrived from America and Europe in the 17th and 18th centuries. Also settling here were Scottish people who had fled the Highland Clearances in the 19th century, which is why some signs have subtitles in Gaelic. The route itself is on hilly roads through sublime scenery. Riders often travel light and overnight in B&Bs or inns.

TransAmerica Bicycle Trail
USA

Distance: 4215 miles (6783km)
Difficulty: 3

The TransAmerica Bicycle Trail dates from the 1970s and was intended as a way of celebrating the bicentennial of the US and the Declaration of Independence. Around 4000 people began the cross-country ride that had been plotted by the founders of what is now the Adventure Cycling Association. They were largely inexperienced long-distance cyclists and rarely riding fancy machines, but the 90-day bike ride was life-changing for many and also kickstarted the remarkable Adventure Cycling Association, today a thriving nonprofit which provides information and inspiration on almost 30 tours around the US. The TransAmerica Bicycle Trail itself starts from Astoria on the Oregon coast and ends in Yorktown, Virginia, by way of Yellowstone National Park, Wyoming's Grand Teton Range, the Great Plains and the Appalachians. You don't have to ride it all in one go.

Index

A

Adriatic Crest, Croatia 120–123
Alps 2 Ocean, New Zealand 58–61
Atlas Mountain Race, Morocco 12–17
Attack of the Buns, Australia 68–71
Australia
  Attack of the Buns, NSWs 68–71
  Goldfields Track, VIC 52–57
  Hunt 1000, ACT/NSW/VIC 78–83
  Mawson Trail, SA 62–67
  Munda Biddi, WA 90–95
  Murray to the Mountains, VIC 96–99
  Otway Rip, Victoria 117
  Tasmanian Trail, Tasmania 104–109
  Tour D'Top End, Northern Territory 110–115
Austria
  Danube Cycle Path 132–137

B

Baja Divide, Mexico 232–235
Bamboo Byway, Thailand/Laos/Vietnam 116
Bartang Valley, Tajikistan 30–35
BC Trail, Canada 236–239
Belgium
  Meuse Cycle Route 160–163
Bergensbanen, Norway 168
Bikamino, South Africa 18–21
bike bags & boxes 6
Bikepacking Kjölur, Iceland 156–159
bikes 8
Bolivia
  Camino dél Puma 240–243
  Salar de Uyuni 294
Border Roads, Tibetan Sichuan, China 36–41
Bosnia & Hercegovina
  Trans Dinarica Trail 224
Burrally, Spain 124–127

C

Cabot Trail, Canada 295
Camino dél Puma, Peru/Bolivia 240–243
camping kit 7

Canada
  BC Trail, British Columbia 236–239
  Cabot Trail, Nova Scotia 295
  Cowichan Valley 8, BC 282–285
  Great Divide Mountain Bike Route (Canada & USA) 294
  Tree to Sea Loop, BC 264–269
canalside routes
  Great Allegheny Passage, USA 270–273
  John Muir Way, Scotland 216–219
Caucasus Crossing, Georgia 128–131
China
  Border Roads, Tibetan Sichuan 36–41
coastal routes
  Adriatic Crest, Croatia 120–123
  Baja Divide, Mexico 232–235
  Bikamino, South Africa 18–21
  Cabot Trail, Canada 295
  Coast to Coast, Cuba 295
  Cowichan Valley 8, Canada 282–285
  East Coast Greenway, USA 294
  Hebridean Way, Scotland 138–141
  Kahurangi 500, New Zealand 72–77
  La Vélodyssée, France 210–215
  Otway Rip, Australia 117
  Shiretoko Loop, Japan 46–51
  Tour Aotearoa, New Zealand 84–89
  Tree to Sea Loop, Canada 264–269
  Twin Coast Mega Loop, New Zealand 117
  Vuelta de Vasco, Spain 220–223
  West Kernow Way, England 178–183
  Wild Atlantic Way, Ireland 184–189
Coast to Coast, Cuba 295
Colombia
  Ruta Chingaza 256–259
Colorado Trail, USA 244–247
Congo Nile Trail, Rwanda 22–25
cooking kit 7
Cowichan Valley 8, Canada 282–285
Croatia
  Adriatic Crest 120–123
  Trans Dinarica Trail 224
Cuba
  Coast to Coast 295
culture-rich routes
  Alps 2 Ocean, New Zealand 58–61
  Border Roads, Tibetan Sichuan, China 36–41
  Camino dél Puma, Peru/Bolivia 240–243
  Cowichan Valley 8, Canada 282–285
  Cycle Route 1, Taiwan 116
  Danube Cycle Path, Germany/Austria/Slovakia/Hungary 132–137

East Coast Greenway, USA 294
Great Allegheny Passage, USA 270–273
Hebridean Way, Scotland 138–141
Isar Cycle Route, Germany 148–151
Kazakh Corner, Kazakhstan 42–45
La Vélodyssée, France 210–215
Meuse Cycle Route, France/Belgium/Netherlands 160–165
Munda Biddi, Australia 90–95
Ronde van Nederland, Netherlands 224
Ruta Chingaza, Colombia 256–259
Ruta Maya de los Cuchumatanes, Guatemala 228–231
Shiretoko Loop, Japan 46–51
Tasmanian Trail, Australia 104–109
Tour D'Top End, Australia 110–115
Trans-Cambrian Way, Wales 170–173
Trans Dinarica Trail, Slovenia/Croatia/Bosnia & Hercegovina 224
Trans Ecuador Mountain Bike Route, Ecuador 290–293
Tuscany Trail, Italy 204–209
Vuelta de Vasco, Spain 220–223
West Kernow Way, England 178–183
Wild Atlantic Way, Ireland 184–189
Cycle Route 1, Taiwan 116

D

Danube Cycle Path, Germany/Austria/Slovakia/Hungary 132–137
desert routes
  Baja Divide, Mexico 232–235
  Bartang Valley, Tajikistan 30–35
  Jordan Bike Trail, Jordan 116
  Oregon Timber Trail, USA 252–255
  Salar de Uyuni, Bolivia 294
Dry Diggings Track, Australia 56

E

East Coast Greenway, USA 294
Ecuador
  Trans Ecuador Mountain Bike Route 290–293
England
  Great North Trail 225
  West Kernow Way 178–183
Eureka Track, Australia 52
EuroVelo 19, France/Belgium/Netherlands 160–165
EuroVelo EV13, Turkey to Norway 224

The Bikepackers' Guide to the World

F

family-friendly routes
Cowichan Valley 8, Canada 282–285
Far North Cycleway, New Zealand 87
filtration systems 7
Finger Lakes Overnighter, USA 286–289
food & drink
Alps 2 Ocean, New Zealand 58–61
Attack of the Buns, Australia 68–71
BC Trail, Canada 236–239
Caucasus Crossing, Georgia 128–131
Congo Nile Trail, Rwanda 22–25
Danube Cycle Path, Germany/Austria/
Slovakia/Hungary 132–137
Finger Lakes Overnighter, USA 286–289
Green Mountain Gravel Growler, USA 248–251
Hope 1000, Switzerland 142–147
Isar Cycle Route, Germany 148–151
Jura Traverse, France 152–155
Kahurangi 500, New Zealand 72–77
Katy Trail, USA 274–277
La Vélodyssée, France 210–215
Mawson Trail, Australia 62–67
Meuse Cycle Route, France/Belgium/
Netherlands 160–165
Mjølkevegen, Norway 166–169
Murray to the Mountains, Australia 96–99
Tasmanian Trail, Australia 104–109
Torino-Nice Rally, Italy/France 225
Tour Aotearoa, New Zealand 84–89
Trans-Cambrian Way, Wales 170–173
Trans-Dolomiti, Italy 174–177
Vuelta de Vasco, Spain 220–223
Wild Atlantic Way, Ireland 184–187
France
Jura Traverse 152–155
La Vélodyssée 210–215
Meuse Cycle Route 160–163
Torino-Nice Rally 225
Tour du Mont Blanc 225

G

gear 7
Georgia
Caucasus Crossing 128–131
Germany
Danube Cycle Path 132–137
Iron Curtain Gravel Trail 224
Iron Curtain Trail 224
Isar Cycle Route 148–151
Goldfields Track, Australia 52–57

GPS systems 6
gravel bikes 8
Great Allegheny Passage, USA 270–273
Great Divide Mountain Bike Route, Canada &
USA 294
Great North Trail, England & Scotland 225
Green Mountain Gravel Growler, USA 248–251
Guatemala
Ruta Maya de los Cuchumatanes 228–231

H

Heaphy Track, New Zealand 76
Hebridean Way, Scotland 138–141
history-rich routes
Adriatic Crest, Croatia 120–123
Baja Divide, Mexico 232–235
Burrally, Spain 124–127
Cabot Trail, Canada 295
Camino dél Puma, Peru/Bolivia 240–243
Caucasus Crossing, Georgia 128–131
Danube Cycle Path, Germany/Austria/
Slovakia/Hungary 132–137
East Coast Greenway, USA 294
Goldfields Track, Australia 52–57
Great Allegheny Passage, USA 270–273
Hebridean Way, Scotland 138–141
Iron Curtain Trail, Germany 224
John Muir Way, Scotland 216–219
Jordan Bike Trail, Jordan 116
Jura Traverse, France 152–155
Kahurangi 500, New Zealand 72–77
Katy Trail, USA 274–277
King Alfred's Way, England 194–199
La Vélodyssée, France 210–215
Meuse Cycle Route, France/Belgium/
Netherlands 160–165
Mjølkevegen, Norway 166–169
Murray to the Mountains, Australia 96–99
Ronde van Nederland, Netherlands 224
Ruta Maya de los Cuchumatanes,
Guatemala 228–231
Tour D'Top End, Australia 110–115
Trans Dinarica Trail, Slovenia/Croatia/
Bosnia & Hercegovina 224
Trans-Dolomiti, Italy 174–177
Trans Ecuador Mountain Bike Route,
Ecuador 290–293
Tuscany Trail, Italy 204–209
Vuelta de Vasco, Spain 220–223
West Kernow Way, England 178–183
Wild Atlantic Way, Ireland 184–187
Wolf's Lair, Italy 188–193

Hope 1000, Switzerland 142–147
Hungary
Danube Cycle Path 132–137
Hunt 1000, Australia 78–83
Huruni Heartland, New Zealand 102
hygiene 7

I

Iceland
Bikepacking Kjölur 156–159
Ireland
Wild Atlantic Way 184–187
Iron Curtain Trail, Bulgaria to Norway 224
Isar Cycle Route, Germany 148–151
Italy
Torino-Nice Rally 225
Tour du Mont Blanc 225
Trans-Dolomiti 174–177
Tuscany Trail 204–209
Wolf's Lair, Abruzzo 188–193

J

Japan
Shiretoko Loop, Hokkaidō 46–51
John Muir Way, Scotland 216–219
Jordan
Jordan Bike Trail 116
Jura Traverse, France 152–155

K

Kahurangi 500, New Zealand 72–77
Katy Trail, USA 274–277
Kauri Coast Cycleway, New Zealand 87, 117
Kazakhstan
Kazakh Corner 42–45
Kenai 250, USA 278–281
King Alfred's Way, England 194–199
kit 7

L

lakeside routes
Camino dél Puma, Peru/Bolivia 240–243
Congo Nile Trail, Rwanda 22–25
Cowichan Valley 8, Canada 282–285
Finger Lakes Overnighter, USA 286–289
Hope 1000, Switzerland 142–147
Mjølkevegen, Norway 166–169
Tahoe Twirl, USA 260–263
Laos
Bamboo Byway 116

La Vélodyssée, France 210–215
Leanganook Track, Australia 56
Lesotho
  Lesotho Traverse 26–29
long-distance routes
  Atlas Mountain Race, Morocco 12–17
  Baja Divide, Mexico 232–235
  Bamboo Byway, Thailand/Laos/Vietnam 116
  BC Trail, Canada 236–239
  Camino dél Puma, Peru/Bolivia 240–243
  Caucasus Crossing, Georgia 128–131
  Coast to Coast, Cuba 295
  Colorado Trail, USA 244–247
  Cycle Route 1, Taiwan 116
  Danube Cycle Path, Germany/Austria/
      Slovakia/Hungary 132–137
  East Coast Greenway, USA 294
  Great Divide Mountain Bike Route,
      Canada & USA 294
  Great North Trail, England & Scotland 225
  Hope 1000, Switzerland 142–147
  Hunt 1000, Australia 78
  Iron Curtain Trail, Turkey-Norway 224
  La Vélodyssée, France 210–215
  Mawson Trail, Australia 62–67
  Meuse Cycle Route, France/Belgium/
      Netherlands 160–165
  Munda Biddi, Australia 90–95
  Oregon Timber Trail, USA 252–255
  Ronde van Nederland, Netherlands 224
  Tour Aotearoa, New Zealand 84–89
  TransAmerica Bicycle Trail, USA 295
  Trans Dinarica Trail, Slovenia/Croatia/
      Bosnia & Hercegovina 224
  Trans Ecuador Mountain Bike Route,
      Ecuador 290–293
  Tree to Sea Loop, Canada 264–269
  Wild Atlantic Way, Ireland 184–187

M
Mae Hong Son Loop, Thailand 116
maps 6
Mawson Trail, Australia 62–67
mechanicals 7
Meuse Cycle Route, France/Belgium/
    Netherlands 160–165
Mexico
  Baja Divide 232–235
Mjølkevegen, Norway 166–169
Molesworth Muster, New Zealand 102
Montañas Vacias, Spain 200–203

Morocco
  Atlas Mountain Race 12–17
mountain bikes 8
mountain routes
  Adriatic Crest, Croatia 120–123
  Atlas Mountain Race, Morocco 12–17
  Bartang Valley, Tajikistan 30–35
  Bikepacking Kjölur, Iceland 156–159
  Border Roads, Tibetan Sichuan, China 36–41
  Burrally, Spain 124–127
  Caucasus Crossing, Georgia 128–131
  Colorado Trail, USA 244–247
  Hope 1000, Switzerland 142–147
  Hunt 1000, Australia 78–83
  Lesotho Traverse, Lesotho 26–29
  Mae Hong Son Loop, Thailand 116
  Mjølkevegen, Norway 166–169
  Montañas Vacias, Spain 200–203
  Ruta Maya de los Cuchumatanes,
      Guatemala 228–231
  Torino-Nice Rally, Italy/France 225
  Tour du Mont Blanc, France/Switzerland/
      Italy 225
  Trans-Dolomiti, Italy 174–177
  Trans Ecuador Mountain Bike Route,
      Ecuador 290–293
  Wolf's Lair, Italy 188–193
Mountains to Sea, New Zealand 117
MTB trails
  401 Trail, USA 246
  Afriski, Lesotho 28
  Beechworth, Australia 98
  Blue Derby, Australia 108
  Christmas Valley, USA 262
  Colorado Trail, USA 244–247
  Cranbrook, Canada 238
  Creswick, Australia 55
  Derby, Australia 108
  Dyfi Forest, Wales 172
  Elan Valley, Wales 170
  Fernie, Canada 238
  Flume Trail, USA 260
  Forrest, Australia 117
  Great North Trail, England & Scotland 225
  Kenai 250, USA 278–281
  Lower Big Chief, USA 262
  Machynlleth, Wales 172
  Melrose, Australia 65
  Melrose to Wilmington, Australia 66
  Mkozama River, Lesotho 28
  Monarch Crest, USA 246
  Mr Toad's Wild Ride, USA 262

  Mystic Mountain Bike Park, Australia 98
  Nelson, Canada 238
  Oakridge, USA 254
  Old Ghost Road, New Zealand 74
  Oregon Timber Trail, USA 252–255
  Peebles, Scotland 225
  Penticton, Canada 238
  Red Ground Track, Australia 70
  Rhayader, Wales 170
  Sawtooth Trail, USA 262
  Tahoe Twirl, USA 260–263
  Tour du Mont Blanc, France/Switzerland/
      Italy 225
  Upper Big Chief, USA 262
multi-country routes
  Bamboo Byway, Thailand/Laos/Vietnam 116
  Camino dél Puma, Peru/Bolivia 240–243
  Danube Cycle Path, Germany/Austria/
      Slovakia/Hungary 132–137
  Great Divide Mountain Bike Route,
      Canada & USA 294
  Iron Curtain Trail, Turkey-Norway 224
  Meuse Cycle Route, France/Belgium/
      Netherlands 160–165
  Torino-Nice Rally, Italy/France 225
  Trans Dinarica Trail, Slovenia/Croatia/
      Bosnia & Hercegovina 224
Munda Biddi, Australia 90–95
Murray to the Mountains, Australia 96–99

N
national parks & reserves
  Akan-Mashū National Park, Japan 50
  Biesbosch National Park, Netherlands 164
  Donau-Auen National Park, Austria 136
  Entlebuch Biosphere Reserve, Switzerland 144
  Fiordland National Park, New Zealand 88
  Gloucester National Park, Australia 94
  Great Otway National Park, Australia 117
  Ikara-Flinders National Park, Australia 66
  Jagungal Wilderness Area, Australia 81
  Kakadu National Park, Australia 112
  Kenai Fjords National Park, USA 280
  Kosciuszko National Park, Australia 78
  Litchfield National Park, Australia 110, 112
  Namaqua National Park, South Africa 20
  Nelson Lakes National Park, New Zealand 74
  Northern Velebit National Park, Croatia 122
  Northumberland National Park, England 225
  Nyungwe Forest National Park, Rwanda 24
  Pamir National Park, Tajikistan 33

Routes by rating

1/5

Danube Cycle Path, Germany/Austria/
   Slovakia/Hungary 132
East Coast Greenway, USA 294
Great Allegheny Passage, USA 270
Isar Cycle Route, Germany 148
John Muir Way, Scotland 216
Katy Trail, USA 274
La Vélodyssée, France 210
Meuse Cycle Route, France/Belgium/
   Netherlands 160
Murray to the Mountains, Australia 96
Otway Rip, Australia 117
Ronde van Nederland, Netherlands 224
Twin Coast Mega Loop, New Zealand 117

2/5

Alps 2 Ocean, New Zealand 58
Attack of the Buns, Australia 68
Bikepacking Kjölur, Iceland 156
Cabot Trail, Canada 295
Cowichan Valley 8, Canada 282
Finger Lakes Overnighter, USA 286
Goldfields Track, Australia 52
Hebridean Way, Scotland 138
Iron Curtain Trail, Germany 224
Kazakh Corner, Kazakhstan 42
King Alfred's Way, England 194
Mjølkevegen, Norway 166
Mountains to Sea, New Zealand 117
Salar de Uyuni, Bolivia 294

Shiretoko Loop, Japan 46
St James Trail, New Zealand 100
Tour Aotearoa, New Zealand 84
Trans-Cambrian Way, Wales 170
West Kernow Way, England 178
Wild Atlantic Way, Ireland 184

3/5

Bartang Valley, Tajikistan 30
BC Trail, Canada 236
Bikamino, South Africa 18
Border Roads, Tibetan Sichuan, China 36
Burrally, Spain 124
Congo Nile Trail, Rwanda 22
Cycle Route 1, Taiwan 116
Great North Trail, England & Scotland 225
Green Mountain Gravel Growler, USA 248
Jura Traverse, France 152
Kazakh Corner, Kazakhstan 42
Mae Hong Son Loop, Thailand 116
Tahoe Twirl, USA 260
Tasmanian Trail, Australia 104
Torino-Nice Rally, Italy/France 225
Tour D'Top End, Australia 110
Tour du Mont Blanc, France/Switzerland/
   Italy 225
Trans Dinarica Trail, Slovenia/Croatia/
   Bosnia & Hercegovina 224
TransAmerica Bicycle Trail, USA 295
Tuscany Trail, Italy 204
Wolf's Lair, Italy 188

4/5

Adriatic Crest, Croatia 120
Border Roads, Tibetan Sichuan, China 36
Camino dél Puma, Peru/Bolivia 240
Caucasus Crossing, Georgia 128
Coast to Coast, Cuba 295
Great Divide Mountain Bike Route,
   Canada/USA 294
Hope 1000, Switzerland 142
Jordan Bike Trail, Jordan 116
Kahurangi 500, New Zealand 72
Kenai 250, USA 278
Lesotho Traverse, Lesotho 26
Mawson Trail, Australia 62
Munda Biddi, Australia 90
Oregon Timber Trail, USA 252
Ruta Chingaza, Colombia 256
Ruta Maya de los Cuchumatanes,
   Guatemala 228
Trans-Dolomiti, Italy 174
Tree to Sea Loop, Canada 264
Vuelta de Vasco, Spain 220

5/5

Atlas Mountain Race, Morocco 12
Baja Divide, Mexico 232
Colorado Trail, USA 244
Hunt 1000, Australia 78
Montañas Vacias, Spain 200
Trans Ecuador Mountain Bike Route,
   Ecuador 290

Parc Naturel Régional du Haut-Jura, France 154
Parco Naturale di Fanes-Sennes-Braies, Italy 176
Parco Nazionale d'Abruzzo, Lazio e Molise, Italy 192
Parco Nazionale del Gran Sasso, Italy 188
Parco Nazionale della Majella, Italy 191
Parque Nacional Natural Chingaza, Colombia 258
Parque Natural de la Serranía de Cuenca, Spain 202
Shiretoko National Park, Japan 46
Tallaganda National Park, Australia 68
Tongariro National Park, New Zealand 117
Walls of Jerusalem National Park, Australia 106
Whanganui National Park, New Zealand 117
Yarra Ranges National Park, Australia 82
Yorkshire Dales National Park, England 225
Þingvellir National Park, Iceland 156
navigation 6
Netherlands
Meuse Cycle Route 160–165
Ronde van Nederland 224
New Zealand
Alps 2 Ocean, South Island 58–61
Kahurangi 500, South Island 72–77
Mountains to Sea, North Island 117
St James Trail, South Island 100–103
Tour Aotearoa, North/South Island 84–89
Twin Coast Mega Loop, North Island 117
Norway
Mjølkevegen 166–169

O

Old Ghost Road, New Zealand 74
Oregon Timber Trail, USA 252–255
Otway Rip, Australia 117

P

Peru
Camino dél Puma 240–243
punctures 7

R

races & rallies
Atlas Mountain Race, Morocco 12–17
Burrally, Spain 124–127
Hope 1000, Switzerland 142–147
Hunt 1000, Australia 78–83
Karapoti Classic, New Zealand 84
Kenai 250, USA 278–281
Lesotho Sky, Lesotho 28

Liège-Bastogne-Liège, Belgium 164
Strade Bianche, Italy 206
Torino-Nice Rally, Italy/France 225
Tour Aotearoa, New Zealand 84–89
Tour Divide, Canada & USA 294
Tuscany Trail, Italy 204–209
rail trail routes
BC Trail, Canada 236–239
Catharine Valley Trail, USA 286
Columbia & Western Rail Trail, Canada 238
Elroy-Sparta State Trail, USA 276
Hauraki Rail Trail, New Zealand 87
Heights Hike-and-Bike Trail, USA 276
Katy Trail, USA 274–277
Kettle Valley Rail Trail, Canada 238
Marquette Rail Trail, USA 276
Murray to the Mountains, Australia 96–99
Prairie Path, USA 276
Rattler Rail Trail, Australia 62
Rainbow Trail, New Zealand 102
Remutaka Cycle Trail, New Zealand 87
repairs 7
Reynolds River Track, Australia 110
Ridgeway, England 198
riverside routes
Danube Cycle Path, Germany/Austria/ Slovakia/Hungary 132
Great Allegheny Passage, USA 270–273
Isar Cycle Route, Germany 148–151
Meuse Cycle Route, France/Belgium/ Netherlands 160–165
Ronde van Nederland, Netherlands 224
Ruta Chingaza, Colombia 256–259
Ruta Maya de los Cuchumatanes, Guatemala 228–231
Rwanda
Congo Nile Trail 22–25

S

saddle sores 7
Salar de Uyuni, Bolivia 294
San Sebastián, Spain 222
Scotland
Great North Trail 225
Hebridean Way 138–141
John Muir Way 216–219
Shiretoko Loop, Japan 46–51
short routes
Alps 2 Ocean, New Zealand 58–61
Bikamino, South Africa 18–21
Bikepacking Kjölur, Iceland 156–159
Cabot Trail, Canada 295

Congo Nile Trail, Rwanda 22–25
Cowichan Valley 8, Canada 282–285
Danube Cycle Path, Germany/Austria/ Slovakia/Hungary 132–137
Finger Lakes Overnighter, USA 286–289
Goldfields Track, Australia 52–57
Isar Cycle Route, Germany 148–151
John Muir Way, Scotland 216–219
Kazakh Corner, Kazakhstan 42–45
Mjølkevegen, Norway 166–169
Mountains to Sea, New Zealand 117
Murray to the Mountains, Australia 96–99
Salar de Uyuni, Bolivia 294
St James Trail, New Zealand 100–103
Tahoe Twirl, USA 260–263
Tour du Mont Blanc, France/Switzerland/ Italy 225
Trans-Cambrian Way, Wales 170–173
Trans-Dolomiti, Italy 174–177
West Kernow Way, England 178–183
sleeping bags 7
Slovakia
Danube Cycle Path 132–137
Slovenia
Trans Dinarica Trail 224
Sounds2Sounds, New Zealand 88
South Africa
Bikamino, Namaqualand 18–21
South Downs Way, England 198
South West Coast Path, England 178
Spain
Burally, València 124–127
Montañas Vacias 200–203
Vuelta de Vasco 220–223
St James Trail, New Zealand 100–103
Switzerland
Hope 1000 142–147
Tour du Mont Blanc 225

T

Tahoe Twirl, USA 260–263
Taiwan
Cycle Route 1 116
Tajikistan
Bartang Valley 30–35
Tasmanian Trail, Australia 104–109
tents 7
Thailand
Bamboo Byway 116
Mae Hong Son Loop 116
Timber Trail, New Zealand 87
Torino-Nice Rally, Italy/France 225

Tour Aotearoa, New Zealand 84–89
Tour D'Top End, Australia 110–115
Tour du Mont Blanc, France/Switzerland/
    Italy 225
touring bikes 8
TransAmerica Bicycle Trail, USA 295
Trans-Ardennes, France 163
Trans-Cambrian Way, Wales 170–173
Trans Dinarica Trail, Slovenia/Croatia/
    Bosnia & Hercegovina 224
Trans-Dolomiti, Italy 174–177
Trans Ecuador Mountain Bike Route,
    Ecuador 290–293
Tree to Sea Loop, Canada 264–269
Tuscany Trail, Italy 204–209
Twin Coast Mega Loop, New Zealand 117
tyres 7

U
USA
    Colorado Trail, Colorado 244–247
    East Coast Greenway, Florida to Maine 294
    Finger Lakes Overnighter, New York 286–289
    Great Allegheny Passage, Pennsylvania &
        Maryland 270–273
    Great Divide Mountain Bike Route
        (Canada & USA) 294
    Green Mountain Gravel Growler,
        Vermont 248–251
    Katy Trail, Missouri 274–277
    Kenai 250, Alaska 278–281
    Oregon Timber Trail, Oregon 252–255
    Tahoe Twirl, Nevada & California 260–263
    TransAmerica Bicycle Trail, Oregon to
        Virginia 295

V
Vietnam
    Bamboo Byway 116
Vuelta de Vasco, Spain 220–223

W
WAG bags 7
Waikato River Trail, New Zealand 87
Wales
    Trans-Cambrian Way 170–173
Wallaby Track, Australia 55
Walpole & Nornalup Inlets National Marine
        Park, Australia 94
waste 7
water 7

West Kernow Way, England 178–183
Wild Atlantic Way, Ireland 184–187
Wilderness Ocean Walk (WOW) Trail,
        Australia 94
Wildflower Route, South Africa 18–21
wildlife-rich routes
    Adriatic Crest, Croatia 120
    Attack of the Buns, Australia 68–71
    Baja Divide, Mexico 232–235
    BC Trail, Canada 236–239
    Bikamino, South Africa 18–21
    Camino dél Puma, Peru/Bolivia 240–243
    Congo Nile Trail, Rwanda 22–25
    Hebridean Way, Scotland 138–141
    Hunt 1000, Australia 78–83
    Jura Traverse, France 152–155
    Kahurangi 500, New Zealand 72–77
    Kenai 250, USA 278–281
    Munda Biddi, Australia 90–95
    Murray to the Mountains, Australia 96–99
    Otway Rip, Australia 117
    Ruta Chingaza, Colombia 256–259
    Shiretoko Loop, Japan 46–51
    Tasmanian Trail, Australia 104–109
    Tour Aotearoa, New Zealand 84–89
    Tour D'Top End, Australia 110–115
    Trans-Cambrian Way, Wales 170–173
    Trans-Dolomiti, Italy 174–177
    Trans Ecuador Mountain Bike Route,
        Ecuador 290–293
    Tree to Sea Loop, Canada 264–269
    Wild Atlantic Way, Ireland 184–187
    Wolf's Lair, Italy 188–193
Wolf's Lair, Italy 188–193

Acknowledgements

It would not have been possible to create this book without a global group of writers, route designers and photographers who share one thing in common: they all thrive on exploring the world by bicycle. Contributors include Matthew Crompton, who photographed and described his travels in Central Asia and the Top End of Australia. Mark Watson photographed and wrote about his adventures in Central and South America. In North America, Miles Arbour designed and described some Canadian rides. In Europe, Samuel Jones, of Cycling UK, contributed route write-ups from Scotland and Iceland. A fleet of fantastic photographers provided images, including Rugile Kaladyte, who photographed several trips, such as Hope 1000 and Ruta Chingaza; and Cass Gilbert, who has bikepacked more of these routes than most people. Stefan Amato of pannier.cc provided us with photos for some of the European rides.

For many riders, designing a route is a labour of love and several people shared both images and their tried and tested routes, including Francesco D'Alessio and Giorgio Frattale (Montanus Wild), designers of the Wolf's Lair in Italy; Ernesto Pastor of Montañas Vacias in Spain; Dan Hunt and Adam Lee, creators of the Hunt 1000 and the Attack of the Buns routes, respectively, in Australia; New Zealand's prolific Jonathan Kennett, who provided the latest amendment to his Tour Aotearoa; Rob Thomson, founder of HokkaidoWilds, who helped with his ride around Shiretoko; and the organisers of several events, including the Tuscany Trail, the Atlas Divide, the Lesotho Traverse and the Bikamino. Many of these threads come together in the unmatched resource of bikepacking.com, co-founded by Logan Watts. There's no better place to pick up the latest advice, information and maps.

Published in February 2023 by
Lonely Planet Global Limited CRN 554153
www.lonelyplanet.com
ISBN 978 18386 9501 9
© Lonely Planet 2022
10 9 8 7 6 5 4 3 2 1
Printed in Malaysia

General Manager, Publisher Piers Pickard
Associate Publisher Robin Barton
Editor Polly Thomas
Designer Ben Brannan
Layout Designer Jo Dovey
Cartographers Katerina Pavkova, Bohumil Ptáček
Image Researcher Ceri James
Print Production Nigel Longuet

Writers include Miles Arbour, Robin Barton, Matthew Crompton, Samuel Jones and Mark Watson

Mapping © Lonely Planet and © OpenStreetMap contributors
NASA/METI/AIST/Japan Spacesystems, and U.S./Japan ASTER Science Team (2019).
ASTER Global Digital Elevation Model V003 [Data set]. Distributed by NASA EOSDIS Land Processes DAAC, https://doi.org/10.5067/ASTER/ASTGTM.003.
NASA JPL (2013). NASA Shuttle Radar Topography Mission Global 1 arc second [Data set]. NASA EOSDIS Land Processes DAAC, https://doi.org/10.5067/MEaSUREs/SRTM/SRTMGL1.003
British Oceanographic Data Centre (BODC) (2015) The GEBCO_2014 Grid [Data set], https://www.bodc.ac.uk/data/documents/nodb/301801/

Cover image © Cass Gilbert

Lonely Planet Global Limited
Digital Depot, Roe Lane (off Thomas St),
Dublin 8, D08 TCV4
IRELAND

STAY IN TOUCH lonelyplanet.com/contact

Paper in this book is certified against the Forest Stewardship Council™ standards. FSC™ promotes environmentally responsible, socially beneficial and economically viable management of the world's forests.